According to Paul

Other Books by Harris Franklin Rall

According to Paul

BY

HARRIS FRANKLIN RALL

NEW YORK

CHARLES SCRIBNER'S SONS

1944

To

HENRY PFEIFFER
in memoriam

and

ANNIE MERNER PFEIFFER

*Wise and generous servants of the Church
My friends through many years*

THE AYER LECTURES OF THE COLGATE-ROCHESTER DIVINITY SCHOOL

The Ayer Lectureship was founded in May, 1928, in the Rochester Theological Seminary, by the gift of twenty-five thousand dollars from Mr. and Mrs. Wilfred W. Fry, of Camden, New Jersey, to perpetuate the memory of Mrs. Fry's father, the late Mr. Francis Wayland Ayer. At the time of his death Mr. Ayer was president of the corporation which maintained the Rochester Theological Seminary.

Shortly after the establishment of the Lectureship, the Rochester Theological Seminary and the Colgate Theological Seminary were united. It is under the auspices of the resulting institution that the lectures are given.

By the terms of the Foundation the lectures are to fall within the broad field of the history or interpretation of the Christian religion and message. It is the desire of those connected with the establishment and administration of the Lectureship that the lectures shall be religiously constructive and shall help in the building of Christian faith.

Four lectures are to be given each year at the Colgate-Rochester Divinity School at Rochester, New York, and these lectures are to be published in book form within a limited time after their delivery. They are to be known as the Ayer Lectures.

INTRODUCTION

THIS BOOK is an effort to answer two questions: What is Christianity according to Paul, and what is the value of Paul's interpretation to us today? Its first task is historical. It seeks to present Paul's thought fairly and objectively: to see him as a man of his day, sharing in its common modes of thought; to know him as a Jew with the background of his people and of their great prophetic faith; to understand him as an individual with a distinctive personality and a profound and unique religious experience; to realize how, to satisfy that searching mind of his and to serve him in his work as apostle to the Gentiles, he became the great interpreter of Christianity; and then, above all, to ask how Paul understood this new faith and what he had to say on the great Christian themes of man and sin, of Christ and his salvation, of life here and the hope for the future.

But our supreme interest lies in the second question: Are Paul's conclusions valid for our day? What help can he give us for our interpretation of Christianity? That is a theological task. The early Church had to face that question. It began, not with a system of doctrine, but as a great spiritual-historical movement. It had its divine side: the eternal God revealing himself in Christ, creating a new fellowship which was soon to spread throughout the word, making men over in the power of a new life. And it had a human side: these men and this fellowship, their faith and experience, and their writings in which they tell of this faith and interpret it for others.

We of today are asking once again what this Christian faith means. The question is especially pressing just now and for two reasons. The Church is facing an aggressive paganism and it must be clear about its message. The Church is divided when it should be united against its common foes, and it cannot achieve unity except as it comes to realize more deeply its oneness in the faith. So the theological task is upon us and we are asking what help Paul can give. We do not turn to the tradition of the past because we have no living experience of the present, for God speaks to us by his Spirit today. Nor do we overlook the fact that the centuries since that first generation have brought both experience and insight. But Christ is still for us central in history and supreme as revelation, and we study Paul as the first, and perhaps the most notable, interpreter of Christ among those who lived in those first creative days.

If there is anything distinctive in this volume it is in the fact that it seeks to unite these two interests, the historical and the theological. Commonly they are separated, and first by the theologians. Traditional theology has not paid much attention to history. Revelation was for it not so much the living God acting in history as the transcendent God communicating doctrine. It was not concerned with Paul but with his epistles, and with these as a repository of proof-texts. The need of historical study has now been recognized, even at the extreme right; but the practice lags far behind. One has only to read Karl Barth's first great work, that on Romans, to see how little his use of Paul differs from the old biblicism, how he treats Paul as infallible theologian, refusing specifically to distinguish at any point between Paul's words and "the mind of Christ." Nor does his later work show change in this respect. As against this attitude, we are trying here to see Christianity as a movement in history, to understand Paul as a man of his day, to note the time-conditioned aspects of his thought, to see his living faith as "a man in Christ," and to study his efforts to interpret that faith.

But it is even more vital to pursue the theological interest, or, shall I say, the religious. That is why these New Testament writings have been preserved; that is why we are studying this history. We are Christians. We believe that the living God has spoken to men in Christ. We want to know what truth may wait for us in the words of this great Christian interpreter. Now, the historical critic asserts that we must keep these pursuits separate, that historical study must be strictly objective and critical, uninfluenced by personal interest and concerned only with facts. The position seems sound, but in fact it is mistaken, and for two reasons. First, history has to do not simply with facts, or even with facts in relation; its distinctive interest is in meaningful facts, that is, in values Secondly, the historian himself does not cease to be a man because he is studying history. Unless he has a narrow or an empty mind, he will have thought about the deep issues of life. His conclusions may be negative; he may take a materialistic or a naturalistic view of human life. In such case, let him not think that this makes his work "scientific." It may simply mean, as is obvious in many cases, that he is incapable of discerning the deeper issues and the greater forces that are here involved. If by theology you mean the study of life's ultimate values and realities as presented in religion, then we must say that the man without theological (religious) interest and insight is not equipped for the study of Christian history.

What is needed, then, is the union of these two interests, of which neither can be pursued with the largest success without the other. As theologians studying this first great interpreter of our faith, we must be historical and critical. We must avoid identifying Paul with our particular system or regarding him as simply the symbol of a system of doctrine. We must see him as a man, illumined by God's Spirit, given great and lasting insights, but still as one, to use his own words, who had his treasure in earthen vessels. Yet in our historical study we must realize that we are dealing with more than the human and limited, and with more than passing forms of thought. Here God was present. Here were men witnessing God's great deeds, sharing in the life which he gave, and concerned with the issues which mean life and death for us today. We want their help. Our primary interest is not with the past event as such, but with the truth by which we can live.

But why should we study Paul in particular? Historically, the reason is plain: Paul has shaped the thinking of the Christian Church more than any other one man. "One could almost write a history of Christian doctrine, under the title, *A History of Pauline Theology*," says Paul Wernle in his work, *Der Christ und die Sünde bei Paulus*. So, if we want to understand the New Testament, we must study Paul. Not merely do the writings ascribed to him take up a fourth of this Christian collection, but his influence, direct and indirect, extends to a large part of the remainder.

But the deeper reason for the renewed interest in Paul is religious. Christianity is not first of all an institution or a system of ideas; it is a gospel, good news about God, about his purpose and his way of life for men. Our Christian Scriptures might well have been called *The Gospel of our Lord Jesus Christ*, instead of *The New Testament*, or *Covenant*. The New Testament is composed of a series of gospels, differing, yet in essential agreement, including not only the Gospels according to Matthew, Mark, Luke, and John, but those according to the author of Hebrews and according to Paul. We are interested in Paul because, like these others, he brings a gospel, the answer to our deepest needs, the old needs felt in Paul's day and now again forcing themselves upon us. Facing imminent disaster, we know that further technological advance will not save us, nor even give security from want or provision against future wars. We have a new recognition of the reality of sin and its tragic power in human society as in the human heart. We need a word which will convict man of sin and bring him to the God who is the source of life and help, which shall bring healing to the individual soul and reconcile man and his brother. Our primary interest in this study is in the gospel according to Paul as an answer to their needs.

This volume is intended for all those who are seeking a clearer understanding of the Christian faith and in so doing wish to unite their belief in the historic faith with an open mind toward every source of deeper insight. It seeks especially to serve the Christian minister in aiding him to a richer and more positive message. It is not intended for the specialist, whether in New Testament or in theology, and so its pages are not burdened with citations of authorities. The brief list of recommended books appended is for the help of the reader; it indicates only in slight measure those to whom I am so greatly indebted. Fortunately the one necessary source for this study is open to all, that is, the letters of Paul himself. It would be well to have one or two modern translations of Paul in addition to such standard version as may be employed. The great need is to immerse oneself in these letters and through them to enter into the inner spirit and the living faith of this man. There are obstacles here for the common reader: the familiarity of words so often read, which dulls our real apprehension; the peculiar language and thought forms of a time remote from our own and in many ways so different; and the identification of these words, which are primarily religious, with the hard and fast forms of a traditional theology which has been built upon them. I shall be happy if these pages may aid in a truer appreciation of the great apostle and a better understanding of the Christian faith.

This book contains the 1942 lectures given on the Ayer Foundation at the Colgate-Rochester Divinity School under the title, *Paul and the Faith of Today*. Due to the limits of time, only a portion of this material could be given on that occasion. I wish to express herewith my appreciation of the honor of the election to the lectureship and of the permission thus to extend the scope of his volume. The biblical quotations are taken from the Standard American Edition of the Revised Version upon permission granted by the copyright owner, The International Council of Religious Education. I am again indebted to my wife for valued aid in the preparation of this manuscript for the press.

Harris Franklin Rall

Garrett Biblical Institute
Northwestern University Campus
Evanston, Illinois
November, 1944

Contents

Chapter One

RELIGION IN SEARCH OF A THEOLOGY

I. THE BEGINNINGS

AN. WHITEHEAD has said that Christianity "has always been a religion seeking a metaphysic, in contrast to Buddhism which is a metaphysic generating a religion." Its genius, he says, is to make the religious fact primary and then to seek for an interpretation. "The Gospels exhibit a tremendous fact." [1] It would be easy to overstress this antithesis, but it suggests the basic consideration on which this study of Paul rests. Christianity today, as in every age, is a religion in search of a theology. It has, indeed, a conviction, a profound belief on which all its life rests, the faith that the Power which rules this world is good and that its character of love and its purpose for man have been revealed in Jesus Christ. But this belief is not a philosopher's deduction or a system of ideas handed down by authority; it is a conviction which has grown out of life, out of historical fact and personal experience in which men have found God. The task of theology in each age is to serve the fellowship of this faith by inquiring what this conviction means for the thought of God and the world and life, by testing its validity as it faces the life and thought of its age, and by asking what it has to offer to its day and to demand of it.

It is from this standpoint that we must approach the study of Paul and of the whole movement of thought in the primitive

[1] *Religion in the Making*, pp. 50, 51.

Church. Of the difficulty of this task, New Testament students have become increasingly aware. The first reason is historical. We do not have contemporary sources for those first years. Our writings come out of the Church of the second and third generations. The thought and life of the Church had already taken form, though its development was only at the beginning. Even where the writers bring before us the historic Jesus, what he said and did, they are at bottom always concerned with what he was and what he meant to them; that is, not with history as such but with the gospel.

The second difficulty comes from our tendency to read back our own point of view. And the sinners are not all in one camp! There are those for whom Christianity is primarily an ecclesiastical institution, with delegated authority and prescribed orders and sacraments. It is enough for these, finding the word "Church" in Acts and Paul, or even in the two doubtful references in Matthew, to read back into the term the ecclesiastical connotation of later centuries when the primitive religious fellowship had become a hierarchical-sacramentarian institution.

A second group conceives Christianity in terms of doctrine, more particularly of authoritative teaching. Christology and Trinity, theories of justification and atonement, with other developed formulations of later times, are found in passing references. When critical exegesis disallows this, we are informed that these doctrines are "germinally" or "basically" present. The sins of the liberals, in making Jesus an ethical idealist of the socially minded type, have been sufficiently castigated of late. But there remain as a third group the critics themselves, who often share the intellectualism and dogmatism of those whom they attack. Their greatest danger is in the failure to see the fact of a great and creative religious movement, whose source was in God, whose center was in Jesus, whose expression was in the primitive fellowship, whose results seem so disproportionate to the humble beginnings. Sometimes they try to explain the movement by tracing out the origin of the elements from which, supposedly, it has been pieced together. Sometimes a single explanation is sought. And there are still very many, to the left as well as the right, who read back their own intellectualistic viewpoint and assume that there was with Paul, or with Jesus, as the basis of all their work and as representing their primary significance, an ordered and consistent set of ideas which it was their chief interest to communicate.[2]

Primitive Christianity illustrates the fact, first of all, that great religious movements do not begin with the reflections of a philosopher or the program of a reformist, but rather with the deep religious experience of some soul that has sought for God, and the conviction that the Most High has drawn near in saving help and with a word of life. Further, these first Christians were Jews. The Hebrew mind was practical rather than philosophical; it moved in the realm of religious action and expectation rather than of mysticism and speculation. The Jews believed in divine revelation, but their God revealed himself in deeds and demands rather than in imparted ideas. Central for them was a divine history and a people of God.

Consider now the situation of the little company of the friends of Jesus who gathered after his death. They had a faith

[2] Joseph Klausner's *From Jesus to Paul* is a current illustration. He discusses almost everything except the main matter, the profound, personal religious experience which Paul underwent in his movement from Jewish legalism to a more spiritual faith.

but not a theology; they were a fellowship but not a Church in the present sense of that term. They had four great posses-sions. (1) As Jews they inherited a great tradition, the belief in the living God who had called Israel to be his people. (2) They had a great memory which was to become the most precious inheritance of the race: Jesus of Nazareth, his word and work, his life and death, above all his spirit and personality which had left its indelible impress upon them. (3) They had a strong and sure faith which had survived the shock of Jesus' death and had, indeed, been changed and enriched by it; Jesus was the Messiah of God, the living Lord, who would return to establish God's kingdom upon earth. (4) They had a fellow-ship, not simply resting upon a past relation and a future hope, but constituted by a common and present religious experience: the sense of the living presence of the risen Christ, of forgive-ness through Christ and acceptance with God, of the gift of God's Spirit, and of a bond of mutual love. In all this the logic of events was their guide, the events whose center was Christ and whose source was God—not primarily a set of principles or directions remembered from Jesus, and quite certainly not a set of directions concerning Church organization and procedure received from the risen Christ before his ascension. They were, like the Thessalonians, waiting for the appearance from heaven of the Christ who was to deliver them from the wrath to come (the judgment).

But the very logic of events, coupled with this faith and experience, brought a compulsion to think. For there was a whole group of questions implicit in this early situation. (1) They concerned their leader. Why did Christ need to die? What was the significance of his resurrection? What of his rela-tion to God, and their relation to him, and his work in the future? (2) There were questions that pressed upon them as Jews: what was the relation of the new and the old, of the Christian fellowship to the old Israel, of the new way to the laws and practices of the old? (3) And more and more with passing years as the separation from Israel became accepted fact, there was the inclusive question as to what was the faith of the Church. Of this movement of thought in its earlier stages we know but little. It was, none the less, the beginnings of Christian theology, that is, the effort of the Church to interpret the faith which it possessed, and to meet the questions raised by that faith, by its task, and by the world of life and thought about it.

II. PAUL AS THEOLOGIAN

The real search for a Christian theology began when, in Paul, the man and the occasion met together. Was Paul a theologian? The profound influence of Paul upon the great Christian thinkers of the centuries we would all recognize. It is not so evident, or at least dominant, with Origen, Athanasius, and Aquinas; but who could understand Augustine or Luther or Calvin without Paul? And who does not appreciate his renewed influence in our day, an influence not limited to Karl Barth and the continental theology. Many, accordingly, have seen him as primarily theologian. Some of these have regarded him as the perverter of Christianity, who turned it from the religion of Jesus to the cult of a Christ, or to a system of doctrine and an ecclesiastical-sacramentarian institution; others have viewed him as the divinely ordained teacher of theology, whose system was not only first in time but final for all time. But, alike to right and left, it was Paul the teacher, the thinker,

the master of logical and consistent system who was emphasized.[1]

Whether Paul was a theologian depends on what you mean
by theology. If by theology you mean a logically consistent and
complete system of thought, then Paul's letters certainly do not
present us with a theology, even if he possessed such. It cannot
be too often called to mind that Paul did not write theological
treatises. The nearest to this is in his letter to the Romans. Half
of this is given to establishing and making plain the thesis
underlying his gospel as to the one way of salvation for men,
the way of God's grace coming in Christ, offered to man's
faith, and bringing the power of a new life. But even this is
more an argument for his gospel than an exposition of doctrine. For the rest we have, in the main, the letters of a pastor
to the people in his charge, little Christian groups composed of
simple folk. We have greetings, praise, exhortations, prayers
for their progress, rebuke, expressions of interest and affection,
and then the discussion of the most varied matters in which
they needed his help, whether concerned with belief, conduct,
religious experience, or the problems of the fellowship. One
might call them Paul's conversations with his friends. They
presuppose the preaching and teaching in which he had pre-
viously set forth for them the new faith and way. We cannot
then argue as to Paul's position from his silence in these letters,
and we must use great care in reconstructing his "theology" on
such a fragmentary basis. Beyond this we must keep in mind
that Paul's primary interest was not intellectual, that he was
not a philosopher in search of the truth but a deeply religious
man in search of life, or rather that he was one who, having

[1] For a statement of the varying views in this matter over many years,
see H. Holtzmann, *Neutestamentliche Theologie*, Vol. II, pp. 9–11.

found life and peace for himself, saw as his divinely given vocation the bringing of this word of life to others.

But something more must be said to complete the picture. You may think of theology not as the work of a system maker but as any man's earnest and persistent attempt to think through the meaning of his faith and to see it in all its relations. In this sense, theology is the concern of every thoughtful man and Paul is perhaps the greatest theologian in Christian history. For Paul was driven, first by his personal experience and needs, then by the requirements of his work, to discover the meaning of this new faith and to make it clear to others. His letters deal with all manner of questions, some at first sight rather trivial; but whether it be a collection, a Church quarrel, a case of pride concerned with precedence, or the matter of a runaway slave, he sees all in the light of basic principles and uses each as occasion for instruction in high ideal and vital truth. For this task he was fitted by unusual gifts of insight joined to deep personal experience and long years of dealing with men. How tragic the loss of these letters would have been! Without them we might not have had an Augustine or a Luther or even a fourth gospel; and without Paul Christianity might have been only a passing reform movement within the Jewish community. For he saw, as perhaps no other of that first generation, the distinctive meaning of the new faith, and in this group of letters that understanding was preserved for later generations.

The outline of our task is thus made clear. We are not seeking to discover a system of Pauline theology which shall be authoritative for our day. The shaping of such a theology is not a once-for-all achievement; it is the recurring task of every generation. But Paul can help us at two points. He can aid us in seeing the living movement which is greater than any interpretation of it, and how there comes out of it that reflective understanding of its meaning which we call theology; and he can help us in our immediate task as Christian thinkers by those great insights with which he permanently enriched Christian thought and gave it direction.

Our first concern is with the historical setting. Religion is the movement of the Eternal in time, and the response of time to the Eternal. At every point in our religion—in Church, Scripture, creed, religious experience, or theological formulation—what appears on earth is conditioned by earth: "we have this treasure in earthen vessels." We must consider then the "time aspects" of Paul's thinking, the elements in which and out of which his theology grew: the man himself, his religious heritage, his religious experience in individual life and as a missionary, and the environing world of ideas and events. No sum of such circumstances can indeed "explain" Paul's theology or the Christian movement; they are, however, necessary to their understanding.

III. THE MAN

As to our knowledge of the man we are exceptionally fortunate. There is no other man of that ancient world whose spirit and character are so fully revealed to us. We owe this to his letters. Not that they are, as is sometimes suggested, an unpremeditated outpouring of thought and feeling; they are, in fact, the thoughtful product of a master of style. But whatever was true of their particular formulation, these ideas had been worked out through long reflection and had taken shape in years of preaching and teaching. They are, indeed, loosely organized, letters, not epistles, sermons rather than treatises; but they are sure in thought, they move skilfully in their approach to others, and they unite friendliness with psychological insight as he deals with the members of his far-flung parish. And there is a transparent sincerity here; Paul is great enough to be honest and his honesty is an element in his greatness. He is not writing with the thought that posterity is looking over his shoulder, or that he is inditing a new sacred scripture. He is writing to his friends, his beloved converts, the people for whom he has adventured his life. He bares his affection. He pours forth praise, indignation, denunciation, entreaty, exhortation, lyrical outbursts, and sustained argument. In it all we see the man with a clearness which no self-portraiture of a Rembrandt, or *Confessions* of an Augustine, or *Journal Intime* of an Amiel has ever achieved. Yet, with all his sincerity, Paul is a complex personality. He is humble, yet there is a consciousness of strength, a sureness as to his calling from God, and an unshaken independence. He shows a fine sensitivity which makes him sympathetic to the feelings and needs of others; yet he can be severe in speech and uncompromising in judgment. If his theology shows a persistent duality, it is the reflection of the man. In his religious life there is a strong mystical element and the ecstatic was not unknown to him; yet it is the ethical which is always determinative in case of conflict. He ranges through high spiritual realms, yet he is realistic in viewpoint and sure in his grasp when he deals with the concrete situations of early Church life, or explores the sin and the needs of that old Roman world. He is plainly of the active rather than the contemplative type; yet it is his keen, independent, and inquiring mind which distinguishes him in that first generation, and enables him to render what was perhaps his greatest service, that of interpreting this new religion to itself.

To understand alike the man and his theology, we must consider more closely his religious faith and life. He was a great thinker, a theologian; he was a missionary and a great Christian statesman; he was a pastor, and no minister can read his letters without a finer appreciation of his own call to the cure of souls; he may fairly be called the pioneer in the field of religious psychology where Augustine was so notable a follower; he was undoubtedly a preacher of power though he disclaimed eloquence; and the secure place of his writings in the literature of religion is the more significant because they were written simply for the occasion. But first and most important is the fact that he was a man of religion, and we cannot rightly understand any of the rest until we understand this.

Next in significance for our study is the fact that Paul's deepest concern in religion was with salvation. Salvation, whether on a lower or a higher level, is a distinctly religious term. In it are operative two powerful elements which belong to all life: the sense of need and danger, and the urge to the assertion of self and the achievement of life. What makes salvation different from the common quest is the conviction that there is a higher Power through which help may come. Salvation means, in simplest terms, life by the help of God. It is not an element that disappears as religion becomes purer and higher; it is indeed most pronounced in the great religious spirits, for it is the inevitable result of religion's highest conviction, God, and of its deepest desire, life. So Christianity is an ellipse which moves about God and salvation as its two foci. Salvation is the point where religion comes alive. High religion rests back, indeed, upon faith and looks forward to conduct, but its vital center is this cry for life and this experience of saving help. In no man is this more true than in Paul. In seeking then to follow his theology in its making, we shall give special emphasis to his search for salvation.

IV. THE FACTORS WHICH SHAPED PAUL'S THEOLOGY

Three elements commonly enter into the shaping of any theology: the historical, the empirical, and the rational. There is the historical, the cultural heritage, without which *human* life is as little possible as without a biological heredity. The empirical includes the whole range of concrete data given to our experience: in Paul's case all that was represented by Jesus and the life of the Church as well as his personal religious experience and his work as missionary apostle. Finally, there is the rational aspect, when, through reflection and insight, interpretation and criticism, a man seeks to understand what has thus come to him, to bring it into unity, and to relate it to the whole of truth and life, utilizing necessarily such thought forms as are offered by the religious heritage and by the culture of the day. Inseparable from all this is the Church, or religious fellowship. The work of the theologian is never merely individual, any more than is the religious life in which it roots. The Church mediates the religious heritage and is the nourishing source and conditioning environment of the religious experience, while its service, in turn, furnishes the real occasion for the work of theology. If revelation is not listed here as a separate source of Paul's theology, it is because it was not a *separate* source for him. Hebrew history was God's action in revelation and redemption leading up to God's work in Christ and the Church. And he himself was conscious that God by his Spirit gave him guidance in the understanding and proclamation of the new f~ith. His gospel was from God. The whole presupposition of the Christian faith was that God had come to men in Christ, that God was dealing with them and speaking to them. Revelation was not an isolated and separate affair connected with sacred writings and revealed doctrines and a few inspired men.

1. In the making of Paul's theology, then, we note first the influence of his heritage. As regards his life before his conversion we must accept his own statement: he was exceedingly zealous for the traditions of his fathers; as touching the law, a Pharisee.[1] Modern Jewish scholars have denied that he was a typical Pharisee. "Typical" he certainly was not any more than Amos or Jeremiah was a typical Hebrew. The important point is that not only was he a convinced and proud and zealous Jew in his early years, but that he remained a Jew all his life. Not only was he devoted to his people, proud of the past distinction which was theirs in God's providence and deeply concerned with their fate, but his Jewish heritage remained basic for his Christian thinking. That was true of Jesus as it was of the whole primitive Church. We are so wont to dwell on the difference between Judaism and Christianity that we fail to do justice to their kinship. We appreciate this only as we note what they had in common as contrasted with the religions of the Graeco-Roman world. At the best the God of Greek philosophy was an abstract ideal or a philosophical principle or a remote and impassive absolute. For the Jew he was the one living and righteous God, working out his purpose in the world, entering into fellowship with men, creating for himself a people here on earth. The religion was personal, ethical, historical, social, and always monotheistic. For Paul, Christianity was not a departure from this but its divinely-wrought consum-

[1] Gal. 1:14; Phil. 3:5.

mation. The Jewish Scriptures were his Scriptures. His God, as
with Jesus, was the God of Abraham and Isaac and Jacob, the
God of the law and the promises.

2. The second source of Paul's theology was empirical, that
is, it was something given historically and in the concrete experience of Paul and the Church. That meant, first of all,
everything which they associated with the name of Jesus, his
life and deeds and words, his death and resurrection, his continued living presence and power. What Jesus meant to Paul
we must consider in a chapter by itself. Here we must take up
Paul's more personal experience. His conversion will naturally
come first, but his total religious experience and what came
to him in his missionary work are equally significant elements.

Paul nowhere gives a direct report on his religious experience, not even in his conversion. The three accounts in Acts
9:1–19; 22:3–21; 26:9–20 throw little light on what his conversion actually meant to Paul and on what led up to it. Paul's
own references, as in Galatians and Romans, are incidental.
Here and in the following studies, Romans 7 and 8 are used as
throwing light on Paul's personal experience, the former in
relation to his conversion, the latter on what he found in the
new life. It has been protested by some scholars that the "I" of
Romans 7 is simply rhetorical. Paul's conversion is depicted as
unrelated to any inner struggle or dissatisfaction with Judaism,
but as simply the act of a man who, having a vision of Jesus,
was persuaded that he was the Messiah and so joined the new
movement. As against this I would suggest that more, perhaps,
than with any other great Christian teacher the man and the
message were one with Paul. His insights were hard-won and
life-tested.

Paul was a man in search of salvation. True, like Luther and Wesley, he was a deeply religious man before his conversion and a loyal churchman. He shared with his fellow Jews the conviction that God had chosen Israel for his people and had given to her the law. The law was not just the Mosaic code, but the whole revelation of God's will as the Old Testament brought it. Individual and national religion were here joined together. Where Paul differed from others was, as with Luther and Wesley, in the earnestness and honesty with which he took his religion. Law and prophets both made plain that God was righteous and only righteousness could satisfy him. Paul saw more deeply what righteousness meant; no outward conformity and no compromise of partial obedience sufficed him. He probed more honestly into the depths of his own heart. So he remained unsatisfied in the search for that righteousness without which he felt he could not come before God. This was the negative preparation for his conversion. There must have been a positive preparation also, through what he had learned about Jesus and what he had seen in those disciples of the new way whom he persecuted. He had submitted his religion to the severest test that can be applied to any faith: the effort to live it. It had not brought him the certainty and joy and peace which these men seemed to have.

Sometimes the increasing pressure of piled-up waters, and the weakened resistance of the dam that seems outwardly secure, may bring a change which is sudden and cataclysmic and yet has been long in preparation. That was undoubtedly true of that Damascus road vision which swept away Paul's resistance and brought a total reorientation of life. It is idle to discuss whether there was something "objective" here or merely spiritual and "subjective." It is significant that he puts this vision alongside those of Peter and the Twelve. The essential items are plain and there is no significant discrepancy between Paul's references and the several accounts in Acts. A figure appeared to him. He recognized it as Jesus, which might imply that he had once seen Jesus "in the flesh." It was a "spiritual" vision; there must have been an aura of light and glory and perhaps a heavenly voice, as in the Acts accounts, for he knew, not simply that Jesus lived, but that he belonged in some way to the divine realm. Finally, Paul declares that with the vision there came his commission, which presumably involved his message.

Now, it is easy to misinterpret the phrase, "theology of experience," and to suppose that concrete experience brings us ready-made ideas. On the contrary, the empirical always requires interpretation. It was so here. A writer like Luke tends to put it all down in specific words. It is not so in Paul's references. It is suggestive that he went first to the Christian group at Damascus and then off by himself into Arabia. He needed to ask, alike of them and of himself, what this all meant. But that it had a meaning and that it was a word from God he did not doubt. He says in I Corinthians 15:8, "He appeared to me." To the Galatians he says flatly that his *gospel* came "through revelation of Jesus Christ." The vision was no mere sight of a man raised from the dead, but "the light of the knowledge of the glory of *God* in the face of Jesus Christ." [2] Whether at once, then, or upon reflection, the experience seems to have meant to him the following: (1) Jesus lived; he was no impious impostor or deluded fanatic, for God had raised him from the dead. He belonged to the spiritual realm, to God's realm of glory; he could therefore be none other than the

[2] II Cor. 4:6.

expected Messiah from heaven. (2) Since he was God's anointed, with God's power behind him, his death must have been according to God's purpose and for some high end; clearly, it was at once a measure of God's love and necessitated by man's sins. (3) Since Jesus had not completed his work, he would return as Messiah in glory and power for that purpose.

It may be then that the conversion experience gave Paul his faith in outline: the living Christ, his death as the deed of God's mercy, salvation as a new way of life in which God's mercy and man's trust meet together, and the hope of Christ's return for the establishment of God's kingdom. But it is quite a mistake to assume, as some have done, that in that first eventful experience there was given to Paul at once the program for his life work and his system of theology. Paul's theology was one of faith. Faith for him meant on the one hand the certainty of an inner conviction; on the other, a life of adventure and experiment. His conviction and his call came at the beginning: the conviction that God was in Christ reconciling the world unto himself and men to each other, the call to preach this gospel to the Roman world. But the theology in which that conviction found its rich expression, like the movement of his life in which that call came to fruition, awaited the experience and reflection of a lifetime. Paul's life meant adventure, and his theology, experiment. His was truly "existential thinking": a thinking in which the whole man was involved and which demanded action for its completion, and an action through which thinking came to its highest insights and deepest certainties. Hence his theology was always a theology in the making, co-extensive with his whole life.

In addition to his personal experience as a man in search of salvation, it was his work as a missionary that gave content to his thought. One might call his the theology of a missionary. His letters give evidence of the varied problems which engaged him, but they are witness, too, to the fact that this work clarified his thinking and enriched it. The religion of the law had failed when he put it to the test in his own life. The religion of the gospel met the test when he took it out into the Roman world. The lofty ideals of Christian love and the sublime confidence in what man might become as suggested to the Corinthians were not the products of a visionary dreaming in his ivory tower. His picture of sin drawn for the Romans was not the work of a bankrupt idealist or a misanthropic pessimist. In the purlieus of Corinth and Ephesus he had looked into the depths of man's depravity and seen the power of sin; and in the men of these same cities he saw what his gospel could do. All this we mean by the empirical quality of Paul's theology.

3. In considering the sources of Paul's theology we have looked at his cultural heritage as a Jew and his experience as a Christian. We must now consider him more strictly as a theologian. We are not entering a different realm here. His theology was involved in his life as a Christian and his work as a missionary. He was not a systematic theologian, but he was a theologian, and we must not underestimate this aspect of his work. He was first of all under compulsion to think through the meanings of this faith for himself. His earnestness, his honesty, and his keen and venturesome mind alike drove him to this. He was a man of action, but he was not one who could borrow his opinions from others or move on unthinkingly in his religious activity.

And he was under the compulsion of his work. Others through chance circumstances had on occasion carried the new faith to non-Jews; he saw clearly that this faith was for all men and that its proclamation was his life task. That compelled him to inquire just where the distinctive character of the new faith lay and what its relation was to his old faith. So his life work became the interpretation as well as the spread of the new faith. He had to make plain its universal and spiritual character to those who would have kept it in bondage to the nationalism and legalism of Judaism. But an even greater task was to bring it to the understanding of that Roman world which did not know the meaning of ethical and monotheistic religion. Consider the themes he had to present to this pagan world: the one living God, his judgment on sin, the revelation of this God in Jesus of Nazareth, the meaning of Jesus' life and death and resurrection, the message of divine forgiveness, the living Christ, the Spirit by which men were "reborn into the eternal" and by which they lived the new life, the Christian Fellowship, the return of this Christ to overthrow the powers of evil, the resurrection from the dead, and finally the kind of life which this kind of God asked of men and gave to men, the life of *agape*, of love according to the spirit of Christ. These truths he had to set forth again and again, and in reflecting upon them, in seeing how his gospel met the needs and experiences of men, his insights were deepened and clarified and enriched. So his life became for him a school; city streets and roads of empire were for him study and classroom. He might well have written *solvitur ambulando* over his theology: his problems were solved in action. His theology as it comes to us, then, is the theology of a preacher, as all Christian theology should be. It comes out of life, it speaks to life, and it concerns itself in the main only with that which has relevance for life.

Something further, however, needs to be said as to the

method of Paul's theology, particularly at the points where it is influenced by what may be called his world view.

Let us begin with his conception of the Scriptures and his use of them. For the Jew the Scriptures were absolute and final authority; the law was the unchanging will of God for men. Paul had found a new seat of authority: the revelation of God in Christ. It was not so much the words of Jesus, though when he had one of these it was final for him.[3] Rather, it was the revelation in Christ of God's saving mercy as a new way of salvation and of his will for man's way of living. In the name of this new authority, he swept aside great sections of the Scripture, in particular those prescriptions the obedience to which constituted the largest part of Jewish religious practice: the system of feasts and holy days, including the Sabbath; the demands of ritual and ceremony, including circumcision; and the important rules as to clean and unclean. The new way made these obsolete by denying in principle the religion of legalism, that is, the idea that religion was at heart the keeping of rules in which the lawgiver God had revealed his will for men, and the receiving of reward for such obedience. Paul stands not only for the idea of grace as against merit, but for freedom as against law and for the spirit as against the letter.

In actual practice, however, Paul the preacher and theologian sometimes reverts to the old authoritarianism, appealing to the letter of the law as if this were final. Women are to be subject to men, "as also saith the law." We are "not to go beyond the things which are written." [4] Over thirty times we find the phrase, "it is written," used quite as it might have been in his Pharisaic days. He even appeals to the law as authority

---

[3] I Cor. 7:10, 25.
[4] I Cor. 14:34; 4:6.

in his argument for the abrogation of the law. Further, Paul follows the practice of his day in spiritualizing and allegorizing the law, leaving its plain historical meaning in order to find types and symbols to support his position. That is quite likely to follow when men give absolute and sole authority to ancient writings and then try to make them cover new insights and new situations. So Philo had read his Platonic idealism into the Old Testament, confident that he was loyal to the faith of his fathers. So the Scriptures, for Paul, have a "spiritual" meaning, hidden from others, discernible by those, like himself, who have the Spirit. Thus when the law says, "Thou shalt not muzzle the ox when he treadeth out the grain," the words were not really written for the sake of the oxen but for the sake of Paul and Barnabas, to show their right to material support in return for their spiritual labors. So it is quite in the old rabbinic style when Paul argues that when God made his promises to Abraham and his seed, the reference was not to the many, that is, the Jewish nation, but to one, that is, Christ, because the word "seed" in the Greek translation of the passage was a singular noun, not plural. That the singular noun could be collective does not disturb Paul in his argument.[5] So Paul allegorizes the story of Sarah and Hagar, and uses this as an argument once more to support his position that the Christians as descendants of Sarah are the real people of God, while the Jews are the children of the servant who was cast out with her son.[6] Romans 7:1–4, and II Corinthians 3 are other illustrations of Paul's reading into the Scriptures for purpose of argument ideas which are foreign to its plain meaning. Paul's position, of course, does not depend upon such arguments. They simply

[5] See I Cor. 2:10–13; 9:4–11; Gal. 3:16. *Cf.* Deut. 25:4; Gen. 13:15; 17:8.
[6] Gal. 4:21–31.

illustrate the fact that Paul at many points was a man of his day and that at such points we cannot always follow him.

Two other elements in Paul's world view deserve more consideration because they affect more directly his teachings. They need only a passing reference here, however, because they will come up later. The supreme problem of religion is that of evil. In seeking an answer to that problem, the men of Paul's day and of Paul's circle had come to what might be called a practical, or ethical, as against a philosophical dualism. (1) They believed in two worlds—not matter against spirit, but two worlds of spirit. Evil was not just human and individual. There was an invisible kingdom of evil; Satan and these other spirits, finite but powerful, were "the rulers of this world." This kingdom God would in due time overthrow. (2) They believed in two ages. That was the distinguishing mark of apocalypticism. This age was one of evil, but it was near its end. Theirs was the generation upon which "the ends of the ages" had come. All their thoughts and hopes moved under this conviction of the great conflict which was impending and the great consummation which was about to usher in the new age.

It has been a common mistake of liberal thought to overlook or discount this time-setting which lies back of the New Testament. It is an equal error to over-stress this, to find here what is distinctive in the Christian movement, and to suppose that a revival of essential Christianity means a reinstatement of this dualistic world view of the two realms of spirit and the two ages, with the corresponding pessimism as to the present age. Here are elements of abiding truth, but here too Christianity brought significant change. We must take account of these elements in Paul's theology but we must not identify the latter with them.

V. ITS MEANING FOR OUR DAY

What Paul's theology means to us today can be determined only as we consider his teachings in order. But certain conclusions should be evident by this time and this first of all: Paul does not furnish us a systematic or authoritative theology. He presents us with a faith, the gospel which he preached; and this, with various modifications of language and form, is the faith and the message of the Church today. He brings us enriching insights, and upon these Christian thinkers will always build. And he has shown us how our day, and every day, must interpret the enduring faith for its age. His theology is one that rests on the realities of history and on faith in a God working in history; so also must ours and that of all true prophetic religion. His theology is one that comes out of experience, out of the concrete situations of life; so must ours, because we believe with him in a God who is known as he comes into human life. But those very words of prophetic and spiritual religion, namely history and experience, necessarily imply the fact that our theology is something human and conditioned and relative. God is absolute, not so our theology. We know the absolute God, but our knowledge is not absolute. For God must become flesh if man is to know him. He must enter this particular human life and this given historical situation. The living God acts, but the meaning of his action must be grasped by our limited minds and expressed in thought forms inherited with our religious culture or taken from other spheres of life. There are only two ways in which this relative and conditioned character of our knowledge could be escaped. One would be the idea that revelation meant a supernatural communication of knowledge; the other would be the assumption, with mysticism or absolute idealism, that the truth was in man himself and that he needed but to look within in order to know God. Neither of these corresponds to fact or to Christian faith.

In a curious way, traditional theology and modern critical research have united in an over-intellectualized interpretation of Paul and his significance. Both have stressed the Pauline "system." The former has made it an inspired and authoritative theology; the latter, a collection of ideas whose various sources have been laboriously traced out. Both have missed what was central in the man and what is most significant for us. Sharing his faith, using his insights, helped by his discussions, we must seek for ourselves to understand this faith, ancient and yet living, and to construe its meaning for our day, with every added insight which the years have brought to us. Nor shall we forget that our faith, like Paul's, is not simply in a God of the past, but in the living God of the present, guiding us by his Spirit into the truth.

Chapter Two

CONCERNING MAN AND SIN

RELIGION embodies the three great quests of the human spirit. The first is the search for truth. That is more than the modern insistence upon facts and pursuit of science. Man wants to know what the facts mean, what is enduring in the midst of change, what is ultimate in the clash of forces, what the meaning of the world is and the goal of his life. The second is the quest for the good, the good which is supreme and which has the right to command. Man lives in a twofold world, the world of fact and of value, of "is" and of "ought." He is concerned not only with goods but with the good, with what is right and just and not merely advantageous, with the good whose authority he recognizes even when he refuses obedience. Man's third search is for help in deliverance from evil and the achievement of the good. He knows his own weakness, his dependence, and the power of the evils that threaten him. He seeks for help from a Power above himself. This is the age-old search for salvation. The truth that we hold, the loyalty that we give, the help that we find, these, taken in their ultimate sense, constitute our religion.[1]

Paul's chief concern was with the question of salvation, and this will furnish our orientation for the study of his thought. But we must begin this study where Paul himself began, with the consideration of man and the condition from which he needs deliverance. For Paul's idea of salvation includes not simply his idea of God and of the way of help, but his insight

[1] See H. F. Rall, *Christianity: An Inquiry into Its Nature and Truth,* Chs. I–III.

into that condition from which man needs to be saved. For primitive man the problem of good and evil lay in the world about him, as it does for most men today. In this he found the goods that he desired—food, shelter, safety; and in this the evils that he feared—peril from wild beast and human foe and lurking spirits, from hunger, cold, disease, and death. Today, through our science and techniques, we are well on the way to solving these problems of the outer world. What we see with increasing clearness is that the real problem lies in man himself. Not religion alone but every approach to social problems is concerned with this matter of human nature.

It was Christianity, and especially Christianity as seen by Paul, which placed this question at the center. It is true that Greek philosophy in the person of Socrates had already bid men turn from speculation about the cosmos to the study of man. But its conception of man was neither sufficiently idealistic nor realistic. Hebrew idealism reached higher than the Greek conception of man as rational; it saw in him a being akin to God, made in his image, destined for divine fellowship. Its realism probed deeper than the Greek thought of error of mind or of the body as prison house of the soul. Not in the rational or physical, but in the ethical and religious, lay the glory of man and his tragedy. Man was a sinner who had chosen evil instead of good, and self instead of God. God was the dimension by which was to be measured alike the true nature of man and the depth to which he had fallen. His real problem was found, not in his world or in his body, but in his inner self: and not so much in his understanding as in his will. No one saw more clearly than Paul how man and the evil in man had to be considered in order to acquire a real understanding of how man could be saved. His teaching here belongs with his doctrine of divine forgiveness to set him apart from current Judaism. For Jewish legalism the answer lay in God's law, man's obedience, and God's award. Paul saw that Jewish moralism, like Greek rationalism, broke down at the point of the power of evil in man and his impotence to do good.

I. PAUL'S CONCEPT OF MAN

It is not an easy matter to understand Paul's teaching on man. He does not have a system of psychology; he employs the same term with varying meanings, and at some points his usage differs widely from ours. His use of such words as flesh, soul, spirit, body, mind, and heart can only be understood by reading his letters again and again, especially Romans and I Corinthians, and by seeing these terms in the light of his gospel as a whole. His faith in God, his personal religious experience of salvation, and what he saw of human nature in his wide contacts as a missionary, these give the background and basis for his ideas about man and sin.

1. Man belongs to the world of nature; that is the first element in Paul's conception of man. He is a part of the physical order, the world of the material, finite, and perishable. The Hebrew Scriptures, Paul's Bible, had emphasized that man was made by God from the dust of the earth. He is under the law of death: "As for man, his days are as grass." He is of the earth, earthy. He is flesh and blood, and flesh and blood cannot inherit the kingdom of God. To suggest this finite, mundane side of man Paul uses three words: flesh, body, and soul. Soul commonly means for us the spiritual and immortal side of man; for Paul it meant the "natural" as against the

"spiritual." The Greek word used by Paul is *psyche*. Like the Latin *anima* it meant first and literally breath, then life. A soul was simply a living creature. God "breathed into his nostrils the breath of life; and man became a living soul." That God created man in his own image refers to another and higher level of man's nature. The word *psyche* is hard to translate into English, especially in the adjective form. So when Paul says "psychic," or "soulish," our translators render it "natural": "the natural [psychic] man receiveth not the things of the Spirit"; "there is a natural [psychic] body [the living, physical organism], there is also a spiritual body." [1] While this psyche, or "soul," is the principle of life which we share with all animals, it is also thought of as the bearer of our feelings and desires and fears, and even as that which may be saved for the life eternal. So in the gospels, Jesus speaks of saving and losing your soul, which the revised version properly renders as life. Indeed, body, soul and spirit are all to be transformed and saved; only the flesh has no place in the final kingdom according to Paul.

2. The second fact about man, as Paul sees him, is that he lives in a world of sin and is himself a sinner. Paul does not elaborate any theories to account for this. The facts about man's sinfulness he presents at some length in the opening chapters of his letter to the Romans. He points to the pagan world with its lusts and vices, and then turns upon the Jews and declares that they are as truly sinners as the others. They have had the law, indeed, but they have not kept it. "Are we better than they? No. There is none righteous, no, not one." Sin is universal. Such a situation raises serious questions for faith if you believe that a good God created this world.

[1] I Cor. 2:14; 15:44.

3. How did Paul explain this universal sinfulness? Was it because man was a creature of flesh? The Hebrew did not think like this. He was not a dualist; the world was one and the Lord had made it all. And man was a unitary being, not a duality. But Hellenistic thought was different; the great contrast was matter and spirit. The first constituted the world of evil. That was the world not only of the material but of all that went with it: time, change, decay, and death—as well as ignorance, lust, and strife. Over against this was the world of spirit, eternal, unchanging, pure, the world of light and truth and peace. Man belonged to both worlds; rather, the true man, the spiritual part of man, was a bit of the world of spirit, imprisoned for a time in the body. At this point, it is said by some, Paul is Hellenist rather than Hebrew.

This Hellenistic conception of the finite and material as evil has certainly had a large influence in the Christian Church. It has led men to think of sin mainly in terms of the fleshly. It has prevented a wholesome and positive treatment of sex relations. It led Augustine to hold that there was necessarily something sinful in the act of sexual union even within Christian marriage. It made men seek salvation by flight from the world and put a low estimate upon the humble tasks of the daily round. It encouraged asceticism and otherworldliness. Now there are passages in Paul which suggest this viewpoint, particularly in his references to the flesh. "The flesh lusteth against the Spirit," he says. He speaks of "the law of sin which is in my members" which keeps him from obeying the law of God in which his inner man delights; and he cries out for deliverance from this "body of death." "In my flesh dwelleth no good thing." To have "the mind of the flesh," to be "in the flesh," means for him to ᴘe sinful, and is the direct opposite of being in the Spirit or having the mind of the Spirit. "They that are in the flesh cannot please God." [2]

But these very passages, more closely considered, point to a different meaning. Sin is not the equivalent of flesh; sin is "a power" which is "in my members." What makes a man a sinner? It is not having a body with appetites and passions which makes man a sinner; it is having "the *mind* of the flesh," or being "fleshly" (carnal).[3] In the literal sense, of course, a Christian is "in the flesh" as well as "in the Spirit;" and Paul does not hesitate to use the phrase of himself.[4] There are many other expressions of Paul to indicate that for him evil is by no means a mere matter of the body or of the flesh. Rather, we are to present our bodies to God as a living sacrifice and our members as "instruments of righteousness." Our bodies, if we be Christians, belong to Christ; they are, indeed, "members of Christ," temples of the Holy Spirit. "The body is for the Lord, and the Lord for the body." Significantly he speaks of fornication, not as a sin of the flesh against the spirit, but as a man's sin against his own body. The life of Christ is to be manifested in the body. Christ himself came "in the likeness of sinful flesh." [5] It is of interest, too, to note that when Paul gives a list of "the works of the flesh" in contrast with the works of the Spirit, he includes not only what we call fleshly lusts like fornication and drunkenness, but such sins as idolatry, enmities, strife, jealousies, and envyings. His catalog, indeed, lists more sins of the spirit than sins of the flesh.[6]

[2] Gal. 5:17; Rom. 7:18–25; 8:5–9.
[3] I Cor. 3:1–3.
[4] II Cor. 10:3; Gal. 2:20; Phil. 1:22, 24.
[5] Rom. 12:1; 6:13; I Cor. 6:13–20; II Cor. 4:10; Phil. 1:20; Rom. 8:3.
[6] Gal. 5:19–23.

Apparently Paul's conception was something like this: The physical as such is not sinful, nor are its natural appetites and passions. It represents, first, the merely natural, just as the "soul" does (the *psyche*) ; and as such there is no spiritual life or power in it. Further, it is the point at which sin can take hold; it gives sin its chance. And when Paul speaks of sin here, he has in mind apparently Sin with a capital letter, an objective and independent force or being, which finds its opportunity in this physical, finite side of our being. This side is not the whole of man, it is true; there is an "inward man" who recognizes God and even "delights in the law of God." But this higher law is "weak through the flesh"; the force that really rules and makes us captive is sin. The "flesh" is not sin; it gives sin its chance and sin enters in and dominates man. The "flesh" is the seat of sin.

Here we must look more closely at the curious and significant phrase, "the mind of the flesh." Mind does not mean intellect here, but rather the inner spirit and attitude. Thus Paul speaks of having "the mind of the Spirit" or "the mind of Christ." The mind of the flesh includes sins of the spirit, selfishness and hate and strife—as well as lust and drunkenness and greed. It may mean simply the mind that is turned to earthly things and does not think of God; or it may mean the mind which, knowing God, refuses him trust and obedience and turns from his spirit of humility and love to pride and selfishness; the carnal Corinthians are men of jealousy and strife.[7]

Modern Christianity has reacted strongly from the old dualism and asceticism which too often saw the spiritual as an escape from the physical, and for which a "religious" vocation

[7] I Cor. 3:3. The word translated carnal is *sarkikoi*, fleshly.

meant giving up the common vocations of family and business. We have come to see how this body with its drives, and this natural world with its concerns as to food and shelter and work, are not of themselves enemies of the spirit but rather a necessary school of training and even a possible means of enrichment for the soul. On this constructive side Paul has little to say. He may have been influenced by the Hellenistic stress upon the inner man as opposed to the outer, of which he makes so much. Probably he was even more affected by that apocalyptic outlook which saw the end of this old world as near at hand, so that the whole realm of the physical, so soon to perish, became indifferent. It was the common mood of the early church. "The world passeth away, and the lust thereof: but he that doeth the will of God abideth forever." [8]

But the real issue with Paul was a far deeper one. He recognized a cleavage that ran through the whole of life. It was not the Hellenistic opposition of matter and spirit. Rather it stemmed from the Hebrew faith in the one righteous God who made this world of things and time, to whom it all belonged, and by whom at last body and spirit, nature and man would be redeemed. Against this God man in his sin had revolted. The dualism was ethical, not metaphysical. Good and evil, not spirit and matter, formed the contradiction. And it was only for this age. The evil was, in its way, a mystery; but God was Lord of the world he had made, and evil would be overcome— in man by God's grace in Christ, in the cosmos by the final apocalyptic conflict. Paul did not think that the material was the principle of evil, or that the physical side of man was in itself evil.

4. But did not Paul hold to the "total depravity" of human

[8] I Jn. 2:17.

nature? That depends upon what is meant by the term. For traditional theology of the Augustine-Calvin type, total depravity has meant two things: (1) man in himself and apart from God's grace has no knowledge of good, no desire for God and the good, no strength to achieve the good; (2) man's nature is evil and wholly evil, so that thought and desire and deed from the hour of birth are actively and exclusively and constantly directed to evil. The latter position illustrates a common fault of theology: to take a principle or abstract idea and then to absolutize it without reference to concrete facts. Paul rightly shares with this traditional theology the desire to emphasize the grace of God and the total dependence of man upon God. He is fighting against a complacent moralism. He emphasizes the fact of human sinfulness. He sees sin alike as wrongdoing which needs forgiveness and as a power in men and over men which needs a higher power to overcome it. The first half of the Roman letter is concerned with painting this black picture in order to make plain the need and the wonder of God's forgiving grace and saving power. Paul's purpose is polemic—he is fighting. For that reason he makes his statements positive and sweeping, and passes by questions which we must face. Grant the evil in man. Recognize it as a power that holds us in its grip. Recognize, too, that there is no vision, no desire, no strength, no good that does not come from God. Nevertheless, we still have to ask whether all the thoughts and desires and impulses of man are evil and only evil. Empirically speaking, we must simply say that it is not true. The very psychological advances of our day which have made us see the power of the impulse-instinct side of man, and all the dangers and evils involved in this, bring at the same time the realization that there is something here to which we must appeal if anything is to be accomplished, and upon which we must build.

But while Paul recognizes man's actual sinfulness and his utter dependence, the man with whom he deals is no such theological abstraction as Calvin gives us in his *Institutes*. Here, too, Paul is empirical. The romanticists, with their naïve hopefulness as to human nature, are no more lacking in "realism" than are those who think they have included all the facts by eliminating everything from man that could make him a rational-ethical being, made for God and able to respond to him. They imagine themselves orthodox to the degree in which they are cynical and pessimistic. Paul knows himself a creature who belongs, not just theoretically but really, to two worlds: the natural world and God. And he has two natures, or two sides to his one nature. On the one side he is not simply physical creature but a sinful creature, a slave of evil and at the same time eagerly following it. On the other side, despite this evil he has a knowledge of God and gives an inner approval to God's law, that is, to the right and good. He "delights in the law of God after the inward man"; he hates the evil, he wants the good.[9] And all Paul's missionary work rested upon the conviction that these men, sunk in evil, whose condition he so graphically depicts in Romans, could hear and know and respond when he brought to them the word of God's grace. Yes, and that down deep in the inner man they really wanted God, just as he did.

Even more extraordinary is the way in which he held up the highest of ideals for these men. He really expected these men, dug from the pit of paganism, to grow up into the spirit of Christ and to live on such a level as is suggested by his great

[9] Rom. 7:15-23.

hymn of love. And this was not a romantic optimism speaking from its ivory tower, but the word of a man in closest contact and constant conflict with the evils of his day. It can, of course, be said that all this has nothing to do with human nature but belongs solely to the grace of God, and that human nature by itself is wholly evil. But human nature "by itself" is a theological abstraction. God is the creator and sustainer of all things. Nothing is left wholly to itself nor could anything exist wholly by itself. Least of all has God left man to himself. Paul is not dealing with a mythical man as he might be in a world deserted by God, but with men made for God, men whom God has never left alone, men to whom God speaks as persons, who by God's grace can hear him when he speaks and make answer to him. Augustine's great word, "Thou hast made us unto thyself, and our souls are restless until they rest in thee," says something significant about man as well as about God. What we need is not simply to emphasize the idea of divine grace, but to have a larger conception of its sphere and a truer conception of its work.

Paul had no occasion in his letters to set forth this aspect of his conception of man, but he recognizes it in his references to the inner man and the spirit of man. He does not use the phrase, "the image of God," but his doctrine of man as spirit (*pneuma*) corresponds to this. It stands for that side of man's nature which marks him as rational, moral, spiritual being. There is a spirit in man to which God speaks and which can know God and spiritual things; and to this spirit God's Spirit bears witness when man becomes a child of God. It is only because man is spirit that he can receive the Spirit.[10] Without this neither revelation nor redemption is possible, nor indeed

[10] I Cor. 2:9–16; Rom. 8:16.

the incarnation itself. This is not "making void" the grace of God; it is simply widening its scope as that which marks God's whole relation to man from creation onward. All this points away from that theological caricature of Paul's teaching, the idea of a total depravity resulting from the fall in which the image of God in man is utterly eradicated, with every desire for God and every capacity to know God or to hear his word; from which there follows logically, as Calvin saw, the idea of irresistible grace and of man as little more than the passive object of divine compulsion.

II. THE ORIGIN OF SIN

1. As to the origin of sin, it is necessary again to differentiate what Paul actually says from the system that has been built upon him. Traditional theology made the fall and its interpretation of it basic for the whole "plan of salvation" and philosophy of history. This one act of Adam produced a total corruption of his nature. All humanity was present in him so that "in Adam's fall we sinned all," and thus human nature in all its members became equally corrupt. And as we had all sinned in Adam, so we were all guilty down to the last newborn babe, who was at birth totally depraved and guilty in God's sight.

It is well to recall certain facts here. The Bible is primarily concerned with God and evil and deliverance, not with cosmic philosophies or theories as to the origin of sin. There is only one clear reference to the fall in the Old Testament. The purpose of the story of Genesis 3 apparently is not to explain the origin of evil—that is already present in the serpent. Rather, it asks why there should be universal toil and pain and sorrow in a world which God had made. The conclusion is that this was due to man's disobeying a definite command which God had given, the answer being clothed in the form of an ancient myth which the writer used for his purpose. Of total depravity and an explanation of the universality of sin there is no suggestion.[1]

Paul's references to the fall, unless we include Romans 16:20, are three in number. One is an incidental allusion to Satan's beguiling Eve. The second is concerned with Christ as the second man, through whom life comes to men as once death came through the first man. The third develops further the same parallel. He uses the accepted belief that sin and death and judgment have come upon men through Adam in order to point out how grace and forgiveness and life "came unto all men" through Christ.[2] Paul connects the fall with the entrance of sin into the world but not with its universality, though he discusses the latter at length in Romans 1 and 2. Nor does he refer to the fall when he discusses, as he does here and elsewhere, the corruption of the human heart. What Paul argues is that the sin of the Gentiles is due to wilful disobedience, because they do know God, and that the Jew with his higher knowledge of God's will in the law is disobedient in like manner. The source of sin to which he thus points is not inherited depravity but responsible choice. The account is not theological-metaphysical but historical-moral. Romans 7 adds

[1] An illustration of the kind of futile speculation which has so often been connected at this point with traditional theology is given by C. S. Lewis in *The Problem of Pain,* pp. 122–124, when he offers a theory of "the Satanic corruption of beasts," a "fall" of the animal world, "corrupted by an evil angelic being." This is intended to account for the evil of pain in the world before the fall of man. Mr. Lewis here seeks to unite traditional doctrine with modern evolutionary theory.

[2] II Cor. 11:3; I Cor. 15:21; Rom. 5:12–21.

an interesting psychological study. As elsewhere, Paul's concern here is not with theory. He is facing facts and arguing for his faith. The tragic fact is sin; not sins, not just individual acts, but sin as a power in our life, sin as something that lives in us. How does this sin come to be? God is good. The law, too, is good and holy. We all acknowledge that and in a real sense we desire to keep the law. But each man is two men. Against the "mind" which "serves the law of God" there stands this other man, fleshly, sinful; and, having sinned, this sin has become the dominant power ruling his life. The law does not help him; it simply reveals his impotence and becomes the occasion for disobedience. Who that has desired the good does not recognize the truth of this picture? Paul's interest, of course, is not in this psychological analysis; it is to lead up to the wonder and joy of the new way, the way of grace and faith and the power of a new life, to the eighth chapter for which the first seven are the preparation. But this great message, as Paul here shows, does not need to go back to theories about the fall or any dictum about total depravity; its background is in these bitter facts of personal experience which all those know who would follow the high way.

2. More difficult for the modern mind is the way in which Paul speaks of sin as an objective Power, a Being which has existence independently of men and of sin in men and which may thus have existed before the fall. Sin lies in wait, he says.[3] It stirs man up and causes him to revolt. When the law cuts across his natural impulses and desires, sin sees its opportunity and comes in. Then man finds himself its slave.[4] This idea of sin as a Power and of its rule over man appears again and

[3] Cf. Gen. 4:7, "Sin coucheth at the door."
[4] "His servants ye are whom ye obey." Rom. 6:16.

again.[5] Hence some scholars have drawn the conclusion that sin for Paul is "something external and objective," a "personified external Force." "And conversely," we are told, "we do not find any indication of sin (in the singular) being conceived of as individual and personal." [6]

It is hard for our modern western mind to follow the men of the east and of that day in their tendency thus to objectify general ideas or qualities, and even to think of them as personal beings. Elsewhere Paul speaks of death in the same way. Christ, he says, is to put all enemies under his feet at the end, and Death will be the last of these. "O Death, where is thy victory?" he cries out.[7] Was this merely rhetorical, after our own manner of speech? It is not easy to tell, nor is it especially important. Here again the question for us is: what were the facts which Paul recognized and what was he seeking to say? The particular image of thought is not so significant. Religion is always clothing its thought in symbol and myth. What Paul saw was that man's problem was not just the matter of having God's forgiveness for certain sins which he had committed, and then proceeding to keep the law. Sin is not a piecemeal affair. It is sin, not sins. It is a spirit, a way of life, something to which we surrender, which we become. When at last we wake up to the fact, we are in its grip and we cannot get free. That is true not simply on the sensual side—as with drunkenness and lust—but with the sins of the spirit: greed, hate, fear, jealousy, envy, and the like.

Here was the problem as Paul saw it, with an insight so much profounder than the moralism of his day and of ours. The

[5] Rom. 5:21; 6:6-22.
[6] C. A. A. Scott, *Christianity According to St. Paul,* pp. 46, 47.
[7] I Cor. 15:26, 55. Cf. Rom. 5:14, 17; 6:9; II Cor. 4:12.

sinner needed deliverance from himself. There was a higher law above him which he approved and desired; but there was this other "law in his members." Paul puts it in this double way: now he refers to what he himself is, to the mind of the flesh, "the body of this death"; then he speaks of sin dramatically as something that is over a man, the Power to which he is in slavery. It is probable that Paul thought, as the modern man does not, of sin as an objective Being, or spirit Power, that invaded man, finding opportunity in the "fleshly nature of man" and its reaction against the law of God. The important matter was that Paul recognized here a power in man's life that had to be dealt with if man was to be saved. And so he presented his gospel as the greater power, the "power of God unto salvation," as he says in Romans 1:16, 17, where he announces the theme of his great letter.

III. THE NATURE OF SIN

Sin for Paul is not simply a Power that invades and enslaves; it is a moral decision, an attitude and quality of man's spirit.

1. First of all, sin, as Paul sees it, is disobedience; it is man's rejection of God's will. For Plato the "disorders of the soul" meant either madness or ignorance. "No man is voluntarily bad; but the bad become bad by reason of an ill disposition of the body and bad education." [1] Socrates preceding him and Aristotle following shared this idea that sin was a defect of reason or insight since a man would naturally prefer the good life. Later Hellenistic thought held that sin necessarily belongs to man as finite being, immersed in the material world, with the soul imprisoned in the body. The Hebrew prophets saw

[1] *The Timaeus,* 86. Jowett's translation.

more clearly. Sin comes neither from ignorance nor finitude. It is man's responsible action, the choice of evil instead of good; it is disobedience to the God of truth and righteousness. Paul was a Hebrew here. He pointed out that even the Gentiles, who did not have the revealed law, nevertheless had a knowledge of God. But, knowing God, they did not glorify him; they "hindered the truth in unrighteousness." That was their sin. It was worse with the Jews; they had the revealed law but there was not one that sought after God or did good.[2] Even with Christians there is this danger of the sin of disobedience. Paul is constantly exhorting the disciples: Do not continue in sin; present yourselves as servants to the obedience of righteousness; do not sin against the weak brother.[3] Sin is disobedience, personal and individual.

2. But Paul sees in sin also an inner spirit and attitude. Obedience and disobedience are "formal" terms; it is the content that is important. We can tell best what sin is as inner spirit and attitude by following Paul's thought form, that of contrast or opposition. Sin is always something negative. "I am the spirit that always denies," says Goethe's Mephistopheles. You can tell what sin is by noting the good which it denies. The highest good for man, at once the will of God and man's true life fulfillment, is the spirit of God as seen in Christ. And this spirit that was in Christ, this "mind of Christ," is first of all love, unselfish, devoted, self-giving, creative. Paul specifically indicates this in Philippians 2 : 2–8; but it is in his great hymn, or lyric poem, I Corinthians 13, that he portrays most clearly and with deepest insight this spirit that was in Christ. The other great element in "the mind which was in Christ" is his

[2] Rom. 1:18–25; 3: 10–18.
[3] Rom. 6:1, 15, 16; 8:1–17; I Cor. 8:12; 15:34

obedience.[4] In humility and devotion he was utterly obedient to the will of God, and that even to death. This, then, is the mind of Christ, this is the heart of goodness: in reverence and humility and trust to offer God the obedience of utter devotion; in faith to receive God's own Spirit of love and to live by it.

It is in contrast with these two qualities that we see Paul's idea of sin. The mind of Christ is humble, trustful obedience. When man sees God as Jesus saw him, sees him as the God of all power and holiness and goodness, the "Father in heaven," then the answer should be that surrender in trust and obedience which Paul calls faith. Man has found the center of his universe and his highest good, and says yes to this God. Sin is the denial of all this. Men know God but do not give him his place.[5] If you ask what is the motive back of this refusal, the answer varies. There is pride; men profess themselves to be wise and lack humility.[6] There are the "lusts of the heart," lusts of the spirit as well as of the body, which assert their lower desires against what is higher.[7] But sin is seen most clearly in contrast with the spirit of love. Sin is selfishness. Paul does not develop this thesis, it is true, because that is not his method; but he makes his position plain. Suggestive is the way in which he deals with the Corinthians. Their sin is pride, pride in their knowledge, pride in their gifts (like the speaking with tongues). There are parties, strife, ambition, with little regard for others. Paul has his word for all this, but his final word is that which he speaks when he points out the opposite of all this in his chapter on love. For him who has the mind of Christ, God is

[4] Phil. 2:8. Cf. Mark 14:36.

[5] Rom. 1:21.

[6] Rom. 1:21–23. Cf. Jesus' reference to having the mind of the child in order to enter the kingdom of God.

[7] Rom. 1:24; Gal. 5:16, 17.

central in faith and obedience and his fellow man in thought and service. Sin is selfishness; it makes self the center of the world as against God and brother. It takes many forms. It is an over-simplification to identify it with pride and rebellion as Reinhold Niebuhr does, following in the Calvin-Barth succession. Yet at its root it is always man turning from God and putting self first. Sometimes it appears as little more than a spiritual indifference or inertia which refuses God's call to rise to higher things. Sometimes it is the physical passions whose indulgence is selfishly put before all else. Sometimes it is pride in our own importance and wisdom, and confidence in our own strength. It may be "anger and malice and railing," or simply preoccupation with our own interests and satisfactions as with the rich at the Corinthian church suppers. But always it is the refusal of God as against humble faith and devotion and the attitude of selfishness as opposed to love. Its philosophy of life is summed up in two words, I and No: No as it thinks of God, I as it looks at life. In its first aspect, as disobedience, sin is the contradiction of faith; and in its second aspect, as selfishness, it is the contradiction of love. Thus sin is the direct opposite of the life in Christ as Paul summarized this in his pregnant phrase, "faith working through love."

IV. PERMANENT VALUES IN PAUL'S TEACHING

In attempting to evaluate Paul's help to Christian thinking in his teaching as to man and sin, we need to distinguish the central from the peripheral, and his basic Christian convictions from particular forms of expression. The task is difficult but cannot be shirked.

1. Christian thought about sin today is commonly marked by a fourfold approach. (1) It interprets sin ethically: sin is the act and attitude of that rational and responsible creature who has some vision of God and right and who has made a decision. It refuses the merely legalistic and ritualistic ideas of earlier religion as inadequate or false. And it does not use the term sin for the status to which man comes by mere birth so far as it is unrelated to his own attitude and action. It does realize that sin reaches beneath the deed to the inner spirit, and beyond the act of the moment to the character which man has attained through the acts and attitudes of the past. (2) It understands sin socially and historically. Sin not only has to do with the individual in his relations, but with man's corporate life, and with this group life as it has developed historically and as it comes to the individual in social mores and institutions. It knows how deeply and constantly the individual is affected by this life of humanity into which he is born and of which he is a part. It sees here a "kingdom of sin" without thereby committing itself to the idea of a dominion of Satan and his angels. (3) It seeks to understand sin psychologically, that is, in relation to the nature of man. It knows, too, that man's nature cannot be fully understood without relation to his past. It considers his biological heritage, those drives and impulses which furnish life its needed dynamic and create its problems. (4) Its supreme and distinctive emphasis is religious. Sin is for it a religious problem, the problem of man's wrongdoing and wrong-being as seen in the light of God.

It is obvious that present-day Christian thinking, as here indicated, has been influenced by certain results of modern science. If we take the three great nineteenth-century names of Darwin, Freud, and Marx as symbols of movements rather

than as representing systems, we must certainly declare that
Christian thought has not been uninfluenced by them in its
idea of man. It sees primitive man as having a biological
heritage, and not as a creature of innocence transformed by
one deed into a totally depraved nature. It recognizes that he
is primarily a creature of impulses, passions, and drives, rising
only with difficulty to the level of a rational being. It knows
how deeply his nature and his problems are affected by the
fact that he never exists as a mere individual, or with a moral-
spiritual life that is independent of society, but, especially
today, in integral relation with a complex political-economic
order which affects his every interest and relation and reaches
his inmost being.

2. But it is also clear that this thinking is Christian at its
center and is determined in its fundamental viewpoint by
Paul. There are points where Paul's first-century thought
forms are not followed, at least in the manner of later theology.
Yet even here in the main it is only the form which is affected.
We do not build up our doctrine upon the traditional picture
of paradisaic innocence and the fall, but we do recognize the
truth which symbol, or myth, here sets forth: that God is not
creator of sin; that knowledge brings responsibility, and responsibility fateful action, and action inevitable judgment. We
do not picture the kingdom of evil in terms of a Satanic realm,
not even all of those who speak of "the demonic"; but we do
know that evil is enthroned in high seats of power, is established in ancient institutions and ideals which dominate and
destroy, and that it touches every aspect of human life. We
may not think of sin as an objective entity—if, in fact, Paul
did so—any more than we think of the Law or of Death in
that fashion; but we do recognize with Paul that he who

lightly gives himself to sin will find himself more and more the slave of sin.

Let us, however, state positively the main insights by which Paul has aided the Christian religion in its search for a doctrine of man and sin. (1) Hebrew, rather than Greek, Paul saw man as a whole, body, soul, and spirit, and as one whose whole life was to be redeemed. (2) Realist, like the Hebrew prophets, he saw the evil in man, saw it in his spirit and nature, not just in passing deeds, saw it as a power which dominated man; yet he knew that man belonged to God and could respond to God, and so he was incredibly hopeful, not with the hope of the romanticist or humanist, with his idealized picture of man, but with the faith of a Christian believing in what God's grace could do in man and through man. (3) As against legalism he saw sin, not as something external in deed or dereliction, not as a legalistic failure in keeping rules of conduct, but as a matter of inner spirit and attitude. (4) As against mere humanism and moralism, he saw the religious meaning of sin, sin as man's central life-attitude, his refusal to take his life from God and yield it to God, the refusal of obedience and faith.

All this was not original with Paul. But his insight went deeper; he fused the scattered insights into unity, related them to his gospel of grace and the spirit, and so gave permanent direction to Christian thought.

Chapter Three

SALVATION THROUGH RIGHT RELATIONS

CHRISTIANITY is first of all a gospel, the good news about God's purpose for men, about what he has done for men and what he will do that they may have life. This is what we mean by salvation: the gift of life through the help of God, and deliverance from the evil which threatens and destroys life. With this question men everywhere are deeply concerned today. It is true that they do not use the religious terms and they do not usually think of God; but in all lands there is a deep sense of evil, present and impending, and a conviction that humanity must find the right way out or be lost. And there is a growing sense that this right way means some high and enduring order which man must discover and obey, and some power above man with which he must relate himself. In any case, the sense of need and the search for help are in obvious contrast with the complacency and self-sufficiency which marked our western world a generation ago. Economically, politically, internationally, we are seeking for salvation. And this is equally true of individual life. It is evidenced by the widespread interest in the application of psychology to personal problems. It is seen in the recourse to all manner of cults—spiritualistic, theosophic, and the like. In this sense of need and search for help, our age is strikingly like that to which Paul spoke.

But the Church of today does not seem ready for this situation. The traditional formulations have largely lost their appeal. They do not dominate the preaching of today or furnish peace and strength for living to those within the Church. And that is the final test of any doctrine, whether it can be preached and whether it brings men help. The idea of salvation, then, is not merely Paul's central theme but should be the point of his greatest value for us. Historically it is quite clear that Paul has had more to do with shaping the Church's doctrine of salvation than any other man in history. Part of our difficulty lies right here, for all the major conceptions of salvation claim him as their sponsor and can, indeed, appeal to one or another element or item in his teaching. That is true of Churchly sacramentarianism, eastern mysticism, the evangelical emphasis on grace and faith and the atonement, pietism's concern with individual experience and the work of the Spirit, and the varied forms of apocalypticism. We need then to consider Paul's conception of salvation, viewed as a whole and in its central emphasis, and seen first of all as the gospel preached to others and the faith by which he himself found saving help.

The Christian idea of salvation, often narrowly conceived, is in fact a very broad concept. It embraces individual and social, the single soul and the new humanity, mystical and ethical, the beginning of the Christian life and its ever-recurring needs, God's movement in history and that which lies beyond history. We may distinguish three main aspects. (1) Salvation is historical and social; it is something which God is working out in history and for the race. This meaning is reflected in such terms as kingdom of God, people of God, and the Church. (2) It has to do with the individual as God reconciles man to himself and creates a new life within him. (3) It deals with the goal of history and with that which lies beyond history: the final consummation and the eternal kingdom. No one of these aspects can be understood by itself; they are parts of one purpose and process of God, of the one life which he gives to men. They are, however, distinguishable and will be considered in order. We shall begin with the second, where Paul's most notable contribution is to be found. Its two main aspects will be treated in this chapter and the next. Avoiding traditional and technical terms, we may state Paul's position in two theses. (1) Salvation means for man right relations, first with God and then in and through this with all his world. "God was in Christ reconciling the world unto himself"; that is the revolutionary fact in which Paul's religion centers, the fact which discloses the God of grace and calls for man's act of faith. (2) Salvation means remaking. To come into this right and living relation with God means the making of a new man: "If any man is in Christ, he is a new creation."

I. SALVATION IN ISRAEL

The search for salvation was as widespread in Paul's day as in our own. The answers were many and varied, for the question of salvation raises all the great problems of life: the good that we desire, the evil from which we seek deliverance, the God in whom we trust, and the way of deliverance. But first of all we must note briefly the answer which Israel gave. For we shall not understand Paul except as we see him against the background of Judaism and consider how much of this was for him permanent foundation, how much he rejected, and what he found new in Christianity.

1. In the faith of prophet and psalmist Judaism had an answer to these questions which lifted it high above the varied cults of the Graeco-Roman world. There is one God and our

hope is in him. He is no mere hero-god, or half-god, like the
saviors of the mystery religions; he is the living God, creator of
heaven and earth, Lord of men and history. Transcendent and
holy, he is yet merciful, knowing man's frailty, remembering
that man is dust. He asks but one thing: that men shall be
obedient to his righteous will. That will he has revealed to
Israel in the Law. The Israelite who keeps this law may expect
to share in the kingdom of righteousness and peace which God
will establish for his people. Here are notable elements for a
doctrine of salvation. It is religious: the ground of its hope is
God. It is ethical: it looks forward to a new and righteous
order and it demands righteousness of men. It is social: the
whole life of man is to be redeemed. It is historical: the world
of ongoing events is the sphere of God's action, though he is
more than this world.

Needless to say, this conception of salvation had undergone
significant and almost constant change through the years, due
alike to changing conditions without and the development
within of the religious thought and life. Here we are concerned
simply with noting those changes which prepared the way for
Christianity. In its earliest form salvation in Israel concerned
the nation: it was historical-social. That was still the dominant
conception when Jesus came. The disciples' great hope was
"that it was he who should redeem Israel." [1] But "Israel" had
come more and more to mean, not a political entity nor the
racial whole, but the spiritual Israel, a people of God within
the nation. More important still had been the emergence of
the individual. Israel shared here in a general movement in
the Mediterranean world, a movement in which the older sense
of solidarity found place for a new awareness of the individual

[1] Lu. 24:21.

personality with its rights and problems, especially in religion. In Israel's case, however, special factors entered in, due to a deeper understanding of religious faith and life by her leaders. The emphasis on the ethical and, even within legalism, upon individual obedience; the deepening of the personal religious life as reflected in the Psalms; the shift from a nation politically viewed to a people religiously considered—that is, from nation to Church; the displacement of the temple by the synagogue as actual center of religious life: these changes not merely brought in the idea of individual resurrection and immortality but prepared men for the quest for individual salvation in this life. At the same time there was the development, under rabbinic guidance, of the elaborate legalistic system, whose observance constituted the daily religious life of the people and with whose ideas of obligation and salvation Paul came into conflict.

2. It is hard for the modern man to recreate for himself the situation which is reflected in Paul's discussion of Christian salvation as against Jewish legalism, or to appreciate the revolution in religion for which he stands. His interpretation of Judaism and particularly of the Pharisaic system has been sharply criticized. Thus the distinguished Jewish scholar, C. G. Montefiore, insists that Paul could not have been a real rabbinic Jew. Paul represents the law as an intolerable burden, finding freedom and joy in leaving it behind; but "the core and essence of the Rabbinic religion are contained in that one familiar phrase, 'the joy of the commandments.' " "It was not, so to speak, God in his capacity as severe judge or as awful master who had given to Israelites his Law; it was God as loving and merciful. It was the grace of God which was made visible in the Law." Its source was a personal and good God.

Its observance meant life, happiness, satisfaction, peace. And as to man's failures, Rabbinic Judaism took a common sense view: man could not keep all the law, but God was merciful and delighted in repentance and would forgive. "Paul must have been less than a Rabbinic Jew, and more." [2] Jesus, we are told, really stood with rabbinic Judaism in proclaiming faith in God and obedience to the law as one, and as the way of salvation.

The historic question is interesting here but not the most important. As Montefiore admits, the sources on which he depends for his account of rabbinic teaching were not reduced to writing until several hundred years after Paul's time, the report having come down through oral tradition. How many changes had taken place in those first centuries of our era! Jerusalem had fallen. Its people had been dispersed. The interest in proselytes had disappeared. Apocalypticism (in the main a lay theology) had gone from Judaism, and there had been the long period of controversy with Christianity by which, we may assume, both had been affected. On the other hand, we need Montefiore's words to help us to a true picture of the spirit and practice of Jewish piety. But Paul is not without appreciation of this or share in it. He has a deep pride in his race: "Israelites; whose is the adoption, and the glory, and the covenants, and the giving of the law, and the service of God, and the promises; whose are the fathers, and of whom is Christ as concerning the flesh." [3] "The giving of the

[2] C. G. Montefiore, *Judaism and St. Paul*, pp. 29–31, 66. So also Joseph Klausner, *From Jesus to Paul*, pp. 496 ff. Klausner's interpretation of Paul falls definitely below his work on *Jesus of Nazareth*. His failure lies in his almost entire disregard of the profound religious experience which Paul underwent and the deeper problems which he faced.

[3] Rom. 9:4, 5.

law" is a part of this pride. But Paul is pursuing a special polemic purpose in Galatians, fighting for the very existence of his gospel. And in Romans he is concerned with bringing out one particular point, for him a vital one. The validity of his criticism of legalism, which we shall later consider, is not contingent upon his giving a complete picture of Judaism.

Our concern, like Paul's, is with the underlying principles of two contrasted systems, and with the significance of his basic conception as to a new way of salvation. For most men religion, in belief and practice, is a matter of compromise and adjustment. Incongruous principles are joined together because no one principle is made basic and determinative. It is characteristic of the great spirits that they strive for some final insight and, having found it, have the courage to live by it while others scoff at them as idealists or dreamers or fanatics. Such was Jesus. His was the great insight that the God of heaven and earth was infinite good will, a free, self-giving, redemptive love. He saw men about him who said this in words, for it was no new thing to call God Father; but they were far from seeing its full meaning and even farther from accepting its full consequence for life. They said our Father, but they were filled with care about meat and drink as though there were no such God; and they refused to live with men in the spirit of this Father. Paul was a consistent and thoroughgoing Jew. He took the basic principle of current Judaism and submitted it to the severest of tests, that of building life on its rigorous application.

3. The basic principle of the Judaism which Paul knew and practised was legalism. That remains true even if one speaks with Montefiore of "the joy of the commandments." Legalism carried with it the high persuasion that God was a

God of righteousness and that he demanded righteousness of his people; without righteousness there could be no right relation with a righteous God. But there are certain searching questions to be raised here, and these apply not simply to Judaism but to all those legalistic compromises into which Christianity has constantly tended to fall, in the early Church, in Catholicism, nascent and full grown, and again and again in Protestantism.

The first question is: what is the righteousness which this God demands? The answer is given for Judaism in the law: in definite and detailed rules God has revealed to men what he desires. These are not ideals or principles; they are specific rules of conduct. They are not limited to the ethical: prescriptions as to ritual, diet, ceremonial purity, crops, and clothing are joined together with lofty moral ideals and religious teaching. No principle of distinction or of relative values is laid down: obedience is demanded for all. Indeed, just as soon as the divine demand is thought of in terms of rules, two results almost inevitably follow: the loss of any principle by which to distinguish greater and lesser, ethical and ritual, and an externalism which misses the essentials of the spirit. Legalism as such tends to subordinate the ethical and the spiritual. The criticism of legalistic religion at this point is found more in Jesus' teaching than with Paul. It was Jesus who pointed out how easy it was to tithe mint and anise and cummin, and to neglect justice and mercy and faith.[4] He showed how the lust in the heart might be present while the law against adultery was scrupulously kept. With the strictest of legalists he demanded righteousness, but he called for a higher righteousness which transcended legalistic observance.[5] Paul does not

[4] Matt. 23:23.   [5] Matt. 5:20–6:18; 23:16–28.

bring out these defects of legalism as an ethic, for his concern was with legalism as a way of salvation; but the higher ethic of the spirit appears clearly with him, as we shall see, when he sets forth the Christian way of life.

The second question to be put to legalism is this: How do you think of God? The God of Judaism was, of course, no mere judge and distributer of penalties and awards. The very giving of the law to Israel was to them an act of grace. And there was a place for repentance and forgiveness, as Montefiore suggests, for its Scriptures had noble passages like Hosea 11, Psalm 103, and Isaiah 55. But as God's great deed was the gift of the law and his great demand was obedience, so the dominant conception of God was that of sovereign ruler. If mercy came in, it was as a concession to human weakness, an incidental modification of the main matter, that of law and obedience.

The third question is that of salvation. What hope does legalism hold out for men, and what help does it offer? For the Jew salvation meant in the main that which God was to give, alike to the individual as to the nation, at the end. But what is the use of a promise of reward when you cannot meet the conditions? Law, obedience, and reward, that is legalism's doctrine of salvation. But that is too simple a solution. It overlooks the crucial point, and that is man himself. The salvation we need is something that will deal with us, and deal with us now. I am two men, says Paul, who portrayed *Dr. Jekyll and Mr. Hyde* long before Robert Louis Stevenson. I know the law and approve it, and then I follow the evil. If salvation is the reward of righteousness then I am lost, for so long as I am this kind of a man I cannot keep the law.

II. THE CHRISTIAN ANSWER: GRACE

Now, Jesus had arrived at a solution of this problem, not by Paul's long and arduous road, but by his own clear intuition of the heart of God. And Jesus had given the answer in his dealings with men and in his teachings, though apparently it was not directly from this that Paul gained the light. You can do one of two things with sinful men. You can say: first make yourself good and then I will admit you to fellowship. Or you can say: come, join our fellowship, that you may become good. Jesus took the latter way and, to the scandal of the "righteous," Jesus received sinners and ate with them. And when the orthodox protested, Jesus, according to Luke, told them three stories.[1] Thus he pointed out a new way of salvation through the creative power of forgiveness and fellowship. It was paradoxical but true: God receives men as his sons in order that he may make them sons.

That is essentially the position at which Paul arrived. How did he gain it? He gained it through Christ, even though it was not from the Master's words. "Who shall deliver me?" he cries out at the close of his tale of moral defeat, and adds, "I thank God through Jesus Christ our Lord." Paul's doctrine of the cross calls for treatment by itself. It is enough to point out here that it was his vision of the mercy of God, coming to men in Christ and manifested in his death, which led him to this idea of salvation.

Let us put this thought in modern terms. Salvation is life. And life is always a matter of right relations, whether you think of the body in relation to food and air, and in inner

[1] Lu. 15.

organic adjustment; or of social man in the relations of home and community, of the economic and political world; or of man as spirit in relation to the world of the Spirit. In all man's relations God is supreme and determinative, underlying all else and transcending all else. "To know God is to live," to have God is to have all else as well. And this God we may have. By earning the right through obedience? No, only by the fact that he is the love which freely gives, and that by his giving he fits us for his love. Paul put it this way: God is a God of saving grace; his mercy comes to us in Jesus Christ and in Christ's death which was for men. What we cannot achieve God gives. By his forgiveness we gain what we had before sought to earn through the impossible way of obedience to a system of law. The one response that is needed is that of faith, faith as trust and decision and devotion. But once this is given, once man enters through God's forgiveness upon this relation of son with the Father, then that is achieved which we had sought before in vain. It is not that righteousness is disparaged or discarded; it is rather that righteousness ceases to be a mere command above us and becomes the reality and power of a new life within us.[2]

There are five words in particular in which Paul sets forth the meaning of this new way of life: grace, faith, love, the Spirit, and the Church. We have here to deal more especially with the first two. The story of words is an interesting one, the tale of their meaning and function, their use and misuse, and the fate that easily overtakes them. They are vessels bringing the insights of the past, gained at the cost of toil and prayers and tears. They bind the living together, just as they unite us with the past and make us its heirs. But we easily forget two

[2] Rom. 8: 1–16.

facts about words, especially in the realm of religion: they do not represent given quanta of truth, nor are they exact in form and definite in content; they are symbols by which we seek to express or suggest what can never be exactly defined, and they are always living and growing and changing, unless they have become dead and useless. It is not easy to state rightly the meaning which these terms had for Paul. They have been worn smooth with long usage and are too commonly identified with the content given them in traditional theology. Our first task is to recover the vital and rich religious content which Paul gave to them.

We begin with the word grace. Paul saw that the great matter in religion was man's relation to God and that it was the nature of God which determined the question of that relation. If we think of God as an indifferent Olympian, then his attention and favor must be won with gifts. If he is an angry ruler, whose subjects have denied his rights, then he must be appeased by offerings or propitiated by sacrifice. If he is the great lawgiver, the administrator of a moral realm, then the supreme requirement will be obedience. But Paul had seen a new light upon the character of God and his attitude toward men. It had come to him through the death of Christ and his vision of the risen Lord. If God had raised Jesus from the dead, then Jesus was the one sent of God. Then his death, though the deed of evil men, lay within the purpose of God. So, long before any doctrine of the atonement had been set forth by the Church, Paul, with the rest of that first generation, saw in that death the deed of a God of mercy and the revelation of his love. Grace is Paul's word for this love of God in relation to sinful men.

Paul uses the Greek word for grace, as we do the English,

with a variety of meanings, two of which may be noted. In a secondary sense, it refers to that which follows from the love of God, to the "gifts of grace" which he bestows, the spiritual help by which the Christian lives. This is grace in us. But its primary meaning for Paul is that undeserved love of God which goes out to man in forgiveness, which receives him in fellowship, and which creates in him the new life. This is grace for us, and here is the heart of the Christian conception of God. It does not exclude the great prophetic doctrine of the God of holiness and majesty and power. This latter remains fundamental for Paul, as it was for Jesus; indeed, here is the wonder of God's grace that it is the holy and righteous God who thus has mercy. This undeserved redemptive love is the distinctive element in Paul's thought of God and the ground of his doctrine of salvation. It is not a matter of an occasional act of mercy which softens the demands of justice. It is not a special favor extended to one people, as in the giving of the law to Israel. Rather, it is that from which all God's action springs in relation to all peoples. Upon this grace alone man's confidence rests, not upon a combination of God's mercy and man's deserving. In this he trusts for forgiveness and acceptance with God. Upon this he depends in all the enterprise of Christian life and service.

III. THE MEANING OF FAITH

If God is this kind of a God, a Being at once of transcendent righteousness and boundless mercy, then the only adequate answer on man's part will be faith, a faith which is confident trust and absolute devotion. Grace and faith are Paul's two great words for the relation of God and man, just as love is his supreme word for the relation of men to each other. And these three terms form a vital unity in which each finds its meaning and completion in the others. Faith for Paul is the total response to God of heart and mind and will and is so basic to every expression of the Christian life that Paul can say, "Whatsoever is not of faith is sin." [1]

The word faith was not new in Paul's day; it had had a long history and it carried various meanings. Paul himself uses it in more than one sense, but the distinctive meaning which it had for him is that just indicated and this is vital for his doctrine of salvation.

1. Faith, for Paul, involves an activity of the mind. It requires apprehension and insight. It is no blind acceptance of authority or passive submission to power. The gospel is a word that is spoken, spoken by a Person to a person, and so it calls for understanding. In his anxiety to escape humanism and to affirm the reality of revelation, Karl Barth tends to eliminate this aspect. He speaks of revelation as a one-way road, of the word that comes "perpendicularly from above," and of faith as the empty room (the vacuum—*Hohlraum*) into which this word falls. He declares that we are not to speak of knowledge but only of acknowledgment. Barth is right in holding that faith involves the idea of a God who speaks, and is submission to this Word. But speech means a word with meaning, and thus involves not merely acknowledgment but insight and understanding. Faith is the obedience of a man who has heard God *speak* and has heard God speak *to him*. That this is the work of God's Spirit does not alter the matter. Faith thus springs from inner conviction and roots in inner certainty; it is free and open-eyed response, not a blind submission. We must,

[1] Rom. 14:23.

however, keep in mind Paul's emphasis, which Barth has rightly taken up: faith is *response* to the word of God as it thus reaches man, a response of awareness and understanding as well as of will, the answer of spirit to spirit. It is neither a conclusion reached by reflective reason nor an act of wishful thinking in denial of reason. Faith is a real knowing, but it is a knowing of insight and imagination such as came to Paul when he looked upon Christ and saw "the light of the knowledge of the glory of God." [2]

2. Faith, with Paul, means trust. In its broadest sense faith is the conviction that the universe at heart is morally sound and dependable, that man has something upon which to build his life. It is the final tragedy of mankind when it concludes that it can depend upon nothing but force and guile. Join that to selfishness, in individuals and nations, and you have the rampant paganism of our day and the ground for its mood of despair. For prophetic religion faith means belief in a righteous, merciful, and faithful God. In the Old Testament, interestingly enough, the dominant reference is not to man's faith but to God's faithfulness.[3] That, indeed, is the crucial matter. But the conclusion is always at hand: the faithfulness of God demands faith of man. Faith and faithfulness belong together. For Paul faith is the answer to the faithful God who comes to us in Christ. When man sees God as grace, then the only right answer is faith as trust. The object, of course, is not a proposition but a Person; faith is person answering to Person. Hence we must call it a perversion of the Christian position when, as has so often happened, Church, or doctrine, or Scripture has been set up as the object of faith.

[2] I Cor. 2:6–16; II Cor. 4:6. Cf. Heb. 11:1.
[3] Deut. 7:9. Cf. I Thess. 5:24; I Cor. 10:13.

3. Faith, for Paul, is an act of will and an attitude of life; without the decision of the will it is not faith. If religion is not unthinking action, neither is it mere intellectual contemplation or emotional mood. It is man making the basic decision on which all his life is to rest. As insight calls for trust, so trust calls for decision, and the decision is the surrender of life to God. Sin is life oriented to the world of things and centered in self. The first denies God, the second refuses him. As sin is man's "no" to God, so faith is man's "yes." Faith as man's "yes" to the highest is essentially ethical; it is, indeed, the basic moral act of a man's life and the spring of all morality. For what confronts man in God is not only the love in which he may trust, but the good which he must obey. The goodness in which he trusts is the goodness which demands at once the initial act of surrender and the life attitude of obedience. The moral deed is not the supplement of the religious faith. Faith does not call for works to complete it; faith is itself a work, a moral decision and the source of all moral activity. As it is a surrender to love in its response to God, so it is necessarily an expression of love in its relation to men. If the second does not follow, then the first does not really obtain. When faith is misconceived in intellectualistic and authoritarian fashion, when it is made to be an acceptance of doctrine by submission to authority, then, having been robbed of its truly ethical element, it must needs be completed by a moral supplement; and so we have the faith plus works of Roman Catholic teaching. But it is not so with Paul. Of the three great words—grace, faith, and love—which might well be called the three points that determine the circle of Paul's religious thought, there is not one which does not have a definite ethical connotation while having at the same time its primary religious significance.

4. There are, of course, other senses in which Paul uses the word faith. (1) In Romans 3:3 he speaks of "the faith of God," using it to mean faithfulness after noble Old Testament fashion; and it may mean this in man when he includes it in the list of the fruits of the Spirit in Galatians 5:22. For the faith which means an act of will involves faithfulness as an abiding attitude of will. (2) He thinks of it as the energizing, or dynamic, source of life. So he speaks of "faith working (literally, becoming active, energetic) through love." "That life which I now live in the flesh," he says, "I live in faith." [4] (3) Because faith is so central for Paul, he uses it sometimes to designate the Christian life as such. He urges the Corinthians to "stand fast in the faith," to see whether they are "in the faith," which he apparently equates with the "Jesus Christ is in you" in the same verse. These, like the "continue in the faith" to the Colossians, do not refer to correct doctrine but to faithful Christian living, as is clear when he speaks of "progress and joy in the faith." [5] (4) Finally, "*the* faith" was used occasionally by him, as we frequently use it today, to represent that which he preached, which he offered to men for their acceptance. So he writes of preaching the faith and of "the word of faith, which we preach." [6] And so faith can be used to denominate the Christian religion as such, as when he speaks of "the household of the faith." [7]

5. It might seem that at this last point Paul paved the way for that misconception of faith which has made it the obedient acceptance of revealed truth, as in Roman Catholicism. Faith, says *The Catholic Encyclopedia*,[8] is first and objectively "the

[4] Gal. 5:6; 2:20.
[5] I Cor. 16:13; II Cor. 13:5; Col. 1:23; Phil. 1:25.
[6] Gal. 1:24; Rom. 10:8.   [7] Gal. 6:10.   [8] Vol. V, p. 753.

sum of truths revealed by God in Scripture and tradition, which the Church presents to us in a brief form in her creeds; subjectively, faith stands for the habit or virtue by which we assent to these truths." But Protestantism, too, has often lapsed into the same position. The Bible as a sum of supernaturally communicated truth, or some particular confession as the authoritative statement of these truths, or even some collection of "the fundamentals" constituted faith "objectively," while faith "subjectively" was the obedient acceptance of these truths. Does not Paul speak of *the* faith in similar fashion? And does he not declare, "If thou shalt confess with thy mouth Jesus as Lord, and shalt believe in thy heart that God raised him from the dead, thou shalt be saved"? [9]

We are confronted here with the whole problem of the place of religious beliefs in Christianity, the answers to which run from a moralistic or romantic "creedless Christianity" to a rigid confessionalism. And akin to this is the question as to the place of the historical. Does Christianity depend on certain historical facts and require belief in them? Certainly the Christian religion involved for Paul the element of belief. What is a "creedless Christianity," a religion without a *credo,* with no "I believe"? If it has no informing content of thought, its essence must be found either in the realm of action or in that of feeling. It may be a vague emotionalism or mysticism. It may be an equally vague search for the good life, lacking definite content or standard, without authority beyond individual opinion or desire, and without assurance of present help or future achievement. Or it may be a shallow "activism," as is charged by continental theology against American Church life. Paul represents the true Christian position. All high religion holds

[9] Rom. 10:9, 10.

the conviction that the Power which rules is a Being that is good; and that means a life in which conviction calls alike for trust and obedience. In prophetic religion this means a personal God, a God of historic purpose and of personal fellowship. In Christianity it means that the goodness of this God, the goal which he has set, and the way of fellowship which he offers are revealed in Jesus Christ. Interpret his significance as you may, bring whatever doctrine of his person you wish, there is no Christianity apart from Christ. And that means the historical Jesus as accepted fact, and the Christ who has for us divine meaning as the one who shows us God and brings God into our life as saving power. That, I think, is what Paul means when he says we are to confess Jesus as Lord and to believe that God raised him from the dead. The alternative to this, for those who cannot close their eyes entirely to history, is a strict relativism, in which Jesus, product of his own age, becomes, not the abiding center, but the occasion or starting point for a historical movement of which we can posit only one definite fact and that is that it moves.

But if there be such an element of conviction or belief, how can this be distinguished from the position which makes the "essence" of Christianity a sum of doctrine, and "saving faith" the submissive acceptance of such doctrine as authoritatively given through Church, Scripture, historic creed, or in the "fundamentals" selected by self-appointed defenders of "the faith"? I think Paul has the answer for this crucial question, and the order of his thought-movement is decisive. (1) The living God has come to men in Jesus Christ; Christ is the word of God which he speaks to men. (2) The Church is here, not to rule over men nor to tell them what to think, but to witness to this God in Christ, so that men may hear, not the

Church, but the living God; and then to exemplify the new life so that men sharing in this fellowship may be enabled to live this life. (3) The object of faith is not an institution or a proposition, but this living God as he speaks to the soul of man; and faith is man's answer in trust and obedience to the God who has thus spoken.

IV. A NEW CONCEPT OF RELIGION

It is very easy, in the study of Paul, to lose oneself in the minutiae of discussion and miss his profound central insights. It is as easy in religion as elsewhere to miss the woods for the trees. Perhaps this is especially true with Paul, for he brings many things that seem curious to the man of today, ideas that belong to his Jewish heritage and particularly to his dualistic-apocalyptic world view. It is all the more important then that we realize that in these central doctrines of grace and faith we have, not just a chapter in Paul's theology, but a new concept of religion. It is not that any one aspect of it is new, but that its elements are freed from the incidental and external and are set forth in their simplicity and unity and depth of meaning.

Here in its central religious meaning is the concept of God, answering the ever-renewed questions of man's heart: Does Power mean Goodness too? Is there in the heavens a mercy which I can trust? Is there forgiveness for guilt and healing of soul? Is there help for my need? And can I say *Thou* to him? Can I lift my heart in prayer, or even, humbly, walk in fellowship with the Eternal? And Paul's answer is in the word grace, or love. He points to Christ and says, Here is God speaking to you, God searching for you, God offering mercy and calling you into fellowship.

And here is the heart of Paul's concept of religion. What is the true response of man to the Eternal? Is it awe before the Holy, reverence and fear before the Most High? Is it obedience to the Lord of life whose ordering will is the condition of all being and the way to all well-being? Is it the trust of one who discerns this goodness, the love of one who dares to believe that God is the Father of men? Yes, these religious attitudes are all needed and are all included in Paul's conception of faith as at the heart of true religion. For faith with him is not something in itself and by itself which man achieves. It is from first to last oriented in God. It has its source and explanation in God. And it is the one answer that must be made to such a God: humility and penitence in place of pride, dependence instead of self-sufficiency, confident and courageous trust instead of dubiety and fear as man faces his world, the surrender to a supreme loyalty in place of a self-centered existence; and all this not as a deed at the beginning, but as the abiding attitude by which one lives. This is faith; and this is religion. We multiply words perforce as we analyze, but faith was not many things for Paul; it was a single attitude and response called forth by the God who had spoken to him in Christ.

There are other aspects to Paul's doctrine of salvation which we will need to consider. It is not solitary; it is found within the Christian fellowship. It involves the idea not only of moral demand but of a transformation into a new moral-spiritual life. It is concerned with available spiritual forces which work to this end, and Paul has much to say about God's indwelling Spirit and something about sacraments. And beyond the individual and the new life in the fellowship, there is the purpose of God for world salvation which moves on in history and transcends history in its consummation. But here is the living center. At some of the points just noted there is dispute about Paul's meaning and even questions as to permanent validity. Here his teaching is clear and valid, basic to Christianity and in the succession of his Master. It is more than the idea of "God the Father and the infinite value of the human soul," in Harnack's phrase. It is at once simple and profound. It is simple because it sees as the central fact a personal relation with God, the relation of Father and child. It is profound because this God is the God of holiness as of mercy, the God who suffers for us and with us, the God who as righteous God makes his absolute demand upon us and who as Savior and Helper gives what he demands, the God who meets man's sense of guilt and need of forgiveness as sinner and man's need of power for the new life. "God was in Christ reconciling the world unto himself"; "by grace have ye been saved through faith"; "ye are sons, . . . crying Abba, Father"; "faith working through love": in these simple religious expressions Paul declares his message of salvation.[1]

[1] II Cor. 5:19; Eph. 2:8; Gal. 4:6; 5:6.

Chapter Four

SALVATION AS REMAKING

IN ITS simplest meaning, as we have seen, salvation is the help of God given to man so that he may have life. In Christian thought there have always been three broadly distinguishable aspects. (1) Salvation has meant God's grace in forgiveness, bringing men into right relation with himself. (2) It has meant, not just forgiveness of sin, but redemption from sin and the remaking of man; it has meant grace in us as well as for us. (3) Salvation has always had a forward look; it has meant the hope of a new world through God's saving deed, alike in terms of a kingdom of God on earth and of a heavenly realm beyond.

The first aspect was basic for Paul and must remain so for us, for the supreme question of religion is how man can come into living and life-giving relation with God. Not so much attention has been paid to Paul's teaching as to the second aspect of salvation. The evangelical theology inspired by the Reformation was too much engrossed with the doctrine of grace, as opposed to the Roman position, to give this the needed attention. Yet this is just as vital as the other for the ethical monotheism of Christianity. For the word of the Hebrew prophets stands: God is righteous and there can be no true religion without rightness of life. Paul's doctrine of grace did not lose this emphasis; he simply pointed out the way, and the only way, by which a man could attain righteousness. He was concerned, not simply that a man by God's mercy should be accepted as God's child, but that he should become a child of God in actual spirit and life. It was wholly in line with Jesus' word: "Love your enemies, that ye may be sons of your Father. . . . Ye therefore shall be perfect, as your heavenly Father is perfect." [1] The sinner needs forgiveness that he may be received into fellowship with God, but he needs remaking in order that this may be a true fellowship of Father and son.

I. THE NEW EXPERIENCE

The conception of salvation as remaking was not so immediately apparent to the early Church. The new-found faith of the first disciples involved a threefold conviction: Jesus had risen and was the true Messiah; as such he would return to establish the kingdom of God; his death was for us and our sins. For them, as for the Jews generally, salvation meant primarily the world deliverance that lay in the future. Thus Paul indicates to the Thessalonians the meaning of their conversion: "how ye turned unto God from idols, to serve a living and true God, and to wait for his Son from heaven, who delivereth us from the wrath to come." This is from what is perhaps our oldest Christian writing, but even later Paul could write to the Romans: "Now is salvation nearer to us than when we first believed." [1]

Meanwhile, however, the logic of events began to enrich this simple faith. Luke's story of the day of Pentecost is more than the narrative of a one-time experience; it is a dramatic representation of a continuing element in the life of the primitive Christian fellowship, and probably more in the Pauline churches than at Jerusalem. They found that they had something more than a wonderful memory and an inspiring hope.

[1] Matt. 5:44-48.   [1] I Thes. 1:9, 10; Rom. 13:11.

What they hoped for from the future was in a measure with them now. So a later writer refers to those who were "enlightened and tasted of the heavenly gift, and were made partakers of the Holy Spirit, and tasted the good word of God, and the powers of the age to come." [2] In a real sense the age to come was already here. This was not a matter of theology. It was not something planned for. It marked the character of early Christianity as a great creative movement in religion. Though the old world still lay about them and they still awaited the coming deliverance, they found themselves living a new life. Theirs was the sense of forgiveness and peace and joy. Christ was to return. Yet in a real sense the Living Christ was in their midst. They had the power of a new life through the Spirit of God and his gifts. They were members of a new fellowship, the *koinonia* of the Spirit; the new and true people of God was already present on earth.

In all this Paul saw the saving work of God in Christ. His teaching can be understood only as we first see what was here happening, first in his own life, then in his churches. Out of this came the great questions with which he dealt and which theology has come to treat under such terms as justification, regeneration, sanctification, the Church, and the Holy Spirit. Here was a living experience demanding to be understood, to be interpreted as part of his message, in relation to which his churches needed guidance. And here is the matter of our present discussion: salvation as a transforming of human life here and now by the presence and power of God.

How did Paul conceive of this remaking of man? He presents it, not in theological definition, but in various pictures and symbols which tend to pass into one another. Four of

[2] Heb. 6:4, 5.

these may be noted here. (1) The Christian is one who has been created again, made over into a new being. "If any man is in Christ [one with Christ], then there is a new creation: the old things are gone, it is all new." [3] He tells the Galatians that the decisive factor in the new life is not the observing of some rite like circumcision, or omitting it, but being a new creation.[4] (2) The Christian experience is one of dying and being made alive. We have died, he tells the Romans, died to sin; in baptism, we were baptized into Christ's death, buried with him, so that in turn we might be raised from the dead. "You, being dead, . . . did he make alive together with him." And as Christ's new life is a being alive to God, so we must think of ourselves as being "alive unto God, in Christ Jesus." [5] (3) The Christian is one who is in union with Christ. There is a mystical identification with Christ, as man dies with him and is raised with him. Baptism is conceived apparently in no merely symbolical fashion, but realistically as indicating an actual spiritual experience. With a more ethical emphasis, he speaks of walking with Christ in newness of life. (4) Closely related to this Christ mysticism is the idea of the indwelling and re-creating Spirit. Man is made over because there is in him a new mind, a new spirit, and this new spirit is the creation of God's Spirit. It is, in fact, the Spirit of God in man. Romans 8:1–17 presents this most clearly, but its meaning is to be seen only against the background of the preceding chapters. These first chapters show man as sinful, guilty, helpless; God's grace received in faith is the only way out. Then, with the eighth chapter, he considers tne new life upon which man thus enters. Here is more than forgiveness for the past and

[3] II Cor. 5:17.
[4] Gal. 6:15.   [5] Rom. 6:1–11; Col. 2:13; Eph. 2:1–5.

gracious acceptance. Here is a new man, one who walks after the Spirit. Once they had "the mind of the flesh"; now they have "the mind of Christ."

II. THE LIFE OF THE NEW MAN

But what is the life of the new man? Just what is the difference which makes the new creature? The answer is not easy, for Paul presents a bewildering mass of material with no attempt to reduce it to ordered explanation, whether psychological or theological. There is, therefore, a constant temptation for the student to select the aspect that appeals to him and make the rest conform to the pattern chosen. In general, his expressions fall into two groups, which may be termed broadly the mystical and the ethical.

1. And first we consider the mystical. The new man is one who is united with God in Christ. The relation is more than that of personal fellowship constituted by man's response of obedient faith. Paul conceives it realistically and vitally. That is especially seen in connection with the Christ mysticism. The believer has the mind of Christ. He is "in Christ." Paul says flatly: "For me to live is Christ." [1] "It is no longer I that live, but Christ liveth in me." [2] Then again he refers to the Spirit. We are in the Spirit; the Spirit of God dwells in us. We have the Spirit of Christ; we have the mind of the Spirit. These varied phrases, all taken from Romans 8, by their very variety make it plain that Paul is presenting no formal doctrinal scheme. He is referring to an indubitable experience, that of a new life; and he is asserting a profound conviction, that this life is God's work in man. While he moves commonly between

[1] Phil. 1:21. [2] Gal. 2:20.

the two forms of thought, referring now to Christ and now to the Spirit, he makes it perfectly plain that he is dealing with the one reality. It is a single experience to which he refers whether he speaks of God or Christ or Holy Spirit or Spirit of God or of man's having the spirit of Christ.

Of course, we do not have infallible theology here or the consistency of logical system. We have a man trying to indicate to others by sign and symbol what surpassed his comprehension though it had entered into his life. As the sinner was one who lived in the "sphere" of the fleshly, or the natural, which might also mean the positively sinful, so the Christian lived in the "sphere" of the spirit. And this spirit realm meant not just the unseen or something vaguely "divine"; it meant God's Spirit, God as a personal presence and inner power. It meant the spirit of Jesus: love, truth, justice, righteousness, strength, and peace. It meant life in the eminent sense of the word. It was the transcendent God, eternal and holy; but it was this God as he had entered history in Jesus Christ. So this Spirit God is present in the living Christ and in the Church, the Church which is human and fallible but which is also the body of this living Christ and the creation of God's Spirit. The Christian is the man who has been transplanted into this sphere. He does not simply believe in it as something that is to be; his faith is not simply "the assurance of things hoped for," though it is "a conviction of things not seen." Rather, faith unites him with this world now in a living and life-giving bond. He does not simply look forward to it as the world of the coming age; he is already living in it. It is not merely the place of his allegiance; it is the source of life and strength, the inner dynamic. God, the Spirit, Christ, the Church, these all express the reality of this world of the spirit, at once transcendent and present with men. The disciple is a new man because his life is made up of these new relations, new loyalties, and new powers, which come to him in this sphere.

This is the first factor in the new life which makes the disciple a new man: he has entered a new world, the world of the spirit; he is vitally joined to it and shares in its life and its powers.[3]

2. From this mystical and transcendental side we may distinguish the ethical. The new man is one who is made over in spirit and character. For this new world is not simply transcendent power; it is goodness. It is essentially ethical. Its God is love, its life is love. Jesus is its supreme expression. He who has the Holy Spirit has, by that fact, the spirit of Jesus, the spirit of holiness and love. Paul cannot think of it in any other way; the disciple has come under this power and is of this kind. Some of you, he says to the Corinthians, were once adulterers, thieves, drunkards, extortioners; "but ye were washed, but ye were sanctified, but ye were justified in the name of the Lord Jesus Christ, and in the Spirit of our God." [4]

III. THE WAY OF REMAKING

But how, in concrete terms, did Paul think of this change as taking place? We are here at the heart of the problem of salvation. How can men be made over? Many of us are deeply interested in the problem as to how the order of our social life can be changed so as to secure peace among nations and freedom and justice for man. It is, indeed, changing rapidly before our very eyes under the influence of economic, political, and

---

[3] Cf. the illuminating discussion of life dimensions by Karl Heim in his volume, *God Transcendent*. German title, *Glaube und Denken*.

[4] I Cor. 6:9–11.

military forces, which are working as certainly in Britain and America as in the Orient and Germany and Russia. But will the changes serve humanity or destroy it? It is well to concern ourselves seriously with these changes, but it is even more imperative that we shall inquire how the spirit of men and of nations may be changed that they may seek the kingdom of God and his righteousness. Paul's own concern had been with this inner and personal problem. He himself had failed and the failure was due not to the law of God but to the nature of man. Of what avail was the holy law above if within himself was the law of sin and death?

It is not easy to state just how Paul conceived this act or process of change by which sinners were made over into new men, or, indeed, the exact result. His theories are efforts at understanding coming after the event; the event itself was the important matter. Of the fact there was no doubt; he knew it in himself and he saw it in these groups of disciples who had come up out of paganism into the new faith and life. The background of the whole matter is Paul's basic faith: there is a world of spiritual reality and power—the eternal and ever-working God; man is saved through right relation with God, for in that relation the powers of this world work in him; and this God we know in Jesus Christ. But he does indicate how men come into this relation, and what the nature of that relation is through which these saving powers work.

In the higher types of religious life men have thought of this saving relation to the higher world under three categories: the rational, the mystical, and the personal-ethical. These do not, of course, exclude each other, though the emphasis differs, as does the way in which each is conceived. All three elements are present with Paul.

1. To speak of the rational is not to assume rationalism, the idea that man can win all needed truth by his own effort of mind. It does not mean the glorification of knowledge, as though sin were no more than ignorance, and salvation came by information. Least of all does it imply that type of pragmatism which knows no truth.but that of natural science, and sees the progress of man in terms of ever more successful adjustment to the world of space and time. All high religion has a rational element because its God is the God of truth, in whom men see the meaning of the world and life as well as its good and goal. It is no religion of blind submission or unthinking emotion. *Prophetic* religion takes the way of moral and spiritual insight and not of philosophical reflection; it makes insight contingent upon action and sees moral obedience as an organ of knowledge. But in its own way it is as deeply concerned with the truth as is philosophy, and finds it as essential to salvation. It is religion which has gained an insight, and therefore has a message and speaks to the mind of men.

So it is with Paul. The cross does, indeed, seem foolishness to men; it is, in fact, the wisdom of God. Paul has a word of wisdom to speak, he declares, even though the babes at Corinth are not yet able to receive it. He warns the Colossians against a "philosophy" based on "the elements" (probably referring to some kind of astrological cult); yet the christology of Colossians 1:15–20 involves a philosophy of history and of the cosmos, in which Christ offers men the clue to understanding and appears as the one in whom all things "hang together"—a passage to which the prologue of John is closely akin. But the real insight of the gospel is simpler than this; it is the realization that the God of the universe is a God of forgiving love, and that in Christ we see this love as well as God's final purpose for the world. And so faith roots in an insight, an inner conviction which comes when man sees this God in Christ. Nevertheless, though the rational is present, it is not the primary category with Paul to indicate the nature of the new relation between God and man.

2. It has been held by many recent writers that the mystical is the dominant element in Paul's conception of salvation. The question demands a separate discussion, but we must at least indicate his position at this point. In its wider sense, mysticism is the immediate awareness of God or, more particularly, the sense of God's presence in the soul of man. As such it belongs to all religion, for whatever the road that is taken the goal of religion is to bring man to this awareness. In the stricter sense, in what may be called extreme or metaphysical mysticism, the goal is a union with God conceived not in terms of an ethical-personal relation, but as a merging of being, a realistic oneness, in which, for the time at least, the distinction of persons disappears and the soul of man is merged into the being of the Eternal. Mysticism of this type is in direct contrast with prophetic religion, whose emphasis is on the personal, the ethical, and the social, alike as to the relation between man and God and between man and his fellows.

So we come to the central issue: what does Paul rely upon for the making over of man? His dependence, of course, is upon God, upon spiritual forces and not upon man's moral effort. But how do these forces enter into human life? Is it through the personal relation established by faith or is it by some type of mystical union? The answer is not so simple. Albert Schweitzer is sure that it is by way of a mystical union with Christ realistically conceived, and that the ethical is never derived by Paul from the righteousness by faith. And there is much in Paul to support this. The modern liberal mind, if it does not repudiate Paul entirely at this point, is prone to interpret as picture and symbol many of the expressions which Paul, in the manner of his day, conceived in quite realistic fashion. In some realistic sense, for Paul, the believer has died with Christ to the world of sin, and in turn has risen with Christ. He is one with Christ, not just in moral obligation and loyalty, but in some actual sense in his very nature. Paul uses various symbols for this union. Besides the being buried and rising, which he relates to the symbol of baptism, he speaks of being crucified with Christ: "we died with Christ" he says flatly. We are made dead to the law in order to be "joined to another." And so Christ lives in us and we in Christ. He speaks of "Christ, who is our life." [1] Something new has come in as presence and power to dominate the believer's life. "For me to live is Christ." [2]

But two very important considerations enter in here. The first is the variety of expressions: being in the Spirit, the Spirit of God dwelling in us, having the Spirit of Christ, and Christ in us. These are alternative terms united by the one thought of the living presence and power of God in the believer. Schweitzer has rightly said: "Paul never speaks of being one with God or being in God." [3] There is no mysticism here of the classical type, where the soul directly apprehends God and enters without any mediation into relation with him. But it is another matter to set Paul's Christ-mysticism over against a God-mysticism, or to find it analogous to the union with the hero-god in the mystery religions. Paul regards Christ and the Spirit as *mediating* God to us; but they are not *intermediaries*

[1] Col. 3:4.   [2] Phil. 1:21.
[3] *The Mysticism of St. Paul.* So Weiss, *Das Urchristentum,* p. 397.

coming between man and God so that man's contact is only with them and not with the transcendent .God. They do not come in place of God, but they bring God to men. God did not simply send his Son; God was *in* Christ, Christ is God in history. So the Spirit is God present and in action. Whatever later trinitarian speculation may have done with the idea, for Paul the Spirit means the presence and power of God himself in man. If he speaks of Christ in us and the Spirit in us, he can also say "it is God who worketh in you." [4] Here is part of Paul's great advance: if for earlier thought the Spirit was a power or force which a distant God sent down to men as a special gift, or for a special task, for Paul it meant the presence of God himself. The Spirit that dwells in us and that gives us life is "the Spirit of him that raised up Jesus from the dead." [5]

As to the analogy with the mystery religions: true, in them, too, there is a union of the worshipper with his god. But there is no thought of any relation with the God of the heavens and the earth, that is, with God in the absolute sense, whereas for Paul Christ brings us into living relation with this God. Better stated, God, sending Christ, present in him and acting through him, unites man with himself. [6] The Christ mysticism of Paul is not a departure from monotheism.

The second consideration is fully as important: Is Paul's mysticism a departure from the ethical? In other words, does Paul think of this process of making men over as something accomplished in some mysterious and directly miraculous fashion, apart from a consciously personal and ethical relation? The mystery religions did so conceive it. So, in principle, does classical mysticism. The world of conscious choice, of moral reflection and decision, the world of the human and social, is

[4] Phil. 2:13.   [5] Rom. 8:11.   [6] II Cor. 5:19, 20.

left behind in the flight of the alone to the Alone, a flight whose goal is not the achievement of moral personality but the loss of individual personality in the depths of the divine. The ethical-personal is not without its place in the life of the mystic, but it is not the highest and not the way to the Most High. And in the mystery religions the ethical had small place, if any, as means, and no place in the goal. We find in them the striking phrase, *in aeternum renatus*, but it does not mean being transformed into a new life in terms of moral character.

3. We consider then the place of the ethical in man's remaking. The striking fact is that you can hardly find a mystical passage in Paul which does not include an ethical reference or implication. Confessedly it would be a total misconception of Paul to take his insistence on high ideals and his constant moral exhortation and from these to conclude that Paul's religion is simply one of ethical idealism and moral effort. It involves an equal misconception to isolate the mystical passages and assume that for Paul salvation is through a mystical union of a metaphysical kind which by that act or experience so changes the nature of man as to produce salvation. Paul does, indeed, go to the limit in expressing the identity of the believer with Christ, and his realistic mode of thinking seems to give to this a meaning we today find it not so easy to hold. But one fact is clear: it has for Paul at every point an ethical aspect. What does he mean when he says that the disciple has died with Christ; that he, Paul, has been crucified with Christ? Is this a matter of mystical identity realistically conceived? Yes, but he also speaks of this dying, like the living, as a daily matter in which we have an active part to play; that is, as ethical. When he writes of "always bearing about in the body the dying of Jesus, that the life also of Jesus may be manifested in our body," he is referring to his daily experiences of labor and suffering, and the

daily expression of the quality of moral spirit which he associated with Jesus.[7] What we have is really a *faith* mysticism. In a very real sense the believer, for Paul, is united with God in Christ; God dwells in him by the Spirit and all his life is from God. But this mysticism is neither an ecstatic experience in which the self is lost in God, nor an impersonal affair in which by some mysterious action the soul substance is transformed. Man is joined to God by an act of faith, that is, by a personal act of obedient trust. The relation is thus both mystical and ethical. For that reason the union must be renewed day by day in a continuing attitude of faith in which man trusts in God and so receives the grace of God in living fellowship.

That is why Paul constantly speaks of the Christian life in two forms of expression which, at first glance, seem quite incongruous. In the one he refers to the new life as an accomplished fact: the Christian has died to sin, has crucified the flesh; he no longer lives but Christ lives in him; the old man is dead, he is a new creation in Christ. In the other there is a constant summons to action: because they have died to sin they are to live to righteousness; because the old man is dead they are to put to death their "members which are upon the earth"; because they live by the Spirit they are to walk by the Spirit.[8]

What we have then in Paul's conception of the remaking of man is that union of the ethical and religious, the active and the mystical, which informs his whole conception of religion. Men are made over by God's deed, by his Spirit given to them, by his power working in them, by union with the living Christ. These are all expressions for the one fact, that it is possible for man so to enter into relation with God that the transcendent

[7] I Cor. 5:7–16.
[8] Gal. 5:24, 25; Rom. 6:2; 7:6; Col. 2:20; 3:5; II Cor. 4:10; Phil. 3:10–14.

world of the spirit and its forces become operative in him. It is salvation with which we deal here, not merely ethical ideals and moral effort. But it is just as important to note that this saving relation is for Paul a personal relation, that this relation makes an ethical demand not only initially in faith, but as that which must constantly be affirmed and expressed, and that its result and its test are an ethical quality of life.

Obviously, it is the central problem of a doctrine of salvation and of religion itself which here appears: how can divine and human be united, how can God and man come together in a life which shall be at once the gift of God and the autonomous and free life of man? Has Paul solved this problem and given us a consistent and clear expression of the Christian position? That would be too much to expect from the first man in the Christian succession who realized the essential place of both aspects and sought to give them interpretation. But he has given us the basic principles and pointed the way to an answer for what will always be a crucial question for Christian thought.

The dominant categories for Paul, then, in interpreting the religious relation and the remaking of man, are those of prophetic religion rather than those of traditional mysticism, while at the same time he gives a much larger place to the idea of a communion with the divine which is intimate, dynamic, and life-transforming.

IV. ABSOLUTE AND RELATIVE

From this position we can best understand what seems at first like a curious inconsistency, or self-contradiction, which runs through Paul's writings. On the one hand, he is always speaking of the Christian life in the absolute sense, as *fait accompli.* The Christian is a new creation, already transplanted into the kingdom of God's Son. He has died to sin, and is now alive to God. His life is hid with Christ in God. He has put off the old man and put on the new man; sin no longer rules over him. He has the mind of Christ, the mind of the Spirit which is life and peace.

But the empirical Christian in Paul's churches seems to be a very different man, as Paul knows right well. The Corinthians whom he addresses as saints and sanctified seem to be a rather sorry lot, with their pride and contentions and relative indifference to sexual immorality in their own number; and the apostle deals very plainly with these defective disciples. Paul speaks in absolutes but he sees clearly enough the relative. What is more important, he makes place for the relative in his conception of the Christian life. That is the meaning of all those moral imperatives which we have been considering. He is always joining with the assertion of the absolute the recognition of the relative. You have put off the old man and put on the new; therefore you must put to death "your members which are upon the earth." The Christian is one in whom Christ dwells, therefore they are to put on the Lord Jesus Christ and to have in them the mind of Christ.

If Paul were dealing here with the categories of substance and essence and impersonal "nature," categories which are common in mysticism and sacramentarianism, then there would be an insoluble contradiction. In that case it would be a clear either—or. It is quite otherwise if you employ, as he does, the categories of prophetic religion, the personal and ethical and vital. Here is no mere change of legal status or of metaphysical substance or nature. Salvation means life. Men are set into a new relation, a new life-giving fellowship; that is the divine deed, that is something absolute. But to have this life you must live it, to receive it you must in turn affirm it and express it; that is the human aspect, that is something finite and relative and growing. Not contradiction but polarity is the mark of this life. Contradiction is a logical term, polarity belongs to empirical existence, belongs to it on every level but most of all on the highest level, that of an ethical-spiritual life which is lived in relation with God. This life has its two sides, independence and dependence, human freedom and God's determination, man's constant decision and effort and God's ever-needed grace and power. It is always, and all of it, God's gift and man's task. And so with present and future: the Christian belongs wholly to God by his surrender and God's deed of acceptance and renewal; but if this is to be a living reality it must be renewed with each day. Such a life is always absolute in demand, relative in achievement. It is related to the Infinite with its absolute demands, but it is lived in the finite with its limited strength and its limiting conditions. And like all life it is under the law of growth. So Paul declares that for him to live is Christ, that Christ is his life; yet he looks forward to the time when he may lay hold of that for which Christ has laid hold of him, meanwhile pressing on as one who has not yet attained. Under the tension of this polarity all Christian life is lived, a life in which unceasing effort is joined to confidence, in which no day passes that a man need not pray, "Forgive us our sins," and no day in which he may not pray with quiet confidence, "Our Father, thy kingdom come."

V. AS TO PERFECTIONISM

Against this background we can answer the question as to Paul's attitude toward the matter of a possible Christian perfection to be achieved in this life. In the history of the Christian Church this doctrine has commonly appeared in two broadly contrasted forms. The first has a marked legalistic and often negative character. Its great text is: "Ye shall be holy; as I am holy." [1] It tends to be rigoristic, puritanic, ascetic. It has appeared in many smaller separatist groups. The second approach is more evangelical. It lays the primary stress upon what God does for man by his Spirit. With Paul it sees that the Christian life means being made over and not simply being forgiven. Its argument is simple: God demands of us a holy life, a life that is free from all sin and that conforms, within and without, to the spirit of love that was in Christ. The Christian does not obtain this with his conversion. He needs then a "second work of grace." For this cannot come of man's will and effort; what God asks he must give. And he will give it by his Spirit destroying the old evil nature in us and creating the new man in Christ. And since this work is all of God and depends solely upon him, we may expect it to be done completely and at once if we ask in faith believing, surrendering ourselves wholly to God. To think otherwise is to limit the power of God.

The first form is clearly a desertion of Paul's great and liberating gospel of salvation by grace alone through faith. The support of Paul for the second might seem at first to be quite clear. He speaks of the Colossians as those whom the Lord is to present "holy and without blemish and unreprovable." The New Testament Greek word for perfect is *teleios*. It refers to those who have reached the *telos*, the goal, or end. He knows that his converts are still babes, but he speaks also of the mature, or perfect (*teleioi*). He says to the Thessalonians, the

[1] I Pet. 1:16; Lev. II:44.

Lord is to "establish your hearts unblamable in holiness before our God" at the coming of Christ. The Corinthians are to cleanse themselves "from all defilement of flesh and Spirit, perfecting holiness in the fear of God." [2]

Nor does he speak of this as a remote ideal, impossible for this life, for back of this is his deep conviction as to those powers of the world of the spirit which are available for every believer. He is thinking of God, not just of man. If he exhorts the Thessalonians to abstain from every form of evil and to live together with Christ, it is always with the emphasis upon the Lord who will establish their hearts unblamable in holiness, the God of peace who will sanctify them wholly, and the law of the Spirit of life which makes men free from the law of sin and death. "Faithful is he that calleth you, who also will do it." [3]

In the end, however, it is plain that Paul is not on the side of this second type of perfectionism. He holds, indeed, to the absolute demand and to the God who works in us by his Spirit and gives what he requires. But he sees clearly the two other elements already emphasized: (1) The saving work of God is in and through a *personal* relationship into which he has lifted us by his forgiving grace. There is nothing magical, nothing mechanical, no unmediated "direct action" here. What is received from God as the spirit and transforming power of a new life comes, not in a once-for-all deed, but in a continuing fellowship, in a daily life of humility, trust, and dependence, and then only as in turn it is expressed in the obedience of love. So, while Paul affirms the absolutes, he recognizes (2) the relative which belongs to the human factor and the human situ-

[2] Col. 1:22, 28; I Cor. 2:6; Phil. 3:15; I Thes. 3:13; II Cor. 7:1.
[3] I Thes. 3:13; 5:10, 22–24; Rom. 8:2.

ation. He sees the limitations of his "saints" at Corinth. He writes of himself: "Not that I have already obtained [and this applies not simply to the resurrection], or am already made perfect: but I press on"; and adds that those who are "perfect" are to be thus minded.[4]

VI. PRESENT AND FUTURE

One other seeming contradiction must be considered here. Here exist side by side salvation as an eschatological hope and as a present fact. This is not true of Paul alone. Throughout the New Testament, beginning with Jesus' own teaching, though salvation appears as the great deliverance that is to come, yet there is a recognition of the fact that the forces of the new age are already at work. Jesus was proclaiming forgiveness, calling men to live as children of their Father, healing and casting out demons. It seemed as though Satan were already "fallen as lightning from heaven." Men were "tasting the powers of the age to come." The fourth gospel with its solemn declaration that those who believe have already "passed out of death into life" gives special emphasis to this side, but it is everywhere present.[5] And it is notable that it is Paul, Paul with his burning eschatological hope, who presents most fully the facts about this new life and about these spiritual forces in which the power and saving rule of God in men and in the Church are already seen.

The way out for the student of the primitive Church is not to try to secure consistency for Paul either by spiritualizing the eschatological hope on the one hand, or by minimizing the facts

[4] Phil. 3:10–15.   [5] Lu. 10:18; Heb. 6:5; Jn. 5:24.

as to God's saving presence on the other. Paul held to the great Christian hope of a coming redemption. He conceived that hope in the eschatological form of his Jewish heritage. But the logic of facts, of his own experience and that of the Church, was too much for an exclusive eschatological scheme. Side by side with this he sees what God is doing now in saving his people and he rejoices in it though he thinks of this as only for a brief period before the end. That both these conceptions represent something valid and abiding in Christian thought must be noted in a later discussion.

Chapter Five

CHRIST AND THE SAVING
OF MEN

THE WORK of Christ for men has often been conceived as having reference only to his death and to this as related to the forgiveness of sin. Paul's conception is certainly far wider. Salvation for Paul is an all-inclusive concept. It is no mere after-thought of God to correct the evil of man's sin, and no mere matter of a present and individual religious experience. It begins with creation and ends with the overcoming of all evil and the establishment of the rule of God over all things. And for Paul the whole work from beginning to end is related to Christ.

We can distinguish here four stages, or aspects, in Paul's view of this work. First comes creation itself. Christ and his salvation give us the key to the meaning and end of all creation and all history.[1] The incarnation is the next step, culminating in Christ's death and resurrection. It is the act of God's love but at the same time it is Christ's deed: his decision to come to earth, his life of humility and self-giving love, his death, in obedience to God and for the saving of men.[2] The third aspect is seen in everything which this crucified and risen and living Christ means to the believer here on earth: the revelation of God, the judgment of God and his mercy, the vision of the life that is after "the mind of Christ," the gift of that life through the Spirit, and the Church itself as Christ's body and his creation. All these are conceived as the work of God for

[1] Col. 1:16, 17. Cf. John 1:1–3.
[2] Phil. 2:5–8; II Cor. 5:19. Cf. John 1:14; 3:16.

men through Christ, here and now. Finally, there is the work which he is yet to do, for which all else is preparation, the distinctive work of the Messiah as viewed by Jew and Christian alike: the overthrow of the forces of evil in final conflict and the establishment of the kingdom of God.

To discuss the work of Christ, then, would be to cover the whole field of Paul's teaching. Our task here must be a more limited one; nevertheless it deals with the heart of Paul's teaching and its most significant aspects. Of the work of Christ noted above, the first element represents in the main a speculative construction of Paul the theologian, inquiring, indeed, what history and experience mean but going beyond these in trying to see what are some of the ultimate implications of his faith in Christ. The fourth aspect also goes beyond the empirical, taking its particular form from the beliefs of the Judaism of his day. These must be considered later. Our immediate concern is with the meaning of Jesus for salvation as a present experience. Just what does Christ do in bringing life to men and how is it done?

I. THE CENTRALITY OF THE CROSS

For Paul, as for the whole of the early Church, the death of Christ was the central fact in his work for men. That does not mean that it was isolated from his life, or that there was a single and agreed interpretation as to its meaning; it does mean that Paul spoke for the whole Church when he said, "but we preach Christ crucified." Here was his gospel, to others a stumblingblock and foolishness, to Paul "the power of God and the wisdom of God." Let us inquire first how this came to be before we consider its meaning.

The death of Christ was first of all a problem for faith. It was so with Jesus himself. Did Jesus anticipate his death? Did he see in it the culmination of his work, and seek to prepare the disciples for it? Or did it come as an inexplicable tragedy to one who thought of his work as that of the Messiah who was to establish the kingdom, and believed, therefore, that God would give him the triumph over his foes? It is not easy to tell from the gospel sources, for their record was inev'tably affected by the way in which the cross was used in the preaching of a later day. Yet certain conclusions seem fairly to commend themselves. There is a series of passages, not the kind which a later day would have invented, which indicate that Jesus had no clear prevision or settled conclusion as to the end. Such are the temptation narratives, the incidents and teachings at Caesarea Philippi, and the Gethsemane narrative. At the same time they suggest that Jesus early envisaged such a tragic end as possible and sought for its meaning. And unless you deny to the Master the insight given to the disciples, it was he and not just the later Church which found help in the Suffering Servant passage of Isaiah 52:13 to 53:12. This supported his teaching about saving life and losing it, about losing and finding, and about giving life for others as the supreme deed of service. Yet in the end, as the Gethsemane account shows, his answer was less that of an intellectual persuasion and more that of trust in God and obedience to his apparent will. At the same time it would appear that Jesus saw the historical causes of his rejection and what the end would be. "The Roman order, the patriotism of the Zealots, the religious zeal in Pharisaism, representing constant factors in human history, were not evil things, but there was so much evil embedded in them, so much of pride and selfishness, malice and cruelty, blindness and hardness of heart, mixed with their very virtues—that they united in the crime of the cross." [1] To these "constant factors in human history" should be added the fateful influence of vested privilege and power, as represented in the Sadducaic-priestly group, as well as in the religious prestige of the Pharisees and the political power of Rome. Jesus saw in all this far more than his individual fate; he saw that Israel's judgment upon him was in reality their judgment upon themselves, and so God's judgment upon the nation. "Confronted with the absolute of the Kingdom in Jesus, the world by its actions pronounced its own judgment by rejecting it and crucifying him." [2] But there was more than judgment. The God who ruled and overruled was carrying out his purpose. If the way of trust and obedience led to death, then that death was part of God's way and work for man's salvation. So Jesus spoke of himself as giving "his life as a ransom for many." [3]

The death of Christ was plainly a problem for the faith of the disciples; a Messiah destroyed by his enemies seemed a contradiction in terms. It remained a contradiction for those to whom Paul preached: "unto Jews a stumblingblock, and unto Gentiles foolishness." [4] And when we reflect upon it, as we rarely do, it remains one of the most extraordinary facts in human history that these followers of Jesus should not simply have retained their faith in him after his execution as a common criminal at the hands of the authorities, but that they should have put this death at the center of their preaching and made its shameful instrument the symbol of their faith. How did it come about?

---

[1] C. H. Dodd, *History and the Gospel*, p. 134.
[2] *Ibid.* [3] Mk. 10:45.
[4] I Cor. 1:23. Cf. Gal. 5:11, "the stumblingblock of the cross."

Several factors operated to produce this radical change. (1) Decisive was the appearance to them of their Master. Jesus lived. God had raised him from the dead. (2) In him and through him they had come into a new and profound religious experience. They felt that he was in their midst as the power of a new life. The gift of God's Spirit had come to them; the powers of that new age to which they looked forward were even then present. (3) In their new-found faith the death of Christ came to be more and more, not just the deed of evil men whom God overruled by the resurrection, or a dark and troubling mystery, but a center of light and power. The Christ whom they remembered was more and more, not just the gracious friend of Galilean days, or the teacher of parables, but the one whose obedience to God and love of men were seen in his suffering and death. They cherished indeed his sayings and all the incidents of his life, but that last week came to occupy the largest place in their thought, as it did in the later written records. In that death they saw increasingly, not so much an inscrutable decree of God, as a manifestation of God's love. And over against all this they saw a revelation of the depth of evil in man, and of God's judgment as well as his mercy. And while they did not try to explain all that it meant, they were convinced of the fact: "Christ died for our sins."

Here was the burden of the Christian message, the heart of the gospel in which the men of the New Testament were all agreed and about which the Church has been in agreement ever since. The death of Christ is the deed of God's love and its measure. It is God's work for the salvation of men. Here God condemns our sins and calls us to repentance. Here God reveals his mercy and calls for our trust and our surrender to him. And this love which did not stop at death calls us in turn to die to sin and to live a new life in the spirit of this Christ.

II. THE MEANING OF CHRIST'S DEATH

It was inevitable, however, that the Church should go beyond this simple declaration and inquire why the death of Christ was necessary and how his death actually served in the salvation of men. It was Paul who led the way in this inquiry, and the various historic theories of the work of Christ have all appealed to him. But when we ask just how Paul thought about the death of Christ, the answer is not easy. Paul is preacher first and theologian second. He has no one theory or explanation. He reaches here and there for analogy and illustration, sometimes bringing different ideas together in the same passage; but no one of his ideas is carried out in full explanation. Five main approaches may be indicated, though these are often merged one into the other.

1. The first and simplest is the idea of reconciliation, not the reconciliation of God to man, of which Paul nowhere speaks, but of man to God. "All things are of God, who reconciled us to himself through Christ, and gave unto us the ministry of reconciliation; to wit, that God was in Christ reconciling the world unto himself, not reckoning unto them their trespasses, and having committed unto us the word of reconciliation." This is fundamental with Paul, underlying all else. In this important passage, II Cor. 5:14–21, he uses the term reconcile no less than five times. He calls his work flatly "the ministry of reconciliation." The cross is God commending his love toward us "in that while we were yet sinners Christ died for us." [1] The cross is God's offer of forgiveness, "not reckon-

[1] Rom. 5:8.

ing unto us our trespasses." Such words, no doubt, are the echo of countless sermons in which Paul set forth the cross as the measure of the love of God and as the appeal of God's mercy. In such sermons he saw the cross as the power of God unto salvation, working repentance and calling forth faith. The mainspring of this conception is the saving love of God; the concrete human situation is the fact that man is at enmity with God and that only in reconciliation to God can he have life. Certainly this conception of Christ's death as God's work of reconciliation brings out most clearly Paul's basic ideas: man's sin (enmity), God's grace, man's answer of faith, and the life of love in the new fellowship ("that they should no longer live unto themselves"). And here the new way stands out in sharpest contrast with older legalistic and sacrificial systems.

2. Satisfaction is the central thought of the second approach. The passage commonly cited is Romans 3:24–26, where Christ is spoken of as having been set forth by God as a propitiation "in his blood, to show his righteousness because of the passing over of the sins done aforetime, in the forbearance of God; for the showing, I say, of his righteousness at this present season: that he might himself be just, and the justifier of him that hath faith in Jesus." This may mean simply that God's forbearance in the past, and his forgiveness now, might be misunderstood as an indifference to sin and raise the doubt as to whether God himself was just, and that thus Christ's death was necessary to show that such was not the case.

More commonly it has been taken in a stricter sense, as represented in Anselm's satisfaction theory. Rightly Anselm holds to a moral order in the universe, but he conceives that order as a legal one: Sin must always be punished; Christ's death is the penalty demanded by the law; Christ suffered this penalty in man's place that God might be able to forgive. If this is Paul's position, then it is a relapse into legalism. Then, if we would hold to Paul's gospel, we must part company here with Paul's theology. There is no gospel of grace here, for when a debt is once paid there is no longer occasion or place for forgiveness. There is not even justice here, for surely it is not just to "punish" the innocent. But it is questionable whether Paul meant this. Paul does not assert that an abstract justice has to be satisfied, and that God punished Jesus to do this. And if, with Anselm, you lay the stress on what Christ did as *man* to satisfy God's demand, then you lose what is in the very forefront of all Paul's thinking, that in all this *God* is acting for man's salvation, as this very passage asserts. Rather what Paul is trying to do is to set forth the meaning of a great fact, that of God's forgiveness coming to man in Christ's death. He is seeking at once to guard against misunderstanding and to make clear its need. But his recourse to legal terms for this purpose certainly does not help us, whatever it may have done for readers who had a legalistic background in religion like himself. It does in fact tend to compromise the position which elsewhere he makes so unmistakably clear. There is a moral order of the universe, an order of righteousness: that fundamental conviction of prophetic religion Paul shares with his Master. Paul's foes conceived that order legalistically, in terms of law and its consequences, whether of award or punishment. Paul conceived the moral order redemptively, one might equally well say, creatively. He asked: how shall rightness of character and life be *created* among men? He found the answer in forgiveness, not as mere remission of penalty but as the creation of a new and life-giving relation into which the sinner enters when he has faith in the God of grace whom he sees in Christ.

3. The ideas of sacrifice and propitiation represent another approach used by Paul. God set forth Christ, he says in this same passage, "to be a propitiation, through faith, in his blood." "Christ died for us." We are "justified by his blood, . . . saved from the wrath of God through him." [2] "Him who knew no sin he made to be sin on our behalf." [3] "We have our redemption through his blood." "Ye that once were far off are made nigh in the blood of Christ." [4]

In traditional theology these passages have been used in two ways. In one case Christ's death has been thought of as a sacrifice, propitiating God, appeasing his anger, averting his wrath, and thus reconciling God to man. For the second interpretation, the analogy of satisfaction is used. Now it is justice which must be satisfied, the law that "the wages of sin is death," an apparently unalterable order to which God himself is subject, so that he cannot forgive until this demand is met. Sometimes the thought was of a substitute victim suffering a necessary penalty; sometimes, as with Anselm, the thought of a payment to be made to settle a debt.

It is not easy, however, to determine Paul's position. The probabilities are that he had not worked it out in any detail for himself. As a teacher he was seeking by figure and analogy to light up a great fact and make plain its truth. Theology has tried to convert his illustrations into doctrine. If the interpretation given above is correct, then Paul contradicts his own teaching clearly given elsewhere. The truth is that Paul has here gone for analogy to an earlier and lower stage of religious thought, that of the sacrificial system; in this older system there

[2] Rom. 5:8, 9.   [3] II Cor. 5:21.   [4] Eph. 1:7; 2:13.

is profound and abiding truth, but if the older and lower standpoint is made determinative, the result is disastrous to the newer and higher Christian view.

Let us look at some of the ideas, or symbols, here involved, and first that of the wrath of God. To us the term suggests the idea of a God who is angry because of personal affront and is only waiting to wreak vengeance, a concept radically opposed to that of God as Father. Paul's conception is most clearly stated in Romans 2:1–16. Here "the wrath of God" means the final judgment (sometimes he simply says, "the wrath"): "the day of wrath and revelation of the righteous judgment of God; who will render to every man according to his works; . . . the day when God shall judge the secrets of men, according to my gospel, by Jesus Christ." So he speaks of "Jesus, who delivereth us from the wrath to come." [5]

But the phrase seems to connote more than merely the idea of an impersonal judgment. The thesis of the opening chapters of Romans is put in Romans 1:18: "The wrath of God is revealed against all ungodliness and unrighteousness of men," against all who have sinned, Jew as well as Gentile. That does not mean anger and vengeance demanding placation, for Paul is here leading up to the thought of the grace of God. It does suggest that a holy and righteous God must stand now and always in judgment against evil, that here is no mere decision of the mind but an attitude of heart and will as well. With such a God there is, and must be, an unalterable condemnation of all evil and an active opposition. The very love of God involves this, for evil is the destruction of man and evil men are the foes of man as well as of God. Humanly speaking, there is an element of feeling here. Unfortunately, we have only im-

[5] I Thes. 1:10.

perfect terms taken from human life with which to denote this
attitude of God. Certainly the wrath of God does not mean to
Paul the kind of spirit which is meant by wrath in man, for
this spirit he condemns flatly.[6]

More important in this inquiry is the question as to the
propitiation of God by Christ's death viewed as a sacrifice, or
the need of his death before God could forgive. It is held that
Romans 3:25 definitely asserts this in the phrase, "to be a
propitiation in his blood"; and further reference is made to
the phrases, "being justified by his blood," "to reconcile all
things to himself, having made peace through the blood of the
cross," and others.[7] Cremer, in his exhaustive treatment of the
words "propitiate" and "propitiation" as used in profane Greek
and in the New Testament, points out that the Greek word
for propitiate in non-biblical usage is directed toward God;
but not so in Old Testament usage.[8] In the New Testament the
object of propitiation as of reconciliation is man. So Paul
points out, in the crucial passage of Romans 3, that God set
forth Jesus to be a propitiation. If, however, you insist that the
Old Testament principle obtains even in the New and that
blood must be shed before there can be forgiveness, then it
should be pointed out that "under the Levitical system *only
sins of ignorance* were capable of being atoned for by sacrifice." [9] But aside from the recognized inadequacy of such a
sacrifice to secure forgiveness, the Old Testament clearly connects the forgiveness of sins with the mercy of God as its
sufficient ground, just as Jesus did.

[6] Col. 3:8; Eph. 4:26, 31.
[7] Rom. 5:9; Col. 1:20. Note also Col. 1:22; Eph. 1:7; 2:13.
[8] *Biblisch-theologisches Wörterbuch der neutestamentlichen Gräcität*,
by H. Cremer, under Ἱλάσχομαι and Ἱλαστήριον.
[9] See the discussion of C. A. A. Scott, *Christianity According to St.
Paul*, p. 87, and his reference to A. B. Davidson.

4. A fourth approach of Paul toward the understanding of Christ's work is represented by the ideas of deliverance and redemption. This is the first aspect of salvation; it may be called the negative side. And this is the first reason for primitive man's search for help: deliverance from danger, from his foes. Even when the idea of salvation is lifted to the highest spiritual-ethical-social plane, and man thinks first of all in terms of a life to be gained, there remains the keen sense of threatening evil, indeed, a heightened sense that comes with clearer insight. The complacently optimistic attitude, whether with reference to man or the world, is at once blind to the tragic realities of evil and ignorant of what is needed for deliverance.[10]

In Paul's thought of Christ's work as deliverance we have, as we might expect, a mingling of the new and the old. His new Christian insights are joined with traditional forms of expression and interpretation which are not always adequate. The great elements in the Christian conception of deliverance are all here. Men are slaves to sin, unable to free themselves from evil, unable to follow the good. Men are in bondage under a religion of law—not Jews alone, but all men, summoned by God's command but unable to keep it, and so standing under judgment. Christ has freed them by bringing them the God of mercy with his forgiveness and the power of a new life. He has freed them from ignorance and darkness, for God has shone into their hearts to give the light of the knowledge of his glory in the face of Jesus Christ. And Paul recog-

[10] Cf. Andrew Carnegie's remark in his *Autobiography,* registering his happy conclusion gained from his first acquaintance with the idea of evolution through Darwin and Herbert Spencer: "All is good for all is growing better," a point of view to which Darwin and Spencer themselves gave utterance.

nizes, with Jesus, the deliverance from anxiety and fear which comes when once men know the God who is above all hostile powers, in whose hands are all things, who is the God of infinite good will, and from whose love no power can separate us.

There is another aspect to this conception of deliverance from the powers of evil which deserves special attention. It is connected with Paul's belief in a realm of evil forces, of spiritual beings or powers, to whom mankind, through its sin, has become subjected. Christ's work is conceived as a conflict with these powers and as the deliverance of man from their dominion. The belief in such an unseen realm of evil was widespread in Paul's day. In Judaism it was qualified by the faith in one supreme God; it was thus a moral and relative dualism rather than a metaphysical and absolute one. Yet it did involve the idea of a kingdom of darkness which ruled this age and had power over men and nations.

Paul shared this general belief. His references to the devil, or Satan, are few; he speaks twice of the devil and eight times of Satan. But he refers many times to these evil spirits. The modern reader pays little attention to these passages. Commonly we take them rhetorically, as when he calls the list of the "creatures" which might separate the believer from the love of God: death, life, angels, principalities, things present, things to come, powers, height, depth.[11] But for Paul these were real, objectively existing beings, wielding power, threatening man, and opposing God. Sometimes we miss the meaning of his reference because of the terms that he uses. So in Galatians 4:3, 9 and Colossians 2:8, 20, the strange phrase which is literally "elements of the world" probably relates to a form of

[11] Rom. 8:38, 39.

the widespread worship of spirits which were supposed to be rulers of planets and stars and to wield great power over human lives—a superstition which has by no means died out in our day. Not the belief in the existence of such spirits, but the service of them is what Paul protested.

The Christian for Paul does not simply oppose evil men ("flesh and blood") and inner temptation; he is beset by a whole host of these unseen beings: principalities, powers, world rulers of the realm of darkness, spiritual hosts of wickedness in the heavenly places.[12] Of course Paul is a monotheist. "No idol is anything in the world." "To us there is one God, the Father, of whom are all things, and we unto him: and one Lord, Jesus Christ, through whom are all things, and we through him." [13] Above all, he wants them, through their faith in this one God and his power over all things, to be free from all lesser and evil powers. But though the idols are nothing, yet there are demons at work in this idol worship, and he will not have Christians have communion with these demons by sharing in this idol worship.[14]

These evil spirits are not merely those lesser beings who lurk everywhere, bringing upon men evils of body and soul; there is some kind of hierarchy in this unseen realm of evil. Paul speaks of "the prince of the power of the air," "the prince of this world," which probably means Satan, or the Devil. He refers to "principalities and powers" which are created by God and subject to him, but also to those which are evil and which were triumphed over by Christ in his death. These are no petty demons, but possessed of real power. It was they who crucified Christ.[15] In fact, they are just now in apparent

---

[12] Eph. 2:11, 12, 16.
[13] I Cor. 8:4-6.
[14] I Cor. 10:19-21.
[15] I Cor. 2:8.

control of this world. Paul speaks of "the god of this world" and "the rulers of this world." [16] These are strange phrases but they are not to be passed over as merely rhetorical. These are the familiar ideas of Jewish apocalypticism. This age is evil. It is under the rule of Satan and his angels, whose overthrow will be brought by the day of the Lord. This world picture was an attempt to meet the problem of evil. For who could look at this world and not see the power of evil working in it, bringing sickness and suffering, tempting men to sin, sitting in places of power and oppressing the peoples, yes, and nailing Christ to the cross? Hence the suggestion that God, in his own inscrutable wisdom, had given over this age to the forces of evil until the time of deliverance should come.

How did Paul conceive of Christ's conflict with these spiritual powers and his victory over them, and how was the death of Christ related to this? The ultimate conflict and victory, we know, was to come in the future with Christ's return, "when he shall have abolished all rule and all authority and power," putting all things in subjection under his feet, death being the last enemy to be subdued.[17] But Paul thinks of the death of Christ as a central event in the present deliverance of man from these powers and in Christ's victory over them. For the insight of Christian faith lay right here: Christ's death was something which he wrought, not just something which he suffered; it was not a fateful defeat by the forces of evil, but a victory over them; and it was the living God whose power was here at work.

But when we go further and ask how Paul thought of this victory as being won, we are once more in difficulty. And again we must realize that we are dealing with a preacher and his

[16] II Cor. 4:4; I Cor. 2:8.   [17] I Cor. 15:24–27.

gospel, rather than with a thinker and his system. Two approaches are possible here. The first centers in the ideas of slavery and ransom. The figure was a familiar one in that Roman world. Men were taken captive by pirates or in war, were made slaves, and were sometimes bought back, or ransomed. The word ransom is not used by Paul, though it occurs in Mark 10:45. But Paul makes frequent use of the figure of slavery, of the believer as being bought back (redeemed), and of Christ as our redemption, which meant originally and literally a deliverance through a ransom.[18] The Church fathers gained their first definite theory of the atonement from these words of Paul. Man by sinning had fallen prey to Satan, they said, and was his subject. God did not use force with Satan to deliver men, as he might have done, but rather persuasion (*suadela*), offering Christ in death for their liberation. Sometimes it was suggested that God used guile, since Satan did not know that Christ, being divine, could not be held by death. In any case, sinners are delivered from their bondage by a ransom paid to Satan. All of which shows what happens when the dramatic language of a great mind like Paul's is reduced to prosaic literalism.

Recently, a Swedish theologian and churchman, Bishop Gustav Aulén, in his volume, *Christus Victor*, has attempted a restatement of this early doctrine of the atonement, which he considers the true interpretation of Paul. He calls this the "classic" doctrine and opposes it to Anselm's "Latin" doctrine. Aulén recognizes that the dominant view of the Church fathers before Anselm involved the ideas of the devil's authority over man since the fall, the death of Christ as a ransom paid to the devil, and the fact that the devil was tricked. But

[18] I Cor. 6:20; 7:23; Gal. 3:13; 4:5; Eph. 1:7; Rom. 3:24; Col. 1:14.

these elements he considers secondary. The essential elements of the "classic" doctrine as he finds it in Paul are threefold. (1) The atonement is the deed of God. It is not something coming from man. It is not Christ as man and on behalf of man offering a satisfaction to God, as with Anselm. He insists rightly that back of Anselm's theory is the legalism involved in the Roman doctrine of penance, from which come the ideas of satisfaction to legal demand and the impersonal transfer of merit. But with Paul everything goes back to God: "God was in Christ reconciling the world." (2) Paul conceives the work of Christ dramatically, that is, in terms of action, of conflict and victory. Christ comes to earth to war with the forces of evil and set man free. Incarnation, atonement, resurrection are all parts of this one great action of God. (3) The background of this teaching is a dualism, not an ultimate dualism, and yet one which recognizes the reality of these spiritual forces. The devil and the mighty evil spirits under him are not figures of speech but actually existent, and the work of Christ is to conquer them and deliver man by so doing. Besides the devil, the outstanding beings to whom man is in bondage and whom Christ overcomes are Sin, Death, and the Law. All four are conceived equally in objective fashion, though there is a certain ambiguity as to the Law.

Aulén's work does far more justice to Paul than the traditional satisfaction theories. It sees the atonement in the larger setting of the whole work of God as salvation. It does justice to Paul's apocalyptic view, with its thought of a God who saves by action, its strong sense of the power of evil and of God's work as a conflict with its forces, and the thought of Christ's death as a central deed while at the same time he looked forward to a final struggle and victory. It stresses rightly the fact that it is God that is acting and that his action springs from his spirit of love. Aulén recognizes at the same time that Christian theology must bring out here the essential meanings of the Christian faith and not simply take over the forms of Paul's presentation.

Aulén's treatment is open, nevertheless, to criticism, due mainly to his own theological position. He thinks that the underlying dualism of Paul, where God and the good are faced with an unseen realm of mighty evil spirits under Satan, is an essential part of the Christian viewpoint. Further, he omits large areas of Paul's thought as to the work of Christ, namely those which have to do with that bringing together of God and man in the vital union by which sin is overcome, not in some transcendent sphere of conflict, but here in the human heart and life, in the Christian fellowship, in the actual transformation of man by the Spirit of God. In the end, with all his apocalypticism, Paul's dominant concern is with a salvation in which man becomes a new creature and God creates for himself a people of his own possession, a Church which is the body of Christ.

5. We need finally to consider the mystical-ethical approach to Christ's death. The Christian life for Paul, as we have seen, is one of union with Christ in which mystical and ethical are inseparably united. The mystical is vividly and realistically conceived; in the believer, and more especially in the Church which is the body of Christ, the living Lord is actually and dynamically present so that the entire life of the Christian is the life of Christ in him. "For me to live is Christ," Paul writes. And this life is at the same time ethical, the active expression of the believer in thought, attitude, feeling, and action. That follows necessarily because this spiritual Presence is not pri-

marily idea or emotion, but something ethical; "the mind of Christ" is love, devotion, humility, obedience, even unto death.[19] This saving mystical relation, into which Christ takes his followers, is his deed as well as man's experience, and in this deed, as in the experience, the death of Christ is central. Conceiving atonement, then, as Christ's work of bringing man into oneness with God, the mystical element has a distinctive place.

In this view, Christ's solidarity with man comes first. It is for Paul something realistic, not simply social-ethical. He becomes one with us in all our life—in humility, weakness, suffering, and death. Philippians 2:5–8 and II Corinthians 5:14–21 are the great passages here. In Christ God enters into all our life so that all our life may be taken up in him and redeemed. Paul even uses here the strange phrase, "Him who knew no sin he made to be sin on our behalf."[20] The statement cannot, of course, be literalized; Christ did not become a sinner in sharing man's life. Nor does it necessarily follow that this is to be taken juridically, as with the satisfaction theory: that God looked on Christ as a sinner and punished him in our place. It is rather a part of God's action, of his entrance into our life; "God was in Christ," "God made him to be sin," "in order that he might reconcile us," "that we might become the righteousness of God in him." This solidarity is the first part of a double movement in God's work of salvation in Christ. (1) There is the movement from God to man. In Christ God unites himself with our humanity. Christ becomes man, sharing not simply human limitations, but all that sin has brought upon man, including death itself—all except sin (for he "knew no sin") and the disfavor of God which sin, and only sin, brings.

[19] Phil. 2:5–8.   [20] II Cor. 5:21.

Central in this action is Christ's death and resurrection (they are never separated in Paul's thought). (2) There is the movement from man's side, a movement of faith and obedience; and so there comes the saving union of God and man, a union which is both mystical and ethical. Of course, this must be taken in a large and vital fashion, not in a point-by-point mechanical parallel. Man dies with Christ in the sense that man dies to sin, that the "old man" is crucified. Man is buried; that is, as he is "buried" in the water of baptism, so the old man is buried. And as Christ is raised from the dead, so the sinner is raised. This time the words have a double reference, neither of them a literal parallel, one referring to newness of spiritual-ethical life in oneness with Christ, the other looking forward to the final resurrection at the end of the age.

III. SUMMARY AND EVALUATION

The study of Paul's ideas as to the work of Christ has suffered under two common errors. First is the mistake we have found in other connections, that of looking at Paul as a systematic theologian, judging each statement of his as a consistent part of a completely formulated doctrine. True, there is nothing vague or uncertain in Paul's convictions or in the great historic facts which formed their basis: Christ and his death and resurrection, the Christian fellowship, and the creative religious experience of the early Church. But this must be distinguished from his efforts at interpretation. The latter reveal to us not a system of thought, but profoundly significant insights; not divinely communicated theology but a human effort limited necessarily by his own personality and the thought forms of his day, even while we note that it was that of a great man divinely led into deep religious experience and illuminating understanding. It is these insights that we must consider, rather than the details of formulation.

The second error is that of isolating the death of Christ from his total work and failing to relate the doctrine of the atonement to a comprehensive view of salvation. The chief responsibility for this must rest with Anselm, for Paul and the men of the early Church thought primarily in terms of the total movement of God for the saving of men. If the death of Christ is viewed, as in the satisfaction theory, in legalistic fashion as a plan by which forgiveness is made possible through an acceptable substitution of payment or penalty, then it can be thus separated. But Paul saw an age-long process in which God was carrying out his purpose for humanity, corresponding with which there was a human process, taking place both in history and in individual experience. Christ was central in this movement. All that was past found its meaning in him, and from him Paul looked forward to the final consummation. But the meaning of Christ himself, the center of all this, was not to be found simply in his death. His coming to earth, his spirit and life, his love and obedience, his death and resurrection, his creative spiritual presence in the Church and in each believer, and his work in the final consummation when, after conflict and victory he should hand over the kingdom to the Father, all this Paul saw as a whole and as one. The eastern Church stressed the incarnation, the western Church the atonement; Paul saw the meaning of each of these in the other and both as parts, central but not alone, of one creative-redemptive movement of God.

In his preaching it was the crucified Christ whom Paul proclaimed. Part of his task was to set forth the necessity and the deep meaning of this strange paradox of a Messiah put to death. In so doing he naturally employed analogies taken from fields familiar to his listeners and built upon what they believed. The first analogy was from the familiar system of the law, with its imposed penalty: Christ, though not a sinner, took our sins upon himself and suffered in our place and for us. The second was from the sacrificial system: Christ in his death was like a sacrifice, offering himself that we might go free, dying for us. The third was from familiar facts of captivity and of ransom through payment. We are captives, fallen prey to the law, to sin, to death; and Christ offered, not a payment of money, but himself, his life, to bring us deliverance. The fourth analogy was from the field of battle and victory: as men go forth to war to defeat their foes, so Christ went forth against the unseen but mighty and evil spiritual Powers who are the great foes of man; and, strangely enough, he defeated them by that very death in which they thought that they had triumphed.

The mistake of traditional theology has been to select now one, now another, of these analogies or pictures in which Paul set forth the meaning of Christ's death, to literalize and formalize it, and then to try to construct from this an inclusive statement of doctrine. The very variety of the Pauline statements should have warned against this effort. Yet, if we have regard to the religious truth which Paul is seeking to express, we shall find that his fundamental ideas have remained basic for Christian thought.

(1) God was in Christ as himself the Savior of men. The death of Christ was more than a tragedy wrought by evil or a supreme example of heroism and devotion. It was the deed of God for man and the revelation of God to man. God is revealed as sacrificial love, and Christ and his cross are the work of this God seeking to reconcile men to himself. (2) The cross

shows what forgiveness means and what it costs. Forgiveness is not the mere passing over of sin and remission of punishment; it means bringing man into living and life-giving relation with God. Justification, reconciliation, and the re-making of man are all aspects of its great meaning with Paul. And its cost is as great as its meaning: the entrance of God into human life, the oneness of Christ with men, suffering that is vicarious and redemptive, death itself. (3) If God and his love are revealed here, here also are made known what evil is and what it does and what is God's judgment upon it. (4) As Christ enters into man's life, so man must enter into Christ's life. The at-one-ment of forgiveness must issue in an at-one-ness of Spirit and life: a death to sin, a rising to a new life by the power of him who is life and who raised Christ from the dead, and a continued "walking in newness of life."

And beyond this there are permanent values in the Pauline analogies of sacrifice and substitution, of satisfaction and vicarious suffering, of conflict and deliverance. All these have entered deeply into the imagery of Christian hymns and devotions. Some of the cruder expressions need, indeed, to be eliminated, just as we must discard some of the traditional theology built upon them; but there is much that must not be lost. There is an ultimate saving power in mercy, but there is a moral order in the universe of God with its inevitable judgment upon evil. There is a judgment upon evil which the innocent may bear for the saving of the sinful. The principle of vicarious suffering begins with God himself and reaches down into all life; life must be given if life is to be achieved. Sin is an enslaving power and man is not equal to his own deliverance when once he has given himself, in his weakness and folly, into this bondage. Evil is more than a single deed or even this enslaving bondage of the individual; it is a power entrenched in the historic and social structure of humanity. And the powers of this evil, as we see clearly today, call for a conflict mightier than any world war which this globe has yet seen. These principles have their being not only in the God of truth and right, but in the self-giving love of this God; and the expression of this is in Christ. But if the Church in which he dwells really shares his life, then its members will need to "know the fellowship of his sufferings, becoming conformed unto his death," filling up "that which is lacking of the afflictions of Christ." [1] And of that the Church of today is giving new evidence in many lands.

[1] Phil. 3:10; Col. 1:24.

Chapter Six

THE MEANING OF CHRIST
FOR PAUL

IN STUDYING Paul's conception of Christ, the common method has been to begin with what are called the christological passages—that is, the passages where Paul moves out beyond the realm of experience to that of theory, where he seeks to explain the Christ whom he knows in personal faith and picture the transcendent heavenly being. True, Christian thought must move on to ultimate questions, as Paul did; but if we are to understand Paul rightly, even in these more speculative expressions, we must begin where he began.

Paul's concern is with religion, with God as the center of man's life and life as lived in fellowship with God. The heart of his gospel is the conviction that the living God had come to men in Christ. He is not primarily concerned with Christ as teacher, though he is sure that any matter is settled when he has a word from Jesus.[1] His first interest is not with Jesus as example, though he sees in the spirit of Christ the one rule of God for man's life. The crucial fact for his gospel is that salvation has come to men through Christ. To understand Paul's conception of Christ, therefore, we must begin, not with the more speculative passages where he pictures the pre-existent heavenly being or indicates Christ's significance in relation to creation, but rather with those which show his meaning for life and salvation. In the language of the schools, Paul's christology comes out of his soteriology.

[1] I Cor. 7: 10, 25.

113

I. THE PLACE OF CHRIST IN CHRISTIAN FAITH

1. We have already noted the place of Christ for Paul in Christian experience. (1) Christ has brought God to men and reconciled men to God, overcoming the separation wrought by sin. (2) Christ is for the disciple the power of a new life, dwelling in him as a living and spiritual presence. (3) Christ is the creator of the Church, of the new people of God; he is the head of this new body and is its life. (4) Christ is the revelation of man. His spirit is the rule for man's life. He is the true goal of man; we are to "grow up in all things into him, who is the head." (5) Christ is the revelation of God, not so much by his teaching about God as by the Spirit of God that was in him and the way in which God worked through him. (6) Christ is Lord, the one whom the disciple obeys. As we hear God's word and receive God's saving help through him, so we meet in him the will of God and his rightful claim upon us. (7) Christ is God's disclosure of the goal of history and the one through whom this will be achieved.

Even so brief an outline shows how Christ fills the whole horizon of Paul's thought and life. What God was and what man should be, what man should do and what he might hope for, all centered for him in Christ and was understood in the light of the knowledge of the glory of God which he had seen in the face of Jesus Christ. And it is in the light of this religious meaning which Christ had acquired for him that we are to understand what Paul says about the person of Christ.

2. To understand the place which Christ has with Paul it will be well to begin with the terms or titles which Paul gives

him, and to consider these not as sharply defined concepts of theology but as expressions of faith indicating what Christ had come to mean to his disciples.

Whatever the influence which Hellenism had in Judaism and the early Church, the basic attitude of the early Christians, as of Paul, was Hebraic and not Hellenistic; that is, it was religious and not speculative. The dominantly religious interest of the Hebrew mind is seen in the Old Testament references to God. Their concern is not to define the nature of the transcendent, but to know the living God in his will for Israel and his power to help. Definitions and arguments are alike lacking. What psalmist and prophet do is to point men to God. They tell men of the mighty acts of this God. They see in these his power and righteousness and mercy. They bid men trust this God and obey him. Their approach is practical. Their terms for God are picture terms in form, and functional terms in their meaning. God is king, captain, judge, savior, shepherd, rock, fortress, shield, refuge, wall, defense, dwelling-place, light, life, salvation. These are signs which point to God, symbols which suggest the meaning of the Eternal for man; they are not definitions which seek to enclose a God whom man's mind has comprehended.

It is from this point of view that we approach the study of Paul's christological statements, and particularly the terms which he applies to Christ. His writings are not devotional, like the psalms in the Old Testament, or sermonic, like the fourth gospel, and so they do not contain the many picture terms which the former apply to God and the latter applies to Christ.[1]

---

[1] Note, for example, such terms in John as bread, water, life, light, truth, way, door, vine, shepherd.

Paul's common names for Jesus are Christ (Messiah) and Lord, the latter used over two hundred times, the former nearly three hundred, besides the three-score times or more in which they are used together. He never employs the familiar synoptic term, Son of Man. He speaks of him as Son (of God) some sixteen times. Once he calls him the last Adam. Only once in the undisputed epistles does he refer to him as Savior; but that simply shows that we must not lay too much stress upon terms, for salvation through Christ is Paul's great theme. He speaks of him often as Spirit, or life-giving Spirit, within us; and once he says flatly, "the Lord is the Spirit." [2] It is well, indeed, to study these terms for their meaning, but we must not expect to find in them hard and fast doctrinal concepts nor are we to assign too much importance to the question of their source. They suggest rather that Paul takes the highest terms which he knows to name him to whom he gives the highest place, and to indicate what Jesus Christ means to the believer.

3. Christ and Lord are the two terms which call for special consideration. The former had become for him a personal name, as with us, while still retaining its original and special meaning. Jesus was the long looked for Messiah of his people. He takes the supreme place in the great purpose that God has been working out. This is the ancient Hebrew faith but it is now universalized. The old hope of a coming kingdom remains, but what that kingdom means is seen in the light of Christ as king. The prophetic monotheism remains basic to this faith. Every aspect of Christ's work is seen in relation to God: he is the Anointed (Messiah or Christos), sent forth from God; he is declared to be the Son of God by God's power, is by God's act set in his place of rule over his foes, and at the end returns

[2] II Cor. 3:17.

the power to God.[3] Most important, however, is the fact that, though it seems foolishness to the Gentiles and a stumbling-block to the Jews, this is a crucified Messiah, one who was exalted to power just because he went thus to his death.[4]

It is not so easy to determine what Paul meant by calling Jesus Lord, a term which he uses almost as often as Christ. The Greek word of our New Testament, *Kyrios,* comes from a root denoting power. In common usage it meant what we mean by master or lord. It indicated rightful authority and rule, as against the dominance of a despot. But it had a special religious usage in Paul's day, and first of all with the Jews. In the Greek translation of the Old Testament, the Septuagint, which was the Bible of the Jews of the dispersion, it was used in place of Jehovah, the name that was too sacred to be uttered in speech. The Lord meant the God of the heavens and the earth. And the translators of the King James version followed this example and set down Lord where the Hebrew Bible had Jehovah. But it was used also in the wide-spread mystery religions of the Graeco-Roman world. Each of these had its hero god whom it called Lord, to whom it brought worship, and from whom it hoped for redemption. The meaning of Lord is, of course, very different here, for in no one of these cults did the devotees for a moment think of identifying their "lord" with the creator of the universe or think of him as the revelation of the eternal God or even as his agent.[5]

[3] Gal. 4:4; Rom. 1:4; Phil. 2:9–11; I Cor. 15:24–28.

[4] I Cor. 1:21–25; Phil. 2:8, 9.

[5] "It must be remembered that 'God' does not mean the same thing in Jewish and in Greek usage. To the Jew the word 'God' means the creator and ruler, omnipotent, omniscient, and unique; beside him there can be no other God. To the Greek the word 'God' means one of a superhuman class of beings, immortal and incorruptible, but not necessarily omnipotent or omniscient." Kirsopp Lake, *Paul, His Heritage and Legacy,* note, p. 122.

Why did Paul use this term and what was its meaning for him? Two answers may be ruled out here. Paul did not borrow the term and its meaning from the mystery religions.[6] It could easily happen that early Christianity, going out into a world which knew many cults and had no background of strict and lofty monotheism like the Jews, should be conceived by some of its converts as another mystery cult, especially since it, too, had a dying and risen lord. But Paul is clear and explicit: for the Christian there is one God, the Father, and one Lord, Jesus Christ, as over against the gods and lords of paganism.[7] And this and other passages make plain also how unfounded the other opinion is that, in using the term Lord, Paul is identifying Christ with the Jehovah of the Old Testament. Jesus is not God; he is the Christ of God, and the God who is our God and Father is the God and Father of Christ.[8] All this does not exclude the worship of Christ or prayers addressed to Christ, though the dominant reference in prayer and worship is to God.

Paul's use of the word Lord must be understood in the light of the religious meaning which it had for Paul, not by reference to what it meant elsewhere, whether in the Old Testament or the mystery religions. More than any other term it summarizes the Christian faith and expresses what Paul found in Christ. For Paul, God is the God and Father of our Lord Jesus Christ. The Christians are those who believe in one God and have one Lord. They are those who call upon the name of the Lord. Paul's vocation is to preach Christ Jesus as Lord, to

[6] So first set forth in extended argument by W. Bousset, *Kyrios Christos,* who was followed, among others, by A. C. McGiffert, in his *The God of the Early Christians.*

[7] I Cor. 8:5, 6.

[8] II Cor. 1:3 and elsewhere.

which corresponds his position, "servant through Jesus." [9] Thus while Messiah (Christ) came to be used as a proper name, the term Lord became the sign and summary of the new faith.

Wherein then does this lordship lie? Briefly stated, in this: Lordship means power, mastery, the right to rule. In religion that can belong ultimately and absolutely only to God, and a Jew like Paul would be the first to declare this. But here was one in whom God had come to them, by whom God had spoken, through whom they had received forgiveness and the hope of salvation. To call him Lord was not so much to define a theory of his person as to acknowledge the facts of their experience and to confess their faith. He was Lord because he had brought the revelation and salvation of God.

II. INTERPRETATION

But beside these terms which are more distinctly religious, there are statements of a more speculative character. It was inevitable that, having said this much, Paul should go further. Jesus meant what he did because he came from God and belonged to God and mediated God to men. What then was his relation to God, the divine aspect of his being?

Paul nowhere answers this question in systematic fashion. It does not belong to the direct presentation of the gospel; for this gospel it was enough to say that God was in Christ and to confess Jesus as Lord. But it is clear that Paul had reflected on this, and in certain passages he reveals his thought. Christ, he said, had been with God before his life on earth; "existing in the form of God," he had "counted not the being on an

[9] Rom: 15:6 and elsewhere; I Cor. 8:6; 1:1; Rom. 10:13; I Cor. 12:3; II Cor. 4:5.

equality with God a thing to be grasped." [1] And because he thus chose to "take the form of a servant," humbling himself and "becoming obedient even unto death," God exalted him and gave him the name above all other names so that every knee should bow before him.[2] Somewhat different is I Corinthians 15. Here, too, Paul speaks of a lordship, or mastery; God puts "all things in subjection under" Christ's feet. But he is thinking here of the conflict which shall bring in the messianic age. The conflict is thought of now as God's deed, now as Christ's. It is, in fact, God in Christ; but in the end the Son turns over the rule to the Father and is himself subjected to God. The full lordship of Christ belongs to the future, and ultimate and absolute lordship belongs to God. Even more striking are certain other passages which speak of Christ as God's agent in creation and as the goal of creation. "In him were all things created, things visible and things invisible . . .: all things have been created through him, and unto him; and he is before all things, and in him all things consist (that is, cohere, or hold together)." [3]

Though not presented systematically, these various passages clearly represent a settled and thought-out position. They have a definitely speculative character; that is, they go beyond what is more directly given in the records of the historical Jesus and in the religious experience of the Church. Yet this is not speculation for the sake of speculation. Its form is that of reason reflecting upon experience, but its source is faith and its intention is to express what this faith involves. Paul is simply trying to

[1] Moffatt translates: "Though he was divine by nature, he did not snatch at equality with God." Goodspeed renders it: "Though he possessed the nature of God, he did not grasp at equality with God."

[2] Phil. 2:9–11.

[3] Col. 1:16, 17. Cf. the entire first two chapters. Note also I Cor. 8:9.

answer the questions which the Church has asked ever since. In Christ he saw man and God, the human and the divine, one who had lived and died on earth and yet still lived and wrought as the power of God in men and for men. In him he saw God's purpose for men, God's agent for their salvation, and the one through whom some time all evil would be overthrown. It was this faith that gave rise to his conclusions. It is no mere speculation when Paul speaks of the cosmic meaning of Christ. If Christ is central in salvation, he will be central in creation; for creation finds its place, and all else finds its place, when in Christ there is seen God's supreme purpose for humanity. Therefore all things are "of him and through him and unto him." In him all things "hang together," that is, have their meaning and end. This world is not chaos and tragedy; "it means intensely, and it means good," and that meaning is seen in Christ. All this follows from the simple faith that God was in Christ. And so with the rest. He does not say that the man Jesus pre-existed. He distinguishes here. God's Son "was born of the seed of David according to the flesh," and "was declared to be the Son of God with power, according to the spirit of holiness, by the resurrection from the dead." [4] But so far as God was present, so far as the Eternal was in Christ and Christ was from God, in so far for Paul's thought there was a Christ who had been with God.

Consider, too, the practical purpose of these references. Those to whom he writes are, like himself, deeply conscious of the mighty forces of evil which threaten them. These forces are not simply human and historical; they are spiritual beings, thrones and dominions and principalities and powers. In such a seemingly speculative utterance as that in Colossians, Paul is

[4] Rom. 1:3, 4.

declaring that Christ is greater than all these, that he is before all these and will triumph over them.[5] Further, he is warning his Colossian converts against the widespread cults, gnostic and astrological, which apparently had seduced some of them to the worship of these "principalities and powers." So he holds up Christ as "first-born of all creation," as the one in whom all the fulness dwells, insisting that the Christian has but one God and one Lord. The practical purpose of the other notable christological statement, that of Philippians 2, is obvious. It is interesting to realize that these few words upon which volumes of theological discussion have been based would probably never have been written except for the need of correcting a spirit of faction and pride by reference to the humility of Christ.

But while the source of these declarations is to be found in the fact of Christ and the experience of the early Christians, the thought-forms used here, like the terms or titles already considered, were not original with Paul or with the Christian movement. The idea of transcendent spiritual beings, of princes and powers in the spiritual realm, of agents of creation, of mediators and saviors and lords, was widespread at the time. Men spoke of beings who imaged God, reflected his glory, who were the "fulness" of God (the *pleroma*). Paul does not shun such terms because they have been used elsewhere. He simply declares that Christ and not these others is *the* Lord, *the* true "image and glory," that in him and him alone the *pleroma* dwells and through him all things were made. His free use of such terms does not mean a borrowing of the idea of the primacy of Christ or of his divine significance, though it indicates an influence of these thought-forms upon him.

[5] Col. 1:16–20; Rom. 8:38; I Cor. 15:24; Eph. 1:21; 6:12.

A more direct influence upon Paul's doctrine of Christ is to be found in the writings of his own people, and this in addition to the distinctly religious terms of Christ and Lord. Two of the more speculative forms of Paul's christology are anticipated in later Hebrew writings. They are the thought of a preexistent heavenly being who is the image of God, and the conception of the agent of creation. In Proverbs we hear Wisdom saying, "Before the hills was I brought forth. . . . When he established the heavens, I was there . . . Then I was by him, as a master workman; and I was daily his delight." [6] If Wisdom here might seem to be just a personification, a figure of speech, in the apocryphal *Wisdom of Solomon* it is clearly thought of as an actual heavenly being. Wisdom is "the artificer of all things, . . . alone in kind, . . . beneficent, loving toward man, all-powerful, all-surveying, . . . a breath of the power of God, a clear effluence of the glory of the Almighty, . . . and an image of his goodness. And she, being one, hath power to do all things: and, remaining in herself, reneweth all things. . . . She reacheth from one end of the world to the other with full strength, and ordereth all things graciously." [7] In the Jewish Platonist, Philo, the idea of the Logos, or "the Word," has a central place, and this is similarly conceived as an objective reality or being. This conception of "the Word" lent itself to various uses and was widely employed, first in Greek philosophy, then in religious thought, and finally in Christian theology. The Greek term *logos* might mean word, truth, reason, wisdom, order, or even, as Goethe's *Faust* translated it, deed. Where the philosophy was that of immanence, as with the Stoics, the Logos expressed the idea of a divine Soul or Life which animated the world, or a Reason which per-

[6] Prov. 8:25–31.   [7] *The Wisdom of Solomon*, 7:22–8:1.

meated it, gave it unity, and held it together. The more common thought of that day was dualistic, not immanental. In Hellenistic thought the spiritual world was set over against the material. In Jewish thought there had come to be an increasing sense of divine transcendence, of the remoteness of the holy God from the evil world. In either case, there was felt the need of a mediating Being, one who bridged the gulf or one who was the agent of this transcendent Spirit in the creation and ordering of this finite world. These were not idle speculations. They were the efforts of men who beleved that this finite world had in it something of the Eternal, or who were trying to understand how the Infinite, in his work of creation and redemption, could come into time.

To sum up: In the crucified and risen Christ Paul had heard God's word to him, had seen God's presence and power, and had received his grace. There was no question: this was the Messiah of God; this was the Savior, the reconciler of God and man; this was the Lord, bringing God's will as he brought God's help; this was the Son of God, in whom God was present and God was known; and here was God's purpose and here man's hope for the future. But now Paul goes further and asks as to Christ's relation to God in the eternal realm, as to his life before the life on earth, and as to the way of his incarnation, that is, his coming into human life. Such questions were inevitable; it was equally inevitable that Paul in answer should make use of those forms of thought which lay at hand. Men do not think in a vacuum. Just so the later Church, when it continued the effort here begun by Paul, made use of terms furnished by the thought of a later day and spoke of nature, essence, substance, and hypostasis, using Greek and Latin terms for some of which it is hard to find clear English equivalents and about whose meaning the Church fathers themselves were not always agreed.

The crucial matter here is not the terms or forms of thought which Paul used, any more than those of the early Christian fathers, which seem even more strange to the modern man. It is what Paul is trying to say. It is not hard to tell what counted most with him, what really constituted his gospel. And when we look at this we see how essentially one we are with him, and how radically he differs from the mystery cults with their hero gods, and from the speculations of Hellenistic philosophy and their abstractions, even when these are united with Hebrew faith as in Philo.

III. HOW PAUL THOUGHT OF CHRIST

What, then, was distinctive and essential in Paul's view of Christ?

1. God was in Christ and Christ was of God. The two aspects are of equal importance. Paul's whole faith rested on the fact that in Christ God himself was speaking to man and dealing with him and entering human life. And for him the converse followed: Christ was of God and in God. Christ belonged in his spirit and life and inmost being on the side of God. So Paul could use interchangeably Spirit of Christ and Spirit of God just because the life of Christ was God's life. In the same way he ascribes the work of salvation, judgment, and creation now to Christ and now to God. To ascribe these to Christ is to ascribe them to God, since there is nothing of Christ which is not of God.

2. Yet for Paul there was only one God. No Jewish opponent ever charged him with being false to the monotheism of

his people. Christ was not for him a second God. The three coordinate Beings of the Athanasian creed and of so much of popular Christian thought, Beings standing in a relation of absolute equality in which, except for the phrases about generation and procession, there is "no before nor after," this for him would have been incomprehensible. "There is no God but one," he wrote. For others, indeed, "there are gods many, and lords many"; yet to us there is one God, the Father . . . ; and one Lord, Jesus Christ." [1] In innumerable passages and in solemn benediction the words are repeated, God the Father, Christ the Lord: not Father God and Christ God, but God who is Father, and Christ who is Lord. Paul holds clearly, as does the whole New Testament, to the subordination of Christ and the dependence of the Son upon the Father. He ascribes the highest of agencies to Christ in creation as well as revelation and salvation, but always in a frame of reference which looks to the one God who is over all. It is God who sends forth his Son, God who is reconciling men in Christ, God who raised Christ from the dead and gave him power that he should be Lord over all. The head of Christ is God. Christ is God's as we are Christ's. The exaltation of Christ is to the glory of God, and in the end the Son shall be subjected to the Father, "that God may be all in all." [2] The suggestion of John Calvin, that the phrase, "Christ is God's," refers simply to Christ's humanity is a misinterpretation of Paul.

3. For Paul, Christ was an historical and human personage, and the fact was vital to Paul's gospel. He did not, like later theologians, think of an abstraction called human "nature,"

[1] I Cor. 8:4-6.
[2] I Cor. 3:23; 11:3; Gal. 4:4; II Cor. 5:18, 19; Rom. 1:4; Phil. 2:9-11; I Cor. 15:27, 28.

which was conjoined with a divine "nature," or of a "humanity" which was "assumed" in some external fashion by a being come from heaven. Christ was not just man; he was *a* man, "born of the seed of David according to the flesh." It is true that Paul's supreme interest was in the living Christ, the Lord present in his Church and in the believer.[3] It is wrong to conclude, however, that he was either ignorant or indifferent in relation to the historic Jesus. There are scores of references to him in the epistles. He refers to Jesus as man, as Jew, born of a woman, with brothers of whom one is named, under the law, sinless, obedient, filled with the spirit of holiness, with a circle of followers, instituting the Lord's Supper, weak, suffering, betrayed, dying on the cross, buried and raised from the dead.[4] And beyond all this, remembering that Paul's letters are written for special occasions and situations, presupposing in most cases his previous teaching in person, it would be unwarranted to assume that in his regular work he did not make use of such materials of the common Christian tradition as are contained in the synoptic gospels.

More important still, the human Christ was a vital part of Paul's faith, essential in particular at three points. (1) Jesus was the revelation of man, the one into whom men were to grow up. In Christ's life and spirit, in his love and truth, his patience and pity, Paul saw the law of life which remained when the religion of law had passed. In his pure trust and utter obedience, and in his fellowship with the Father, he saw that to which God called men. Only as man could Christ be this

[3] II Cor. 5:16, 17.
[4] The references have been fully collected, together with the many parallels in which Paul, while not quoting, shows the dependence of his teaching on Jesus, by Paul Feine, *Jesus Christus und Paulus.*

revelation of man. (2) And, paradoxical as it might seem, only as man could he become the revelation of God. For in Paul's thought, the supreme revelation of God was the disclosure of his *love*, and this was seen in the love of him who in humility and suffering went to the cross. The power of God might be seen in the heavens but his character had to be revealed in a man. (3) Most important is the fact that for Paul the humanity of Jesus was essential to God's way of salvation. If it was needful that Christ should be from God and one with God, it was equally needful that he should be truly man and one with us. How strongly Paul felt the need of this identity with us is seen in his daring phrase about God's "sending his own Son in the likeness of sinful flesh." In Jesus God had actually become one with sinful humanity. Jesus had shown in his own person as man how the law might be fulfilled in those who walked "not after the flesh, but after the Spirit," how the Spirit of God might dwell in man. In his person Jesus as man was "the last Adam," the beginning of a new humanity, "the first-born among many brethren," the one to whom these others were to be conformed. In this human Jesus, in his life and death and resurrection, God's purpose of world redemption was being wrought out. Paul's idea of salvation, both individual and racial, demanded this conception of Jesus as a man. Upon this the Church has always insisted in its doctrine of salvation.

4. For Paul, Christ is not only the center and culmination of human history, but the final purpose and meaning of all creation is found in him. This is the explanation of those passages which relate Christ to creation. The modern man finds it hard to understand Paul when he declares, "all things have been created through him, and unto him; and he is before all

things, and in him all things consist." [5] Paul is not here giving
up his Hebrew monotheism or displacing God as Creator. God
is still for him the world ground. But there is a telic explanation of things as well as a causal one. The "cause" of all things
may be sought in the goal which lies ahead as well as in the
power which is behind all things. In Christ Paul sees not only
God's act of revelation and salvation and his final goal for
man, but the meaning of creation itself. Hence he sees in
Christ the why of all things and so the real cause of creation.
Creation finds its explanation in salvation and both in Christ.
So "all things have been created through him, and unto him."
To this end all things were made, visible and invisible, in the
heavens and upon the earth. And he gives unity to all, to the
things of creation as to the events of history. That ideal unity
is revealed in Christ; it will be achieved when through him
God "reconciles all things unto himself." This is the meaning of
the pregnant phrase of Colossians 1:17: "in him all things
consist," that is, hang together, or have their unity. As Pascal
said: "He who knows him, knows the meaning of all things."

IV. FINAL QUESTIONS

So we come to two closely related and equally difficult questions which Paul does not raise but which have concerned the
Church ever since Paul's day. And first, how can God and
man belong together in one life? How could Christ be human
and divine? Paul gives us no direct aid here; he simply leaves
divine and human side by side, affirming now one, now the
other. He sees Christ now "according to the flesh" and as such
"born of the seed of David"; then he sees him "according to

[5] Cf. Col. 1:15–22.

the Spirit" and as such "declared to be the Son of God with power." [1] He certainly knows nothing about an amalgam or addition of human "nature" and divine "nature." Such abstractions belong to the later theology which used these impersonal categories of substance and essence taken from Greek thought. Paul, *per contra*, is essentially Hebraic, thinking of both God and man in terms of the personal. Jesus for Paul was not just man; he was *a* man, this particular historic personality.

So we face the related question: how did God become man in Christ? Faith accepts the fact of the incarnation; that, we must always keep in mind, is the primary matter. Now we are asking as to the how of the incarnation. How can the divine, the transcendent, enter the human and finite and sinful? Paul's conception of the pre-existent Christ does not solve this problem. What of the relation of this divine being, "this second man," who "is of heaven," to the man who was born of the seed of David, who believed and obeyed, who was tempted and prayed, who hungered and thirsted and died? There is no suggestion with Paul of such later theological devices as an alternating consciousness, human and divine, or of the ancient heresy of docetism which denied a real incarnation by asserting that Christ's humanity was merely a kind of visible mantle, an external guise. The Christ of Paul was a man. Equally foreign to him was the conception of a union of "natures" as noted above, which is in fact only a verbal solution. Nor can we follow that other verbalism, the so-called kenotic theory, building on the Philippian passage and holding that the divine Christ temporarily "laid aside" such attributes as his omniscience and omnipotence when he came to earth, so interpreting Paul's "emptied himself." The idea of loosely attached "attrib-

[1] *Kata sarka, kata pneuma.* Rom. 1:3, 4.

utes" or powers which can be laid off and taken on like a garment corresponds to nothing in our knowledge of the personal life, nor does it do justice to Paul whose concern is here clearly, not with a speculative explanation, but with a moral fact, with an act of pure love, of humblest service, and of obedience unto death.

There is, however, another possible approach to this question besides the idea of a union of "substances" or "natures," or the appearance on earth of a heavenly being in the disguise of humanity. The category which is basic for Paul in his thinking about God and man and religion is the personal-ethical. Though God is the holy and exalted One while man is finite and sinful, yet God and man belong together. There is kinship, as well as otherness. Man is made in the image of God. Man belongs to God and God in his grace comes to man; and that is possible because both are personal beings. It is sin which holds them apart. But when God comes with his grace and man answers with a repentant and believing "Yes," then they are joined; then God dwells in man by his Spirit and man shares in God's life and nature so far as the finite can thus share. Whether then Paul speaks of God or man or salvation, this personal-ethical quality and relation is basic.

And it is this which makes incarnation possible. Let us keep in mind what incarnation means: the living and eternal God himself is present in this human life, present in a man, and so present that this life is one, not two, that this is God's life here on earth so far as the limits of the finite can receive it. Revelation, salvation, incarnation, these all belong together in God's gracious action; and all are made possible by this basic personal-ethical relation. In the end, of course, we deal with a mystery, with what must transcend our human grasp. All this

is not explanation; it is simply a signpost pointing the way
which our thought may travel. And it is the gospels which
bring this sign. They indicate the human side of the incarnation as clearly as the divine. They reveal not simply God's coming but the human response: that vision and trust and perfect
obedience which Jesus brought to God. This was the way by
which God entered this life. Only by this way is a true incarnation possible. In the perfect oneness of his life with God, Christ
was indeed unique, yet in the manner of that oneness, in that
life of utter faith and love and devotion, he showed to us the
only way of sonship.

What goes beyond this is rightly to be seen as theory or
theology. That does not mean invention. It rests upon two
great facts: God was in Christ, and what is of God is eternal.
So men will keep on trying to set forth by picture or symbol
that which we can never fully comprehend, as Paul tried in
Philippians 2. But we must keep in mind that this is not the
fact itself but only our attempt at explanation. The important
matter is the fact and the faith: the fact of Christ, and the
faith that God was in Christ for our salvation and that thus
there is opened the way for God to enter our life today. It is
this gospel which counts with Paul. Even in his more speculative expressions, it is the gospel which he seeks thereby to make
plain. His concern in Philippians is not to define a theory but
to summon men to live in the spirit of him who humbled himself and became obedient unto death. It may even be true, as
has been suggested, that this passage, and some others in the
New Testament like Matthew 11:25–27, are lines from primitive Christian hymns.[2] It must always be kept in mind: the
New Testament writings are not concerned with theological

[2] See B. W. Bacon, *The Gospel of the Hellenists*, pp. 312–314, 319.

formulations but with the proclamation of a gospel and the witness to a faith.

Our discussion may well close with the words of Luther with which Harnack prefaces the study of the Reformation in his *Dogmengeschichte:* "For Christ is not called Christ because he has two natures. What does that concern me? He bears this glorious and comforting name because of the office and work which he has taken upon himself; that gives him the name. That he is God and man by nature, this he has for himself; but that he uses his office to this end and pours out his love and becomes my Savior and Redeemer, that is for my comfort and my good." To this may fittingly be added the oft quoted words which Melanchthon prefixed to the first edition of the first evangelical theology, his *Loci Communes:* "To know Christ is to know his benefits, not to contemplate his natures or the modes of his incarnation."

Chapter Seven

THE INDWELLING SPIRIT

I. THE IDEA OF THE SPIRIT

OF ALL Paul's concepts that of the Spirit is perhaps the most constantly used and the least clearly defined. Heinrich Holtzmann says that it "is at once the most comprehensive, the most difficult, and the most variable concept which Paul has produced." [1] The reason is not far to seek: Paul shared with that first Christian generation the profound sense of a new and mighty working of God in their midst. Spirit denoted this presence and action of God in history and in human experience; it included not only the special and extraordinary gifts such as "tongues" and healings, but what was more important, the new life of the believer seen as a gift of God and the life of the Church viewed as a divine creation and indwelling. Within this sphere Christ himself belonged, so that Paul could say of him, "Now the Lord is the Spirit." [2] This great enlargement of the sphere of Spirit activity was accompanied by a notable enrichment and ethical deepening of the idea. The problem of understanding Paul's concept of the Spirit does not come, therefore, from the confusion which belonged to a sudden outburst of ecstatic religion, as is sometimes suggested, but rather from the extension of sphere and enrichment of content of religious experience in the early Church which Paul is seeking to express on its divine side by this term.

The conception of a spirit of God, or a spirit from God,

[1] *Neutestamentliche Theologie*, Vol. II, p. 155.
[2] II Cor. 3:17; cf. Rom. 1:4.

working in men is a very ancient and widespread one. It was used to explain unusual experiences such as vision, trance, and ecstatic speech; that is, whatever transcended man's ordinary powers. It did not involve necessarily any moral quality. The distinguishing idea was that of a power coming from a source above man. The exploits of Samson and the frenzied enthusiasm of a Saul were both thus explained. The man who received this power was to that extent "beside himself"— the Germans say "outside himself," *ausser sich*; that is, for the time being it was not he who saw or acted but this higher Being, or Power, which had invaded his spirit from without and dispossessed it. The idea is also employed to explain the special skills of Bezalel and Oholiab in their work for the sanctuary.[3]

Not a little of this more primitive conception lingered on in the New Testament. It is illustrated especially in the ecstatic "speaking with tongues" as referred to in the first Corinthian letter. The idea of biblical inspiration as absolute control of word or idea insuring infallibility also belongs here. To much of this, the pentecostal groups of today are successors, as is evidenced by their idea of a coming down in sudden and overwhelming fashion of "the power" and their emphasis on the gifts of healing and tongues.

The conception of the Spirit depends evidently upon the conception of God. The three conceptions of God which are most common in religion (leaving philosophical theory to one side) are those which stress in turn sovereign power, spiritual substance, and moral personality. With the first there goes the thought of the Spirit as a force, external and compulsive. It is

[3] Ju. 14:6, 19; 15:14, 15; I Sam. 11:6; 18:10; 19:23, 24; Exod. 35:30–35.

the more primitive viewpoint. The second conception marks the religion of extreme mysticism, for which the distinction of persons between God and man is something to be overcome by the absorption of the human into the divine. Here the divine is conceived in terms of spiritual substance, or essence. Sacramentarianism as a way of salvation is akin to this; for here again God is conceived first of all as pure and incorruptible essence. The sacraments show a double miracle: first, when the material and corruptible elements are transformed into the spiritual and incorruptible (the "miracle of the mass"); second, when the corruptible human "nature" is similarly transformed by the taking of the elements. Throughout, it is not a question of personal relations and moral quality, but of substance or essence. The third conception is a development of the first. It retains the idea of personal will, of power, and transcendence; but the will is ethical and not arbitrary, and the ethical dominates the idea of power. And as the concept of God is more fully ethicized and personalized, there is a corresponding change in the concept of religion; that is, of the character of the relation between man and God, which becomes necessarily more personal, ethical, and inner.

It is in this third setting that the Christian conception of the Spirit comes to its true and full expression. This was the line on which prophetic religion developed. God is a moral personality entering into personal relation with his people, a relation in which faith and obedience are the dominant requirement, whose fruit is a higher moral and spiritual life, and whose gifts are conceived as ultimately coming to all the people. Here belong such great passages as Isaiah 11:1–5; 32:15–17; 42:1–4; Micah 3:8; Jeremiah 31:31–35; Ezekiel 36:26, 27. Here are the beginnings of the higher concept of the Spirit. It still means power from on high, but the power has moral and spiritual quality; it is the spirit of wisdom, the fear of the Lord, courage, righteousness, devotion to justice, faithfulness, pity, mercy. It is to the New Testament, however, that we must turn for its developed form and it was Paul who gave it its fullest expression.

The sources for Paul's idea of the Spirit are the same as for his whole body of thought of which this is so important a part. (1) There is the underlying faith of his people in the one God; the Spirit is God's Spirit, God himself present and at work with men. That is why the term Spirit includes so much; it is the total expression of God's presence and work. (2) There is the historic fact of Jesus. As Paul's conception of God's character is determined by the spirit which was in Christ, so is his conception of the divine Spirit. From one side he sees Christ as belonging to the realm of Spirit; from the other side he sees Spirit as having the moral quality of Christ. "The fruit of the Spirit is love, joy, and peace," and love first of all. And the idea of love with Paul gains its content from the spirit of Christ.[4] Generically Spirit, for Paul, means God; specifically, or qualitatively, it means Christ. That is perhaps the greatest single advance made in the Christian doctrine of the Spirit. (3) Paul's doctrine of the Spirit was shaped by Christian experience, his own experience and that of the Christian community. Here was a period of extraordinary religious vitality, a creative epoch which was the more notable because, in Paul's words, "not many wise, not many mighty, not many noble" were called. The outstanding creative results of this movement were three: (a) a lofty spiritual faith joined to a high ethical ideal; (b) the transformation of men and women, often of the

[4] Gal. 5:22; I Cor. 12:31; Phil. 2.

lowest social strata, whose lives were morally remade and who often exhibited high spiritual gifts; (c) a fellowship which secured a notable unity with the minimum of organization, and which was able to bring into this unity the most diverse elements of race and class. The explanation of all this Paul found in Christ and the Spirit, that is, in the God who had come to men in Christ and whose redemptive power was present with men in his Spirit. This Spirit Paul understood by seeing how it worked in the gift of insight, in the transformation of life, and in the creation of the fellowship.

We can now summarize Paul's conception of the Spirit at those points in which it marks the Christian advance over the more primitive viewpoint. (1) The Spirit is for all men and not for the few. There is no aristocracy of the Spirit, with special gifts for priest or prophet, pastor or bishop, king or pope. "For there are diversities of gifts but the same Spirit; . . . the same God who worketh all things in all." Indeed, he is not even a Christian who does not have the Spirit.[5] (2) The presence of the Spirit is not the mark of unusual experience or exceptional endowment; it is rather the source of all Christian life, of its every gift, every virtue, every expression. Even the simple Christian confession, to say *Jesus Lord*, is possible only in the Spirit.[6] What Paul emphasizes, in fact, is just this work of the Spirit in the normal Christian life as over against the speaking with tongues which so impressed the vain Corinthians. And he did this "on the basis of his experience, which showed him that the Christian himself was the greatest miracle." [7] (3) The Spirit is ethical in its nature and its fruit,

---

[5] I Cor. 12:4; Rom. 8:9.
[6] Gal. 5:16–25; Rom. 8:1–17; II Cor. 12:3.
[7] H. Gunkel, *Die Wirkungen des heiligen Geistes,* pp. 80, 81.

and we see its nature when we consider the spirit which was in Christ. The Spirit is the Christ spirit. "The fruit of the Spirit is love, joy, peace, long-suffering, kindness, goodness, faithfulness, meekness, self-control." The use of the singular, fruit, is suggestive. Dealing here with the central, ethical-spiritual aspect of the Spirit's work, Paul transcends the idea of particular gifts, or powers, separately and more or less externally bestowed. There is one life of the Spirit given us, and these various qualities are but the expression (the fruit) of that one life and of its essential nature. To have the Spirit is to have a given quality of character: "the mind of the Spirit" which is "life and peace," the spirit of a son "whereby we cry, Abba, Father." It is the same as having the spirit of Christ, or as having "the mind of Christ," which means the self-sacrificing love that led Christ to earth and to the cross.[8] (4) The Spirit is still conceived in terms of power; now, however, this power is ethical, not mechanical or magical or externally compulsive. A man can only have the Spirit as he "walks" by the Spirit. That is, he can only receive it as he lives it out in obedience.[9] (5) Finally, it must be added that with all the emphasis on the Spirit as ethical and as indwelling, the element of transcendence remains. There is no suggestion of pantheism here. This is *Holy* Spirit and *Holy* is used in its primary sense, not as ethical, but as denoting the transcendent.

II. THE WORK OF THE SPIRIT

The Holy Spirit for Paul is God in action. Nothing could be more misleading than to seek in Paul for a sharp division of

[8] Gal. 5:22; Rom. 8:6, 14, 15; Phil. 2:1-8.
[9] Rom. 8:2-4; Gal. 5:16, 25. Cf. also Rom. 15:13 with Lu. 4:14.

function as related to Father, Son, and Spirit. The transcendent God, the Holy One, Creator of heaven and earth, is the forgiving God who comes to us in Christ and the self-giving God who is present with us in the Spirit. Whatever God does with men and in men is done by his Spirit. That remains true whether the reference is to God or Christ or the Spirit. In the main Paul thinks of the work of the Spirit in five aspects.

1. The Spirit brings truth and light to men. He brings insight to the believer and the true wisdom of God, making him see the meaning of the cross and of God's way of salvation. So especially in I Corinthians 1:17 to 2:16.

2. By his Spirit God transforms men. The Spirit of God in man becomes man's spirit, his new life. Through this Spirit men become sons, as Christ is Son, growing up in him who is the head. There are many "gifts of the Spirit" which enter in to make this new life but "the greatest of these is love." [1]

3. God's Spirit in man is the power of a new life. Here is deliverance from the old impotence and the servitude of sin, from "the body of this death." "The Law of the Spirit of life" makes us free. Men have now "the mind of the Spirit," which is life and peace. Now the law of God can be kept because it has become the life within.[2]

4. The Spirit is the Spirit of fellowship. It is the "togethering" Spirit, the power that heals and unites. First of all, it makes the individual whole; the divided self of Romans 7:15–21 is now one in the new spirit which forms its life, one in a new and single loyalty. But Paul's special emphasis is on the Spirit as a Spirit of fellowship. It joins men in one body, of which all

[1] Gal. 5:22, 23; Rom. 8:14–17; Eph. 4:15; I Cor. 12:31 to 13:13.
[2] Rom. 8:1–11.

are members. It fills them with one Spirit, though the gifts
may vary. It unites them, above all, as the Spirit of love, that
love which is "the bond of perfectness"; that is, the love which
at once perfects us and binds us together. Thus it breaks down
all the old divisions which have separated classes and nations,
as well as those personal hostilities which come from such sins
as selfishness, fear, hate, greed, bitterness, and anger.[3]

5. Finally, Paul sees in the Spirit the source of all the special
"gifts" of the disciples. A good deal of attention has been given
to the exceptional gifts of the Spirit which appeared at Corinth.
Throughout the history of the Church there have been recur-
rent groups, from the Montanists on, who have felt that the
Church's great need was the renewal of these special gifts,
particularly those of prophesying, healing, and speaking with
tongues. It is important here to clear up certain misunderstandings. The gift of tongues must be understood in the light of
Paul's account, not that of Acts. Paul gives us first-hand knowledge; Acts is a late report, already with legendary features.
Paul makes clear that this "tongue-speaking" (*glossolalia*) was
an ecstatic utterance, incoherent and unintelligible even to the
speaker. It was not a speaking with understanding and it did
not instruct. Prophesying seems to have been an earnest and
searching presentation of the truth which brought men to
repentance and faith.

The Corinthian emphasis on ecstatic experiences and on the
speaking with tongues was a return to earlier and lower conceptions of the Spirit and was akin to what appeared in the
mystery cults of that time. There was the same stress on the
emotional, the same absence of the rational and ethical. In
their frenzy some even shouted, "Jesus is anathema." Outsiders

[3] I Cor. 12:4 to 13:13.

coming in thought them mad. In any case, it neither expressed the spirit of love nor served to build up the life of the fellowship but tended rather to pride and self-assertion. Paul does not rule out such gifts entirely. He was here a child of the Hellenistic world and his contrast at this point with Jesus must be recognized. He himself had ecstatic experiences and spoke with tongues.[4] But at the crucial point, what he emphasizes is that which brings truth and appeals to the understanding, which builds up the fellowship, which unites rather than divides, and which evinces humility and love and service rather than pride and selfishness. So he puts "tongues" at the end of his list of the offices in the Church and declares that love is the most excellent way.[5]

III. HOW THE SPIRIT IS GIVEN

How does Paul conceive of the way in which the Spirit is given to men? Here, as so often, we lack direct discussion; yet the Pauline answer to this question is evident and is important.

There was an older conception, to be found in the Old Testament, which made the coming of the divine Spirit as mysterious as was its operation. It was supernatural and the supernatural as such was inexplicable. In similar fashion unusual and baffling forms of evil, such as insanity, or epilepsy, or even a sudden and stubborn rheumatism, were ascribed to demon possession. Familiar in the history of religion is the method by which, through loneliness, vigils, and fasting, or through such rites as were provided for the initiate or the group by the mystery religions, the ecstatic experience was induced, which was in turn taken as evidence of the presence and power of the

[4] II Cor. 12:2; I Cor. 14:18, 19.   [5] I Cor. 12:29, 31; 14:1-33.

Spirit.[1] A third conception is that of the sacerdotal-sacramentarian way. It was the Church's answer to the excesses of the ecstatics, and it brought it all safely within the control of the Catholic Church, conceived as the repository and dispenser of the means of salvation. The gift of the Spirit is channeled through the Church. Through the sacraments, ranging from baptism to extreme unction, and under the hands of priest and bishop, the sacred power flows out in its appropriate form for the particular need.

Paul does not discuss the question at all, partly, it may be presumed, because there was no special occasion, but in the main because there was no special method or medium for receiving the Spirit. It is an eloquent witness to the simplicity, the spirituality, and the depth of Paul's conception of the religious life and the experience of salvation. His position can be outlined in five simple statements. (1) The God of grace comes to man in Christ. (2) Man answers this God in penitent and obedient faith. (3) Man lives the new life with God in the fellowship of faith, with man in the fellowship of love. (4) In that fellowship God gives himself to man—this is the gift of grace, of the Spirit. (5) Through the power of this fellowship man is transformed. All this, it is to be noted, moves in the sphere of personal relation, ethically conceived.

In all this the required human response is faith, faith as Paul sees it, faith as insight and conviction, as the answer of trust and obedience, faith working through love. And this is all that is needed to understand how men receive the Spirit: the God who gives, the disciple who lives in faith with this God. "God giveth his Holy Spirit unto you," he writes the

[1] Interesting parallels from varied sources in F. M. Davenport, *Primitive Traits in Religious Revivals*.

Thessalonians; you received the Spirit, he tells the Galatians, "by the hearing of faith." [2] Men receive the Spirit as by faith they live the Christian life. There is no Christian living without God's Spirit. The disciple's life, in every form of experience and expression, is at once God's gift of the Spirit and our response to God, and all in the form of personal relation: the I and Thou in the relation with God, the I and you and we in the human fellowship.

This does not mean, of course, that there is no movement in the Christian life. The faith may be weak, the obedience imperfect, the knowledge that of babes, the humility mingled with pride and the love with selfishness and strife. Then the fellowship is a broken one and the tides of the spirit run low. And here Paul's letters are full of suggestions, not directed to a technique for the reception of these spiritual forces, but telling the Christian about the new life and what it requires; for the receiving of the Spirit is not a matter apart but belongs to the whole Christian life. That life, as Paul presents it, has a duality of movement: first, dependence upon God and the constant taking from him of forgiveness and grace and the Spirit; second, the active expression in love and service of what God thus gives. In order to live you must have the Spirit; in order to have the Spirit you must live by it. "If we live by the Spirit, by the Spirit let us also walk." [3] There is great aid to be gotten, without doubt, from the example of the saints, the counsel of the wise, the use of rightful helps, the practice of mediation and prayer, the sharing in public worship, as well as from the simple ways of love and service. But the philosophy of the matter is found in the simple Pauline principles indicated above, and they are the principles which underlie the whole

[2] I Thes. 4:8; Gal. 3:2, 5.   [3] Gal. 5:25.

Christian life. That life is a unity, for all of which the presence of God's Spirit is basal—basal, not something apart.

IV. THE PERMANENT VALUE OF THE DOCTRINE

Perhaps no other doctrine of the Christian faith has been as subject to misunderstanding and abuse as has the doctrine of the Spirit. With this, and in a measure because of this, has gone the not uncommon neglect of this teaching. For the average churchman it is vague, mysterious, and unmeaning. Traditional orthodoxy used it to secure infallibility for Scripture writers and creed-forming councils, and thus made it externalistic and mechanical in its operation. With special groups within the Church, its work was seen in individual and subjective experience, emotional and non-ethical in character. In Catholicism it took on a narrowly ecclesiastical and sacramentarian meaning. But all this should not hide from us its important place in the Christian faith. Let us look at it first functionally, less in terms of exact formulation of doctrine, which it certainly did not have with Paul, and more with reference to the truth which Paul was seeking to express and to the ends which this concept served.

1. Paul's doctrine of the Spirit unites the ideas of divine transcendence and nearness, of otherness and kinship. Immanence does not rightly express Paul's idea of the latter. With his many and varied phrases, he never speaks of God in us. The nearest he comes to this is to say: "It is God who worketh in you," and "Your life is hid with Christ in God." [4] Nowhere does he approach the mystical thought of the merging of the

[4] Phil. 2:13; Col. 3:3.

soul with God in a metaphysical union. God and man always stand as persons over against each other, and the Spirit which he gives us is *Holy* Spirit, that is, transcendent and other. Yet this transcendent God becomes the intimate God. His Spirit, creative, makes over our life, informs our spirit, and constitutes its deepest and truest nature. It becomes our life and strength; we live by the Spirit and walk by the Spirit. And it is to this same experience that Paul refers when he says, "For me to live is Christ." Paul is equally removed from that one-sided emphasis on the otherness of God which sacrifices the idea of kinship between God and man, and that immanentism which has lost the personal God and all thought of transcendent holiness and power.

Perhaps the greatest point of weakness in Barth's theology appears here. He "has no theology of the third article," as one of his earlier critics puts it.[5] That is true despite the longer discussion of the Holy Spirit in Barth's *Dogmatik*, Vol. I, Part I, pp. 470–489. Hence he can find no place for a union of God and man by which man in any measure is made over by the Spirit of God into the likeness of Christ, into the spirit of a true child of God through the dwelling in him of faith and truth and love, wholly the gift of God and yet at the same time the true life of man. The Spirit in us, so far as this life is concerned, means for Barth our recognition of the Word when God speaks to us. But even this seems dangerous to him, destroying in a measure the creatureliness of man, so he hastens to add that in reality we do not know or recognize God's word to us; it is God (the Spirit) who thus knows. God, as it were, hears himself speak. Beyond that is the vigorous insistence that "everything which can be said about man's receiving the Spirit

[5] *Zeitschrift für Theologie und Kirche*, 1926, p. 471.

being driven by the Spirit, and filled with the Spirit, is in the meaning of the New Testament an eschatological expression"; that is, it is viewed as belonging to the *eschaton*, the end, to another age, not to this. What man has here he has in faith, which means as a promise. It is not in the least degree fulfilled or accomplished in the present. We have it only as the expectation of what is to be. "We assume this future completion because it speaks of God's act, though the hands which we stretch out to God are empty." [6] Does he mean that, except for a hope, our hearts are empty, too? There seems to be no place in Barth for salvation as sanctification, that is, as a real making over of the believer.

2. In Paul's doctrine of the Spirit, the individual and the social in religion are brought into unity. In the gift of the Spirit religion becomes individualized. The infinite God is present to each individual soul; through the Spirit God dwells in him and works in him, making him a son of God. Here is no great or small, no male or female, no bond or free, no cleric or lay. Each has his task from God and his gift; "to each one is given the manifestation of the Spirit to profit withal." For each there is a final place of meeting known only to God and himself, where "the Spirit himself beareth witness with our spirit, that we are children of God." [7] Yet this Spirit is a Spirit of brotherhood as well as of sonship; it is a Spirit of love; there is no Spirit of God in us if there is not a spirit of love uniting us to men. Here, long before men talked about whole-making, integration, or the principle of organicism as basic to all life, Paul, discussing the Spirit, wrote about the body and its members. We are members of a Body, of the Fellowship, whose life is the Spirit, or the living Christ. There is no such thing as reli-

[6] *Op. cit.*, p. 486.   [7] I Cor. 12:7; Rom. 8:16.

gious atomism, or pure individualism. We share the life of the Spirit in the life of the whole which the Spirit creates. "Ye are the body of Christ, and severally members thereof." [8]

3. In this conception of an indwelling Spirit Paul secures the unity of religious and ethical, and in securing this meets the severest test to which life submits religion. Religion signifies for Paul both utter dependence upon God and the greatest freedom and activity. It is neither moralistic activism, nor passive mysticism or fatalism. The Christian life in all its range and depth is wholly the gift of God: "We live by the Spirit." But as the Spirit of love and truth and righteousness, it demands active expression in life; hence, "by the Spirit let us also walk." [9]

4. Paul's doctrine of the Spirit asserts and assures the more inner and spiritual aspect of religion. Religion, like every other form of social life, easily tends to become identified with its more formal and institutional expressions. The prophets advanced the inner and personal aspect of religion by their insistence upon the ethical. This necessarily brought increased emphasis on the individual, stressed the personal spirit and attitude, as with Jeremiah and in the Psalms, and so moved from the idea of a holy nation to that of a people of God within the nation. The New Testament, following Jesus, emphasizes the fact that the higher righteousness must be that of the inner spirit, and that this inwardness must mark all religion. The doctrine of the Spirit is the constant reminder of the need of this inwardness in religion.

[8] I Cor. 12: 1–31.   [9] Gal. 5:16, 25.

Chapter Eight

THE CHURCH

IT IS very difficult for us of the present day to understand what the first Christians meant by the word which we translate "Church," for almost inevitably we read back into their references some of the varied meanings which the word has gathered through the centuries. Our first task then must be, not so much a discussion of Paul's idea of the Church, as the inquiry how there came to be a Christian community and how its members thought of it.

Christianity was a fellowship from the beginning, a company with a leader. That much is plain. Did Jesus go farther? Did he announce the establishment of a "Church" and place Peter at its head? Did he contemplate an ecclesiastical organization directed by the twelve apostles, with their successors ruling the Church of the future? All this is asserted by the Roman Church on the basis of Matthew 16:18: "Thou art Peter, and upon this rock I will build my church." The word Church occurs in the gospels at only one other place, Matthew 18:17, which suggests a method of procedure in controversy between Church members. We face the double question: Did Jesus speak these words? If he did, what do they mean?

Many scholars have questioned whether Jesus spoke these words. The latter passage clearly reflects a later time when the Church had lost something of its early spirit of brotherhood and Church discipline was a necessity. As to the former, would Jesus, feeling that this age was near its end, talk about the establishment of an institution planned for the centuries?

Present-day scholarship, dating our gospels in the second generation after Jesus' death, holds that they are concerned with what affected the faith and life of the Church of that day and are inevitably colored by this. In any case if Jesus had thus formally established an independent ecclesiastical body, it would be hard to explain why the primitive Christian community did not from the first recognize its independence of the Jewish Church.

But if we assume that Jesus really used these words, what do they mean? What did Jesus refer to when he spoke of his "Church"? Certainly not an ecclesiastical-legal institution as Rome has supposed. Nor even what Protestant orthodoxy has assumed. That would have been unintelligible to the disciples and unrealistic for Jesus in that situation. What Jesus probably meant, as we shall see later, was a fellowship, or company, or community, represented by this group, in which he saw the real remnant of Israel, the true people of God.[1] Every picture of Jesus shows him with his followers. The group varied in its composition. Apparently there was a nucleus of those who were in closer and more constant association with the Master, with a larger number, including some women, who were present during the last days at Jerusalem. After his death we find a fairly large company at Jerusalem, their faith made strong by his appearance to them, their life enriched by the experience of divine presence and power through the Spirit, while a deep sense of mutual love bound them together. They believed in Jesus as Messiah, they looked for his return to establish God's rule; but they did not think of themselves at first as standing

---

[1] An extended discussion is given by K. L. Schmidt, under *ekklesia*, in the *Theologisches Wörterbuch* edited by R. Kittel, Vol. III, especially p. 530.

over against the Jewish community. They were rather a community within that community.

Paul played a leading part in making the Christian community see that there was in it something new and different which set it apart from Judaism and made it universal. The direction of the Christian movement was alike extensive and intensive. There was a multiplication of the Christian groups, or communities, as the new faith moved out into the Roman Empire and at the same time an increasing realization of what the new fellowship signified. The geographical extension and the deepening understanding went hand in hand, and each affected the other. Our concern is with the latter. How did these first Christians in general, and Paul in particular, think of the Christian community? Why did they give it the name Church (*ekklesia*), and what did they mean by that name?

I. THE CHURCH AS THE PEOPLE OF GOD

What did the word Church mean in this primitive Christian usage? Words have histories; meanings change with the years and the same word may have many differing connotations at the same time. Thus the word Church may mean with us a building, a local congregation, the act of worship ("going to church"), a particular religious denomination, the sum of the various Christian communions, or the invisible and inclusive fellowship of the followers of Christ. The English word Church, with the corresponding German *Kirche* and the Scotch Kirk, probably comes from the Greek *kyriakon,* an adjective meaning the Lord's, first applied to the house used for Christian worship and then coming to mean the congregation meeting there. We must go back of this to the Greek word of our New

Testament, *ekklesia,* a word carried over into the Latin as *ecclesia,* appearing in French as *église,* and giving us our English word ecclesiastical.

The earliest use of the word *ekklesia* in Greek was secular. The word means literally called out, and it referred to some special or regular assembly of the people. Thus in Acts 19:39 the town clerk suggests to the mob at Ephesus that their cause should be brought before the regular *ekklesia,* or town meeting. The Christian use of the word, however, is to be traced in its origin to the Septuagint, the Greek translation of the Old Testament which had become the Bible of the Jews throughout the Graeco-Roman world. There it is used to translate the Hebrew word *quahal. Quahal* meant literally assembly, just like *ekklesia*; but it came to have a distinct religious meaning, first as indicating a religious gathering, the solemn assembly, then as meaning the people themselves as the people of Jehovah. There was another Greek word which literally meant much the same as *ekklesia,* namely syngogue (literally, a bringing together and so an assembly). This, too, was used in the Septuagint to translate the Hebrew *quahal.* But synagogue came to mean more particularly the *local* religious gathering of the Jews or the building in which they met, while *ekklesia* was used when the reference was to Israel as a whole conceived as God's people. Finally, when Israel ceased to count as a nation politically, *ekklesia* came more and more to denote the faithful Israel, Israel as a believing and worshipping people—a Church.

Now we can see how significant it was that the Christians chose the word *ekklesia* as the name for their fellowship instead of the word synagogue, though the latter is used once, in James 2:2. There is a claim involved in the very term and it represents the first important element in Paul's conception of the Christian fellowship. The Jews had many synagogues, that is, groups meeting regularly for worship, like those referred to in Acts 6:9, to one of which Paul and Stephen may well have belonged before their conversion. But the Christians were not just another among these synagogues. They were the Christian *ekklesia,* the Christian communion, or fellowship, or people. But there is more implied here, and Paul makes it plain. They were not just *an ekklesia,* a Christian one; they were *the ekklesia, the* people of God. The Old Testament word for Israel, *ekklesia,* now belonged to them. The God of Israel was their God and they were the true Israel. Once Israel had meant the nation. When the nation proved false to God then Israel meant the faithful remnant, the Jewish *ekklesia,* or Church. But the Jewish Church had refused the Messiah Jesus and now his disciples held themselves to be the true Israel.

Here then is the first meaning of the Church in Christianity. It is not a newly established institution. It is not primarily an "institution" at all; it is a people, God's people. It reaches back in history. It carries on the historical purpose which began with the nation Israel, God's purpose of creating for himself a people upon earth.

But if the word *ekklesia in* Christian usage stands for continuity with the past, it also stands for something new; and we have now to consider the new and rich content which Paul finds in this term. In referring to it we shall commonly use the word Church. But it needs to be said here very definitely: there is no one word in English which gives the real New Testament meaning of *ekklesia.* It may be rendered church, community, fellowship, people; but it is more than any one of these in its common meaning.

II. THE BODY AND ITS MEMBERS

We cannot do better in studying Paul's conception of the nature of the Church than to begin with his picture of the body in I Corinthians 12. "As the body is one, and hath many members, and all the members of the body, being many, are one body; so also is Christ [that is, so it is with the Christian communion]. For in one Spirit were we all baptized into one body. . . . Now ye are the body of Christ, and severally members thereof." The figure which Paul uses is not original with him. The Stoics especially had made use of it. Humanity, declared Seneca, has the unity of a living body, and in that body each individual is a member with his corresponding obligation to the whole. In its broadest sense, this organismic conception has been effectively used in modern philosophy also as a principle of interpretation, not simply of human kind, but of all reality and process. This is, of course, a figure, or analogy, to be used as such and not to be pressed too literally. But when all is said, it remains true: here is Paul's central idea for the understanding of the Church, or Christian community, and it is for him and for us the most fruitful single concept. The Church for Paul is a living, an organic whole.

This idea of Paul's is to be clearly distinguished from two other conceptions which have been very common in Christian history, and first of all from the institutional concept. The clearest example of this theory is the Roman Church. For Rome the Church is something formally established and legally prescribed. To its proper and necessary form as determined by God there belong ecclesiastical orders with delegated powers, including infallibility of teaching (under certain conditions) and the administration and control of the necessary means for salvation (the sacraments). Paul has nothing to say about clerical orders or episcopal authority. The items of organization where differences of opinion have often blocked the way to Church union are absent from his writings. He knows nothing of an authoritative head of the Church and vice-regent of Christ in the person of the Apostle Peter, nor of a college of bishops (the Twelve) at Jerusalem with Peter at their head. He recognizes the acknowledged leaders at Jerusalem—Peter and James and John. But these are not the Twelve, and James was not even a member of the Twelve. Moreover he regards himself as an apostle and not a whit behind the "pillar apostles." Barnabas, too, is an apostle, and Andronicus and Junius are "of note among the apostles." [1] But Paul's thought is equally removed from the conception which sees the Church as simply a voluntary association of Christian individuals uniting for common religious ends. His concept of Christianity is neither humanistic nor individualistic. It is historic-social, or corporate (the people of God), and it is divine as well as human. These two aspects, as contained in his picture of the body, we have now to consider, and first the corporate.

The first and obvious significance of the analogy of the body is that the Christian fellowship, or community, has a common life. It is not a mere sum of individuals each separately joined by faith to God. There is a unified life which no individual by himself can fully express. It will help us to note how this principle of the whole and the part belongs to life everywhere. Life is always a mysterious, inexplicable bond which unites individual parts and creates a whole that is richer than any mere sum of what the parts as such possess. And the parts in turn, by belonging to the whole, share in this more significant

[1] I Cor. 15:5–10; Gal. 1:6 to 2:21; Rom. 16:7.

life. So the cells unite to form an organ—the skillful hand, the seeing eye. So the organs, or the members, using Paul's term, unite to form the body with its varied activities of sensation, perception, purposive movement, reason, and social relations. There are social wholes as well as biological: at every step the higher life of humanity depends upon family, community, church, state, friendship groups, and associations in industry. Without these man could not rise above the level of the brute.

The Church illustrates this principle upon the highest level of human existence, considered both in man's relation to God and to his fellows. Paul has no occasion to work this out in detail. His Corinthian argument was brought forward for practical purposes. As against the individualism and pride and divisiveness of the Corinthians, he shows how dependent each is upon the life of the whole and upon every other member, and in turn how each is needed for the life of the whole and is under obligation to contribute to that life. Paul's illustration, which is both corporate and social, makes clear that he is dealing not with something mysterious and wholly different, but with something akin to common experiences of life, though on a higher plane. Paul is not deserting the categories of the personal-social-ethical for something wholly foreign and inscrutable.

But does not the mysterious enter in when we turn to the other side of Paul's idea, the divine aspect? Yes, but only in the sense in which there is mystery present in all divine action and in the religious life of the individual, where human and divine are similarly joined. As in the case of the individual, Paul pictures God's life-giving work in the Church under varying forms. The Church is God's creation. It is the body of Christ, and Christ is the head of the Church. Anderson

Scott says flatly that Paul "equated Christ with the society of redeemed men of which he was the Head" and quotes approvingly, "There was no Christ apart from his people." [2] The statement is extreme, and shows the danger of literalizing and absolutizing the symbols or pictures of religious language. (One might as well say, Paul knows no Holy Spirit apart from the Church.) There is significant truth here but it is of the same kind as in Paul's other statement, "It is no longer I that live, but Christ liveth in me." [3] The Church in a very real sense is a continuing incarnation. The God who entered human life in Jesus of Nazareth is visibly and actively manifest to men in the Church of Christ. Here Christ's spirit dwells and works. Here his reconciling word is heard. Here he unites men in faith and love and service. If the Church in its life does not make Christ visible to man then it is not the Church of Christ; so far as it does, it is his body, and his spirit is its essential and motivating life.

Similarly Paul makes the Church the seat and organ of the Holy Spirit. The Church is "the communion (*koinonia,* fellowship, community) of the Holy Spirit." "In one Spirit were we all baptized into one body." [4] The Spirit forms the life of the whole and the Spirit works in each individual member. There is only one life of the Church and that is the Spirit: "there are diversities of gifts, but the same Spirit." As we have seen before, however, these references to God and Christ and the Spirit do not have to do with three distinct types of life or aspects of the divine work in the Church. In almost the same sentence Paul speaks of "diversities of gifts, but the same

[2] *Christianity According to St. Paul,* p. 157.
[3] Gal. 2:20.
[4] II Cor. 13:14; I Cor. 12:12. Cf. Eph. 2:11-22: "in whom ye also are builded together for a habitation of God in the Spirit."

Spirit," of "diversities of ministrations, and the same Lord," and of "diversities of workings, but the same God who worketh all things in all." [5]

What we have here then in relation to the Church is what we find everywhere else where Paul treats of God's work of salvation. There is a human side and there is a divine. These two sides we have now to consider, together with the paradoxes or apparent contradictions in Paul's references to the Church which arise out of their relation.

III. THE CHURCH AS DIVINE AND HUMAN

Paul's conception of the Church seems at first in hopeless contradiction. On the one side he presents the Church as a divine creation set apart from a sinful world, realizing God's plan for a holy people. It is Christ's body, and its life is God's own life, his creative presence. Paul addresses its members as "them that are sanctified in Christ Jesus, called to be saints," literally, "called saints." Not only is the Spirit the essential life of the Church, but it is also the life of each member, and all their activities in the Church are the gifts or the workings of the Spirit. "It is God that worketh in you." [1]

It is equally apparent that Paul has no illusions as to the kind of members who compose his scattered congregations. That is especially apparent in the Corinthian letters. He has hardly greeted "them that are sanctified" before he takes up the matter of their endless quarrellings. He declares that Christ has been made to them "wisdom from God, and righteousness and sanctification, and redemption." He says of them, "Ye were washed, ye were sanctified." Yet he calls them carnal, censures

[5] I Cor. 12:4–6. [1] I Cor. 1:2, 3; 12:4–11.

the jealousy and strife which is in their midst, and refers to a case of flagrant sexual immorality which had remained unrebuked by the Church.[2]

What we have here is the problem which we faced in our consideration of "Salvation as Remaking." How can the Christian life be at once divine and human, the work of God and yet marked by imperfection? How can the Church be holy and yet composed of sinful men? Mere moralism is untroubled by such a question; it knows only the human, which is confessedly limited. And there are ways of conceiving God's work in salvation which seem to escape this difficulty, as when God's action is conceived as direct, independent of man and his response, and strictly determinative. Similarly you may conceive of God as working by a sacramentarian instrument in which the divine potency is present objectively in the elements of the eucharist, working necessarily, in scholastic phrase *ex opere operato*. And you may think in this connection of a divine ecclesiastical institution in which the ruling hierarchy is made infallible in its official actions by direct divine determination, and to which is given the dispensation of the sacramentarian saving forces. Or you may stress divine sovereignty working by irresistible grace. But not so in the Christian way of salvation as Paul conceives it. For here you have united the God from whom all saving help comes and the life of personal relation in faith in which and through which the divine help is given. God's grace and man's response both have place in this continuing relation.

This double aspect is expressed in the word holy as used by Paul, and in other terms which contain the same root, namely

[2] I Cor. 1:2, 3, 30; 3:3; 5:1, 2; 6:11; and note the whole section, chs. 1 to 6.

saints, sanctified, and sanctification. In its primary sense when applied to men, that is holy which belongs. Such is the Church and such are those of its fellowship. The "saints," or "holy ones," at Corinth are those who belong to God, who have surrendered themselves to Christ in the act of saving faith. But this belonging is no mere external affair; it means being made over, and that gives its second sense. The saints are those who are *being* sanctified; the "holy" are being hallowed, or "holied." The "belonging" means an active and creative and ongoing relation with a God who is holy and who makes holy. The holy Church, just because it belongs to God, is the seat of these transforming spiritual powers and, as a human fellowship, is itself being made over. The Holy Spirit dwells in it, the Spirit of love and truth and righteousness, and those who belong to it are in the sphere of this saving power. Here is holiness in its more distinctively Christian sense. Holiness as the mark of the transcendent God, and so as applied to that which belongs to him, is, as Rudolf Otto has showed, an almost universal religious concept. But holiness as the character of love and righteousness, pertaining supremely to God and given by God's grace to his children, is the distinctive idea which came with the prophets, had its fulfillment in Christ, and was made clear by Paul in its vital meaning for salvation.[3]

The Church then is holy in this double sense: it belongs to God and is the place in which the Holy Spirit dwells and works; it is the fellowship of those who belong to Christ and are being made over in holiness of character and life. In the first sense the holiness of the Church is something ideal and absolute; in the second sense it is something relative and im-

---

[3] See articles on "Holiness" by N. Söderblom and R. H. Coats in the *Encyclopedia of Religion and Ethics*.

perfect, because it pertains to what is human and finite and to an ongoing process never absolutely complete. Nevertheless this second aspect is something very real; indeed, it is the very heart of Christianity as a living religion, for it is the place where God and man come together for the saving of men.

This is the paradox of the Church as that which is at once holy and imperfect, as that which unites the absolute with the relative. Relative and imperfect is not only the life of the Church and its people, but all that in which the Church expresses itself. The empirical Church has tried to escape from this. Knowing itself as holy, it has assumed that it must be able to point to something in its life which was absolute and perfect. The separatist groups, taking one side of Paul's affirmations, have tried to establish this quality of perfection, first by a doctrine of sanctification of the individual, to be attained through a special work of the Holy Spirit; then by the exclusion of the imperfect from the fellowship, limiting the Church to the truly saintly, or sanctified. Those of the churchly tradition have also sought for some point of absoluteness where they could escape this limitation. This appears in the claim of infallibility, whether of a governing hierarchy, a creed-making council, or in relation to the Scriptures. Evangelical Protestantism has erred in failing to see that while the Absolute, the eternal God, speaks to man and comes to him for his salvation, neither creed nor Scripture as such can be identified with this Word of God in absolute fashion. For these are man's apprehensions of the Word, his understanding of the living God and how he has dealt with man. Catholicism has even more plainly sought to put itself in the place of God and give to the empirical Church an absoluteness which belongs only to God himself.

IV. ORGANIZATION AND FUNCTION

There are a number of other questions which the modern man puts to Paul concerning the Church and which can only be answered if we realize how different Paul's approach is from ours. We need here to keep constantly in mind that Paul conceives of the Church as being essentially a divinely created spiritual organism, while still recognizing its empirical-human character.

1. Does Paul think of the Church as one or as many, in terms of one body or of many local congregations? A survey of Paul's references to the Church shows clearly both usages. He speaks frequently of "the Churches" or of "all the Churches." He mentions the Churches of a group ("the Churches of the Gentiles"), or of an area (Galatia, Asia, Macedonia, Judea). Especially interesting is his reference to some particular group of disciples meeting in a given house as a Church ("the Church that is in their house," viz., the house of Prisca and Aquila).[1]

Yet Paul's dominant conception seems to be that of the Church as one body. The reason is not ecclesiastical or institutional. He is not thinking of a central control, as at Jerusalem. Rather it is his basic spiritual concept which appears here. Christ is the head, not of many bodies, but of one body. The disciples are joined in one fellowship, and one life and Spirit animates the whole. The immediate application of Paul's figure of the body was, it is true, to the local congregation at Corinth, but the references to this body as the body of Christ and such phrases as "the Church of God" or simply "the Church" make plain the fact that for Paul the Church was in a real, and not merely collective, sense one body.

If this spiritual sense, however, is kept in mind, then there

[1] Rom. 16:3-5. Cf. I Cor. 16:19; Col. 4:15; Philemon 2.

is no contradiction in Paul's thought as to one and many Churches. It is not only that the one spiritual body of Christ takes visible and empirical form in local congregations of believers, but these are all joined in vital union to Christ. Christ dwells in them and any one of these would be the Church of Christ if all others should disappear. Indeed, each one of them is the Church of Christ in that particular place. Similarly each individual disciple is first of all a member, not of the Church at Corinth, but of the one Church of God. So the Churches of today, when they act rightly, receive men and women not into a particular denomination (the Methodist Church) or into a local congregation (the First Presbyterian Church), but into the Church of Christ. The division into local bodies is a necessity in this finite-temporal existence; the division into ecclesiastical groups is a defect which comes from the imperfect and sinful character of the empirical Church, just as the real unity of Christ's body is only partly realized in the local congregation. But to the degree that we are Christian we are also one; and that is measured by the degree in which Christ's spirit, which is God's Spirit, is incorporated in us.

2. What has Paul to say about organization and orders? That question, too, can be answered only through a similar approach: that is, making the spiritual (mystical-organismic) conception basic but at the same time dealing with the empirical Church. Paul's letters, by their silence as well as by what they say, would seem to indicate the following. The spiritual life of the Church is the crucial matter. Unity in the fellowship comes from within, from the one Spirit of God giving this life and from the one spirit of love which flows from God's Spirit, the love which is "the bond of perfectness." [2] There is no suggestion that there is a particular type of Church organization

[2] Col. 3:14.

which is necessary to the being of the Church. Ministry (service) is an essential element in the life of the Church, but Paul does not suggest a ministry of recognized and uniform clerical orders. He recognizes many different forms of ministering; he refuses to put one above another except to apply the test of spiritual edifying.[3] In his list of forms of ministry he puts at the head apostles, prophets, and teachers, that is, the witnesses to Christ and his gospel and those who bring out its meaning. "Government" (administration) is low on the list and "tongues" last of all. It is not the order followed by either the "sects" or the "Churches." Paul is not indifferent to the needs of order and administration, and he speaks not only of "gifts of governments," but of the gift of "the word of wisdom."[4] Corinth herself illustrated the dangers which went with the "enthusiastic" type of Church and the need of such practical gifts. The later Church illustrated to the full the danger of finding in clerical orders and ecclesiastical administration something divinely absolute and unchanging, the essence of the Church instead of an instrument in its service and for its well-being (*esse* instead of *bene esse*).

3. How did Paul conceive the function of the Church? Again we must discriminate between the Church as seen in its divinely given life and the empirical Church regarded in terms of its varied activities, bearing in mind, of course, that the two cannot be separated. In the ongoing life of the empirical Church, "ministration" is a big word with Paul, as I Corinthians 12 indicates. The Church is here to serve. The ministry of truth comes first, represented by apostles, prophets, and teachers, which we might render missionaries, preachers (not what we should mean by pastors), and teachers. The first

[3] I Cor. 14.   [4] I Cor. 12:8, 28.

function of the Church is to preach the gospel and to teach the truth. The sacraments are referred to but the doctrine and the mode of administration are not discussed. Common worship was clearly important in the life of the community, and this was apparently quite free in its form.[5] But beyond this it is plain that for Paul the Church was a community filled with God's Spirit and, in the spirit of love, ministering to its members in the whole range of their needs, spiritual and material.

4. Did Paul think of the Church as necessary for a man's salvation, and if so, how did he conceive this? The question is one that Paul would hardly have raised. The idea of a purely individual or solitary religion was wholly foreign to him. That does not imply the later idea of an institution with exclusive control of the means of salvation in terms of indispensable sacramental channels. Salvation was something very personal, the soul of man to whom God had spoken responding in faith to God's mercy as seen in Christ. But this salvation was more than an individual affair, certainly more than the mystical idea of the flight of the alone to the Alone. This God was one who was carrying out a purpose in history. That purpose involved a people of God. In that historical succession Jesus himself came, and against that background Paul understands him. From Jesus the movement goes on in the making of a new people. The message comes to the individual through this people, and the Christian life is lived within this fellowship and nurtured by it. Here is the tie of love, here the place of service, here the worship, here the abiding place of the Spirit. Paul is not concerned with abstract questions. It was enough for him to recognize that this was the way in which in fact God was at work saving men.

[5] I Cor. 14.

Chapter Nine

SALVATION IN HISTORY AND BEYOND HISTORY

WE HAVE BEEN considering salvation from the standpoint of the individual. It is, indeed, one of the great advances in prophetic religion that it concerns itself with the individual man. For long ages the life of the individual was almost wholly merged in the life of family or clan. As prophetic teaching turned more and more to the inner and ethical and personal, it made increasingly plain the significance of the individual and so prepared the way for the Christian gospel. But the concern with the individual has sometimes tended to exclude that other and earlier aspect of salvation which has to do not simply with the individual and the moment but with the social and historical. Salvation is something that God is doing for man and is working out in history.

I. ISRAEL'S PHILOSOPHY OF HISTORY

It is significant that the first philosophy of history appeared in Israel, not in Greece. In his *Legacy of Israel*,[1] Edwyn Bevan summarizes this philosophy as follows: "(1) an apprehension of God as righteous will, Some One who does 'mighty acts' in a world-process; and hence, (2) a conception of world-process as process in Time, which embodies a Divine plan beginning in God's mighty act of creation and leading up to a great consummation in the future; (3) an association of the Divine plan

[1] P. 50.

166

with a Divine community, a 'people of God' chosen to be the vehicle of God's purpose, so that the ultimate consummation is a communal bliss, the community redeemed, blessed, and glorious." To this we might add (4) the belief that this God had made a special revelation of himself and his will to Israel, and that this revelation came in and through history.

To appreciate the importance of this great conception one must contrast it with that of Greek philosophy of which Professor Bevan speaks in the same context. As against the living God of Israel, for the Greek thinker (1) God "tended to become an immovable Being to whom men might indeed strive to attain, but which did not particularly act in the world-process; (2) the world-process was a vain eternal recurrence, a circular movement, leading nowhere: and (3) deliverance was attained by the individual when he detached himself in soul from the world, not through his incorporation in a Divine community of the blessed." And if one turns to the third great world culture of antiquity, that of India, one finds its mysticism and world-denial equally unable to reach any philosophy of history or indeed to find meaning in the human world of time and toil.[2]

Here as always, however, it is necessary to distinguish between the underlying faith of Israel and the form of its expression. The faith is that of a living and righteous God who is working out a gracious purpose for man in history, a purpose which means the destruction of evil and the establishment of a reign of justice and peace, and which is to be realized in a people. That faith remained constant in its essentials; yet there were important variations, mainly at three points. (1) Who was this people of God to be, this object of God's gracious

[2] See Albert Schweitzer, *Indian Thought and Its Development.*

purpose? Was it the nation Israel? Or a spiritual Israel within the nation? Or was it God's aim to include all the nations of men in a universal kingdom? (2) What was to be the nature of the coming rule? Here the thought moved from the material and political up to the moral and spiritual. The significant fact was, first, that the moral and spiritual dominated; second, that with true Hebrew realism the prophets saw life whole and looked to a redemption which should include the material with the spiritual and nature with man. (3) What were the means by which this end was to be brought about?

In general, this third question was not consciously raised since the common conviction was that it was to come by the deed of God and it was enough for faith to affirm this. Our modern concern with secondary or natural causes, with the human and historical, did not enter into their thinking. Yet obviously, so soon as the coming rule of God was conceived in ethical and spiritual terms and not merely as external control, this question was bound to arise. One fact at least was clear: God's revelation and God's action implied a demand. The prophetic purview includes not only a past of divine action and a future of divine consummation but a present of human action. They are always speaking in terms of crisis and decision, with a call to repentance. Here are the human and ethical elements. And then there is the profound insight of the Servant of the Lord passages in Second Isaiah, especially that of Isaiah 53, suggesting the need of redemptive suffering. At both points the philosophy of divine action in history means more than sheer omnipotence.

As to the form in which this faith was envisaged, this was inevitably in picture and symbol with each writer a law to himself. More important was the change which came with changing social and political conditions. This is especially evident in the apocalypticism in which Israel's hope was expressed, popularly at least, at the time of Christ. We are familiar with this through the little apocalypses of the gospels, the references in Paul, and the book of Revelation, but it had already had several centuries of development in Judaism when Paul wrote. Daniel is the outstanding Old Testament example, but there were numerous non-canonical writings in Judaism running well through the first Christian century. For many years Israel's situation, humanly speaking, seemed utterly hopeless. How could there be a national deliverance and a new life for this people in the face of the mighty empires which in succession had dominated the Mediterranean world? So, as the historical probability diminished, the religious hope took a more and more strikingly supernatural, or miraculous, form. Not from within history, nor in relation to history, but from without, by a compelling divine deed from above, was the deliverance to come.

Apocalypse means literally an unveiling. The anonymous writer, taking the name of some ancient worthy like an Enoch or Ezra or Daniel, presents in dramatic form a program of coming ages and events as predetermined by God. The practical purpose is to serve the saints of the latter days of trial by pointing out that all is according to God's plan, who has determined that this shall be but who has also prepared the deliverance which is now at hand.

Religiously, apocalyptic is an expression of faith in God with whom is the power over men and nations. Theologically, its stress is on the transcendence and absolute power of God and in this is its hope. It tends to a marked dualism which appears at several points. (1) God in his transcendence and holiness is set sharply over against this world in its utterly and hopelesly evil character. This is not the metaphysical dualism of matter and spirit which marks Hellenistic thought, but there is (2) a certain dualism in its conception of evil spirits, to whom this earth and the present age are subject. Hence the final conflict between good and evil is often transferred to the world of the invisible where at the end of the age these powers of darkness led by Satan will be destroyed. In this realm, rather than in history, the decisive conflict takes place.[3] (3) There is a dualism in history. Apocalypticism is a doctrine of two ages: this age, evil, hopeless, under bondage to Satan, in which at most God will gather out the elect and preserve those chosen; the coming age, when he will have destroyed the forces of evil in the final conflict and his saints will reign in power and enjoy the blessings of the new earth.

Apocalypticism flourishes especially in periods of acute distress. Its writings are "tracts for bad times." It comes out of a world where history has lost meaning and evil forces seem dominant. The only hope seems to be in direct action through irresistible force, not so much building upon the good which is, as overturning the evil that a wholly new order may appear. There is a certain analogy here with the Marxian revolutionary philosophy, except that the saints put their hope in God and in a new Jerusalem coming down from heaven. The purpose of apocalypticism was to strengthen faith in such times of distress by pointing to the living God and by declaring that now the day of his saving deed was at hand. It was, in fact, a form of theodicy. In an age when the world about them, in its rampant evil and its oppression of the saints, seemed to contradict all faith in a good and mighty God, it pointed men upward

[3] Cf. the discussion in Chapter V.

to a realm of transcendent glory and power, and forward to the coming age when this power would be manifested, declaring that what was happening was in God's plan and that the coming deliverance was sure.

II. OLD AND NEW IN THE PRIMITIVE CHURCH

It seems quite certain that Jesus believed in the imminent end of his age, that the judgment of God was at hand, and that God would establish his rule upon earth. It is, however, a great mistake to assume (1) that this was his one message and (2) that he shared the apocalyptic system as a whole. There was, indeed, no "apocalyptic system." These was a core of religious conviction, essentially that of prophetic faith, faith in the living God who would overthrow evil and establish his reign. There was the current form which this hope took, due to special conditions of the times, a form which involved despair of the present, a stress on extreme supernaturalism of action, and a sense of the imminence of the coming crisis. And finally, with the literary apocalyptists, there was the speculative and imaginative development of elaborate schemes as to the order of events in a succession of "ages," with pictures of the final conflict and the new age.

Vitality is a matter of emphasis, and the emphasis of Jesus is significant. It did not rest upon the calculations and depictions of the apocalyptists, which by their very elaborateness suggest the wavering between faith and fear; it was rather a quiet and sure faith in God, with whom rested alike the time, the manner, and the issue of the event. The coming judgment meant a summons to repentance, as with the prophets; the fact of such a God, of his love and his power, was a call to faith and obedience, to quietness and confidence. And this God and his help were not simply for the future; his power and love were a present fact, men were here and now to trust that power and live as his children by that love. And while the day of deliverance had not yet come, even now the forces of evil were yielding to his power.[1]

For the early Christians and for Paul, two great facts entered in to give new form to these Jewish hopes. True, the general framework of expectation did not change. Paul shows no special originality in his apocalyptic utterances: the world under the dominion of evil forces, the imminent end of the age, the destruction of the "principalities and powers" in the coming conflict, these were familiar ideas. But the significance of Paul, as of Jesus, is to be sought in his distinctive ideas rather than in what he shared with his contemporaries. There was first the fact of Jesus, of his life and message, his death, and that he had been "declared to be the Son of God with power, according to the spirit of holiness, by the resurrection from the dead." [2] And this was now the mark of his followers, "to wait for his Son from heaven" to complete his messianic work.[3] The Jewish apocalyptic writings were not at all agreed in their picture of the last days and especially as regards the rôle of the Messiah. For some, God was himself the leader of hosts in the last world conflict. For Paul the risen Lord was to return, "with the angels of his power in flaming fire" to lead the conflict against the forces of evil, to "abolish all rule and all authority and power," to "put all his enemies under his feet," death himself

[1] I am accepting here the critical conclusion that the little apocalypses of the synoptics, with their elaborations of detail, are not the words of Jesus.

[2] Rom. 1:4.   [3] I Thes. 1:10.

being the last foe, and then to yield up to God the kingdom which he had thus established.[4]

But there was more to Paul's message than resurrection, messiahship, and return; and this something more constitutes the second great fact which went to set the Christian faith apart from Jewish apocalypticism. Life has its own way of dealing with our theories. The apocalyptic hope was not, indeed, surrendered, and it furnished for a long time a feeling of tension between the life lived in the presence of the Eternal and the world which was so soon to pass away. But more and more there came the realization of the presence and power of the Eternal in their midst. (1) There was a gospel of grace and forgiveness. The death of Christ was changed from a stumblingblock for faith to the center of a message of divine mercy: "Christ died for our sins." And this was a message whose promised gifts of acceptance with God, and peace, and joy, did not need to wait for the coming of a new age. (2) There was the realization that the powers of the new age were already here. Men did not theorize about it. They did not have to struggle, like some modern scholars, to make this fit in with an "eschatological standpoint." They simply recognized with joy the fact that God had given them his Spirit and that men were becoming new creatures and were walking in newness of life. (3) There was the fact of the Christian Church, a fellowship to whose presence as existing actuality they had awakened. It was human, an association of the followers of Jesus. It was divine; God had created it by his Spirit. The new life which anticipated the new age was here in this communion. This was God's people, the true Israel, the place of God's indwelling. (4) There was a task given to this Church.

[4] II Thes. 1:7; I Cor. 15:23–28.

Apparently it was Paul who first clearly grasped this fact in its full meaning; but increasingly the Church realized that it had more to do than to await the end of the age.

The old framework remained, but the course of events was developing a new situation. The letters of Paul make plain that situation. Paul continued, it is true, to speak of the Lord's return; nor do I think that the end of the decade within which his generally accepted letters were written shows any material change in this respect from the beginning. But it is not the Lord's return with which he is primarily occupied. It is interesting to note that the longer references, in the Thessalonian letters and I Corinthians 15, are due, not to a desire to emphasize this teaching (which was generally accepted), but to special circumstances, the first called forth by misunderstandings which Paul corrects, the second in incidental relation to his discussion of the resurrection. Whatever his theory, the years were passing, the gospel had to be preached, and the Church was slowly moving out through the Roman world. Paul had his plan of a Christian empire.[5] His whole mind was taken up with the winning of men for his gospel and with building them up in the new life. And the field of his work made some difference with his thought. What this Roman world needed was not the discussion of the future—enough if he declared this hope; it was the gospel as the power of a new life. And just as in that preaching it was easier to present Jesus as Lord rather than as the Jewish Messiah, so it was more pertinent and more convincing to present the universal gospel of a present salvation than the thought of the coming consummation which made its more special appeal to those of Jewish background.

[5] Rom. 15:19–28.

It has been the contention of these chapters that Christianity deals with something divinely given in terms of historical fact and religious experience, and that in that *Given* its faith discerns the living God of redemptive love and love as the way of life. But theology itself is not a part of this *Given*; to interpret, to relate, to formulate its faith and message, this is the Church's never-completed task. Nor has it any "Given" moral code; to apply its ethical insight to the changing situation, individual and social, demands unceasing reflection and experimentation. All this needs to be recalled in connection with the problem of a Christian philosophy of history.

Christianity thus began with an apocalyptic philosophy of history, resting back upon a prophetic faith, oriented to the person of Christ, and with a living experience as its dynamic source. We can put these three elements briefly in summary: (1) The living God, working in human· history and through a chosen people, moves toward his redemptive end in· which evil shall be overcome and he shall reign on earth. (2) The revelation and redemption in Christ form the goal to which this history moves and in which it finds its meaning; and the Christian fellowship, the Church as the body of Christ, becomes the new people of God, the true Israel. (3) The present is a time for proclaiming the gospel, for calling men to repentance, for gathering them together in the new fellowship. (4) But this is just an interim stage with an interim task. The consummation of the purpose is not through this but through a supra-human and supra-historical victory, which will be won over the spiritual forces of evil when Christ returns. Only thus will the kingdoms of this earth become the kingdom of the Lord God.

III. TOWARD A PHILOSOPHY OF HISTORY

What was expected did not happen and what happened compels the Church of today to reconsider and reformulate this primitive philosophy of history. The simple fact is that the new faith and the logic of events disrupted the apocalyptic scheme. The revelation of God in history, centering in Christ, did not end with the resurrection. The new data that compel us to frame the new philosophy are obvious. (1) The forces of spiritual regeneration are at work here and now in men and in history. Men are being made over. There is a fellowship of Christ. We are not waiting for an entrance of God from above at the end of time; he is here and is acting now in time. There is a Church and it lives and grows in history. (2) The few days or few years have become nineteen centuries. You cannot revive the apocalyptic mood, with its sense of fateful imminence, by appealing to Scripture passages or the undoubted fact of the apocalyptic temper of that time. (3) There has come a new conception as to how God works. It is not, of course, a question of the calendar, a matter of mere duration; it is the basic question whether time has meaning, and how the Eternal enters into time. The logic of the new philosophy appeared, in fact, in what Paul himself was the first to see and appreciate: God's way of working with men and what God through Christ was even then doing for men. He saw the power of forgiving love reconciling man with God and man with man; the presence of God in his Spirit as the transforming power of this new life; the association of men of faith and good will in a fellowship transcending all the old divisions of sex and station and race, a fellowship which is itself a divine creation as is the new man who finds his life within it; the power of God's word of truth in the gospel to win its way with men everywhere and to become to these men the power of God unto salvation. The emphasis on the ethical, the social, and the historical is not a modern innovation; it belongs to prophetic religion and is implicit in the gospel which Paul preached to his churches. The fault of the modern man is that he has lost faith in the reality of the living God, present and working in history, and in the power of the spiritual forces coming from this God and entering into human life.

We need then to recognize the implications for a philosophy of history which were present in Paul's gospel and in the facts of primitive Christian history, implications for which the apocalypticism of that time offered no adequate expression. We need to join to these the insights gained from the succeeding centuries of history. I am not thinking of actual achievements first of all, though there is no ground for despair at that point. True, the brief optimism of a generation ago has fallen upon evil days; but the current pessimism, social and theological, is no nearer to the truth, and the reading of such volumes as those of Kenneth Latourette [1] should aid us to perspective in our historical outlook. If we stop to realize that man has been on this earth for a possible million years, then the slow progress of the last two thousand years should hardly impel us to conclude that our only hope is in a divine intervention which will put an end to the tragic farce which we call human history and by sheer force, apart from man, accomplish what has been excluded by human folly. But the ultimate basis of our hope, and so of a Christian philosophy of history, is not in any estimate of human achievement. It lies in our faith in the God and Father of our Lord Jesus Christ, in our experience of the

[1] Cf. the summary in his *Anno Domini*.

forces set free through Christ in this world, and in our larger insight gained by the Church through the years as to God's way of work in the world.

The development of a philosophy of history is one of the most urgent tasks for Christian thought. Once more, as in Paul's day, the world situation seems to contradict all faith in the meaning of human life and history and in the existence of a God who alone can give such meaning. Roughly speaking, the theories of history fall into three classes.

1. There are the naturalistic theories which leave out any direction and control by a supreme Power who is good. Time and change alone are real; we have nothing but man and the finite scene. Sometimes there is an effort to secure ground for hope within this framework. So we had from Herbert Spencer a philosophy of evolutionary optimism, the idea of an inevitable though impersonal cosmic trend to goodness; but the course of events has proved too much for this. Somewhat similar has been the fate of the religion of naturalistic humanism, putting its trust in human effort and growing knowledge, holding that, though we came out of darkness and death, and though life and light would again disappear in these, yet for a brief time at least man might build a kingdom of light on this earth. For the most part, however, naturalism is simply the denial of any real philosophy of history. Time has neither meaning nor goal. Change, impermanence, and death alone are real. Relativism rules. Goods are relative. Right is merely the course of conduct indicated for the moment. There is nothing above us, nothing higher than man, nothing more enduring than the moment, nothing to give meaning to life, or direction to change, or certainty of goal. The ancient Order is gone and Chaos is king.

2. All Christian philosophies of history are marked by faith

in a living God whose purpose and action shape the course of human events and determine their issue. But there is a marked difference as to the way in which God's action is conceived and his relation to man and the world of time. So we note as our second form the apocalyptic idea of history. In radical contrast with all naturalism and humanism, it rests its hope on God; but it tends to conceive of God as acting in external and compulsive fashion. God does not so much enter into time as act from without time. Infinite and finite, the Eternal and' time, are so set over against each other that it is hard to see how they can be related. And this dualistic tendency is sharpened by belief in the total depravity of man and the hopelessly· evil character of all history. Hence, strangely enough; the result is much the same as with naturalism, that is, a denial of a real and saving presence of God in history and so of a creative meaning for what takes place in time. God does not achieve his ends in and through history; he brings history to a ·close in order to attain his ends. So history becomes a more or less unmeaning interlude between creation and the concluding act of redemption.

3. But there is another approach to the Christian conception of history and this constitutes our third theory. This latter recognizes at once the otherness of God and his kinship with man, the sinfulness of human nature and its capacity to receive the grace of God, the dependence of man upon God and the working of God through man, the transcendence of God and his immanence as purpose and power and redemptive love giving meaning to this human scene and working out his ends creatively in history. Its task is to see how divine and human can thus be related and how God achieves his ends in time. To do this is to construct a philosophy of history. Nominally Paul's philosophy was apocalyptic and as such fitted in with the

second position: history had come to an end, the Lord was at
hand, and salvation was to be achieved at his return by divine
and all-decisive action. As a matter of fact, however, though
Paul did not draw the full consequences, his teaching furnishes
the material for the third viewpoint. It is involved in his ethical
interpretation of the kingdom of God, which is "righteousness
and peace and joy in the Holy Spirit." [2] It is given in his
realization that the powers of the new age are already at work.
The Holy Spirit is present with his gifts and transforming
power. Men by God's grace are even now in fellowship with
him and know the law of the Spirit of life which is overcoming
sin and making new creatures. And the Church is here, a
fellowship of the people of God, a divine creation, called to
spread the gospel, to win men to Christ, to spread throughout
the world. The meaning of this is not altered in principle
because Paul envisaged at most a few years or a generation
instead of the ongoing centuries The imminence of the end
was an incident to Paul's faith. And we who believe that the
revelation of God is in history, through action rather than
through doctrines communicated in words, should find no difficulty in seeing the continuing revelation of God as to the meaning of history in the centuries that have elapsed since Paul's
day. Would it not be a form of atheism to rule God out of these
years?

IV. A CHRISTIAN PHILOSOPHY OF HISTORY IN OUTLINE

There is no place here for the development of this third
philosophy of history, but its constitutive elements may at least

[2] Rom. 14:17.

be indicated, and they will give us the grounds for our belief in a salvation *in* history and not merely one at the end of history as contemplated by apocalypticism.

1. There is a living God, a God of will and action, a God of righteousness and mercy. His goodness is no abstract ideal or static perfection; it is dynamic and creative. It is not a holiness which removes him from the finite and evil, but a self-giving love. The creative presence and self-giving love of God are always and everywhere present in human history, but their supreme revelation and expression are in Jesus Christ. Christ is at once the disclosure of the meaning of history and the instrument of divine action for the achievement of its end. The creative presence of God in human life is expressed in the Christian conception of an indwelling Spirit.

2. History is meaningful event, moving in the realm of free human action and concerned with values and their achievement; the kingdom of God is the Christian conception of the goal of history. Literally it means the rule of God, but it is that rule seen as man's supreme good, as the achievement of his highest possibilities, of the end for which God created him. It is no mere power to which man submits, or arbitrarily imposed authority; it is a divine life which is given to man and a way of life which man accepts as his own. It is thus the sway of an inner and all-controlling spirit, God's Spirit of self-giving and creative love, in which man shares the life of God and achieves the true life of fellowship with his brothers. The goal of God, his kingdom, is thus a new humanity, achieved here on earth and in the movement of history.

3. The method of God in relation to his kingdom is determined by the nature alike of God and of man and of the goal which God has set. It cannot be accomplished by sheer power

whether in the course of history or at its end. Its goal is in the realm of the ethical-religious-social; the means must be found in the same sphere. (a) God's way, then is ethical; his dependence is upon the forces of the spirit. Central is the power of forgiving and self-giving love, *agape,* seen as God's love in the cross of Christ, effective in society as the great fellowship-building power. (b) With love goes truth, truth as revealed in the gospel, coming to man not simply as moral demand but, through the Spirit, as God's gift of light, convicting of sin, setting free man's mind, and revealing God and man and the way of life. (c) God's way is social. He works in and through the group. The Church is central here as the fellowship of man on the highest level of life, the communion of faith, of witness and worship, of love and service. But God is concerned with all the other associations which make up human life. They do not belong to a merely secular order without spiritual significance, or a demonic order necessarily opposed to the divine. The home, the world of work and wealth, the state, science and education, these are at once a part of the life which is to be redeemed and instruments of God in the achievement of that life. (d) God's way is historical. Time is not meaningless succession, for God or for man. It is not the all-destroyer, spelling only change and decay and death; it is the medium for God's creation and conservation of values. Men do not find the Eternal by fleeing time, or achieve life by escape from the world of change. History is time become meaningful and creative. Historical and social are here inseparable. History is time seen as an organic whole, its parts united in a living process achieving that which is not possible for the moment. Society is mankind seen in organic unity, achieving in the whole what is not possible to the individual in isolation. This life of humanity in social relations can be achieved only in history, just as the goal of history is achieved in a divine society. Here the insights and attainments, with the social expressions which they shape, are passed on from generation to generation. Only in history can God create a new humanity.

V. BEYOND HISTORY

So far we have considered the kingdom of God as something being achieved in history. By kingdom is here meant the kingship, or the rule, of God. But this rule is one which comes only with the free response of man; therefore it is at no time absolute or perfect. There is a certain incongruity here between the thought of a God of all power and a rule which is incomplete. The explanation lies partly in the fact that God's rule over free spirits can only come with struggle and growth, moving through failure to achievement. But the paradox is not finally solved except as faith looks beyond history. This it does in two ways. First, it sees a God who as transcendent God is even now Lord of his universe. Second, it sees a consummation of the kingdom of God beyond history. This twofold outreach beyond history is shared by Paul with the Bible as a whole.

1. The men who pray, "Thy kingdom come," believe in a rule of God which now is. They believe in a God who is Creator and Lord and Ruler of heaven and earth. It is because they believe in the rule that now is that they so confidently pray for the rule that is to come here upon earth. The realm of freedom is of deepest importance, for here God achieves his highest goal in creation. Yet the rule of God in this realm

is possible only because there is even now a rule of God which at once transcends this finite life of ours and supports it. Without this faith in the God who is more than history there is no ground for hope of a salvation in history.

This sovereignty of God we sometimes speak of as the cosmic order. It is the realm of the fixed and unalterable, within which all our life moves, which sets limits to all our freedom. It is the moral order which underlies all human life, as well as the order of nature which rules the process of the suns. It is not, however, something abstract or impersonal. It is the direct expression of the mind and will of God and of his sustaining power. Apart from this there could be no science, no purposive and effective action, indeed, no reason in man or freedom for man or any life at all. This sovereign rule of God is thus not so much a barrier to human action as a necessary condition, through its all-including order, of any free and effective life.

But it is more than this: it is the power and purpose of God active in the restraint of evil and in the support of good. It holds before men the unchangeable values which give meaning to life, at once rewarding our loyalty and judging our disobedience. It is as surely a part of God's creative-redemptive process as is his reconciling love. In its light alone can history find meaning. It sets its sure limits to the power of evil and works against this. George Meredith, in his "Lucifer in Starlight," tells how once the prince of evil, leaving his dark domain and mounting upward, reached at last the point whence he surveyed the "stars, which are the brain of Heaven," and then, looking, sank, while

> "Around the ancient track marched, rank on rank,
>   The army of unalterable law."

2. But there is another way in which history points beyond itself. It is this which apocalypticism seeks to express and this we must here consider, whether we be apocalyptists or not, as we think of the "last things." For history, with all its achievement, remains the sphere of time and the finite; it is under the law of imperfection and change and death. The good is achieved in the historical process (time plus society plus moral freedom), but never in perfection; it is conserved, but not finally. Nor is evil ever wholly overcome. So we need, not simply that which is above history, the supra-historical, and that cosmic order which undergirds history and permeates it, but the transhistorical, the consummation which lies beyond history.

What are the elements which enter into a Christian eschatology? There is the idea of conflict and judgment. Between God and the forces of evil there is eternal opposition. The free achievement of the good in a process of history makes inevitable the existence of evil and the fact of conflict. But just because the movement is in the realm of freedom, there are possible limits to God's redemptive activity as he works to complete the imperfect and to overcome the evil with good. And here that order comes into play which we considered above. Evil cannot be the last word if there be a cosmic order which is the righteous God. The ultimate end of evil in such a cosmos must be restraint or absolute destruction. We look beyond history at another point. If the good that is achieved in history comes through the God who is more than history and expresses his purpose, then he will conserve this good. And that must be in a realm beyond history, for time by itself means the destruction of all that it produces: each individual life moving on to inexorable death, and the universe itself running down at the end, if science be right, in the utter stillness of some *Wärmetod*. Faith in God means, therefore, some belief in a final conflict and judgment in relation to evil, and in a security for the good that has been achieved at such cost.

Paul held this hope and expressed it in apocalyptic form. He saw a final conflict in which the forces of evil were to be destroyed, and a resurrection of the saints to dwell with Christ. There is no special point in inquiring as to details in Paul's picture. We do not know whom Paul meant by "the one that restraineth" or "the lawless one" whom Jesus was to slay with the breath of his mouth. We do not even know whether Paul thought of others than the saints in connection with the resurrection. Of an intermediate millennial reign of peace on earth, the thousand years of chiliasm, there is no suggestion. What we have is simply a necessary period of conflict in which evil is to be destroyed in order that, all other things having been subjected to God, Christ himself might now take his place as subject also, and God be all in all.[1] Paul's significance for us is not in these details; this general outline has nothing original or distinctively Christian. It is a dramatic setting-forth of basic Christian convictions whose particular form was given by current apocalyptic belief.

Our own eschatology will of necessity be more modest. It will not attempt to unveil the course of events as Jewish apocalypticism did. One thing, however, it must do and that is to assert the continuity between the historical and that which lies beyond history. The principle of discontinuity, and the stress on the apocalyptic, mark the Barthian type of continental theology. They rest back upon the dualism which

[1] II Thes. 2:6-12; I Cor. 15:24-28.

determines Barth's whole conception of the relation of God and man, of the Eternal and time, of this age and the next. They emphasize the sovereign power of God and stress direct action, and tend to deny to history any creative meaning. But it is the values won in history that are to be conserved in the world beyond history, values won in the free and convinced response of man to the word of God's redemptive love and through the surrender of human life to the rule of this spirit of love. No destructive final conflict, no exercise of sheer power, not even of divine omnipotence, can of itself create such values, or, in other words, be the means of salvation.

This discussion of the philosophy of history will seem to many to have departed from Paul and the primitive faith. But that is true only if we persist in conceiving revelation as communication of doctrine and hold to an externalistic authoritarianism. That position is most consistently represented today by popular premillennialism. Unfortunately, in its insistence on the letter, the vital Christian elements are endangered and an impossible mixture of Judaism, divine militarism, and speculation results. Neo-apocalypticism nominally gives great weight to the early apocalyptic tradition; in fact it is deeply influenced by its underlying theological or philosophical viewpoint, alike in its emphasis and its omissions.

It is the basic principles of the gospel according to Paul which have in fact given direction to the philosophy of history suggested above. These pillar principles may be noted here in closing, and they must be determinative for all theology and not simply for this field: the God of our faith, the Father of our Lord Jesus Christ; the way of this God in man's salvation as revealed in Christ and his gospel of grace and faith and love; the significance of the Christian Church and of the historical-social aspect of salvation; the Christian conception of man and of that relation between God and man in which freedom and dependence, grace and faith, divine action and human responsibility, are joined together; and, finally, the deep sense that all our life here in time is lived in the presence of the Eternal, that it is the life of sinful men in the presence of the holy God, and that the consummation of God's purpose and of our hope lies beyond time in the realm of the eternal and rests in the hand of God. And this last phrase gives the source and seal of our Christian confidence as to history and what is beyond history: We believe in the God of righteous love whose goodness is matched by his power: "Fear not, little flock; for it is your Father's good pleasure to give you the kingdom." "Faithful is he that calleth you, who will also do it." [2]

[2] Lu. 12:32; I Thes. 5:24.

Chapter Ten

CONCERNING ETHICS

IT IS a revealing fact, to which justice has not often been done, that the major part of Paul's letters is concerned not with matters of doctrine but with the concrete problems of human living, whether in relation to God or to men, most of it dealing with the life with men. In studying Paul's ethics our interest is not in finding a system of rules. It has been the common mistake of the past to seek in Paul's words, as in those of Jesus, an authoritative code of conduct and thus to bring in a new legalism in denial of the very gospel for which Paul fought. Christianity is not a new system of laws and Paul is no more an inspired lawgiver than he is an infallible theologian. Nor shall we find in Paul a system of ethics. We may, however, find light on two questions of great importance. (1) What is the relation of religion and ethics in Christianity? (2) What has Christianity to offer us as a way of life? Granted that it is not a set of rules, does it give us basic principles or ideals as a guide to conduct, and are these valid and adequate for us today?

I. RELIGION AND ETHICS

1. Religion in the stricter sense is the life of man as seen and lived in relation to God. Ethics has to do with human conduct and character as seen in the light of ideals or standards, and with the good that is to be the goal of man's effort. Both are concerned with human life and with that life as having a sig-

nificance through relation to something higher than itself. But religion is God-centered: it begins in God, sees all in the light of God, and is wholly dependent upon God. Ethics begins with man and is concerned with his conduct and character and goals.

2. But though distinguishable, religion and ethics are not separable. The ethical demands the religious for its completion. That is seen in its distinctive problems. (1) Ethics requires an authority, a ground for its unconditional demands, something that will lift these demands above the relative and individual and hedonistic. That which commands us must itself be good; for a moral personality cannot give its supreme allegiance to a non-moral power, whether from prudence or under compulsion. Ethics thus involves a cosmic belief, a faith in the ultimate unity of goodness and power. (2) Only with such a belief can ethics be sure that its devotion is not unfounded and that its goal will be realized. (3) Ethics requires a dynamic. We need not merely the demand to summon us, but the help to fulfill the demand, the transforming power which will change the law that is above into a life within.

3. The religious, on the other hand, demands the ethical if it is to be truly and fully religious. That applies to the God whom it calls men to worship, to the hope that it holds before them, to the life which it offers men as a gift from God, and to the life which it bids them lead with their fellows.

This relation of religion and ethics is not a matter of speculation; it is the great prophetic tradition which reached its consummation in Christianity. Here religion and ethics have been brought into complete unity; religion is through and through ethical, and ethics takes its form and strength from religion. This is not to say that historic Christianity has always seen the meaning of these principles or worked them out in practice. That is the unending task of the Church, and history shows how often it has failed and at what important points. Thus in its concept of God it has sometimes put sovereign power above moral character. The Church itself has often been made an end instead of an instrument of God's purpose for man's service and salvation. It has assumed at times an external authority instead of resting its authority upon its message of truth, its holiness of life, and its ministry in mediating divine things. It has violated moral integrity and evangelical freedom by demanding acceptance of doctrine upon authority without reference to inner conviction. Its concept of salvation has sometimes been a magical sacramentarianism or an emotional mysticism with no essential ethical element. Legalism has been a constant peril, and not merely in Roman Catholicism. It has dropped from the high conception of the relation of God and man expressed by Paul's words of grace and faith and has restored the ruler-subject relation. Nominally stressing works in order to conserve the ethical, it has endangered what is truly ethical in the Christian sense, namely the inner spirit and attitude. And the genuinely ethical freedom of the Christian spirit, facing new situations and gaining new insights, has been imperilled by closed static systems.

II. RELIGIOUS AND ETHICAL WITH PAUL

How are the religious and ethical related in Paul's teaching? How does the ethical enter in to shape his theology, and how does his theology issue in ethics?

1. The place of ethics in religion rests first of all upon the concept of God. Here is the very heart of prophetic religion: a

God who is righteous and faithful, who demands righteousness
of men and whose goal is a rule of righteousness upon earth.
But to speak of an ethical conception of God or to say that God
is righteous is not enough. That might mean a God who was
merely lawgiver and judge. Or one might, stretching the word
ethical, think of an equitable but impersonal cosmic order in
which conduct would always be followed by appropriate consequences. Paul's message is ethically far richer.

(1) God is love, love as seen in Jesus Christ. His goodness is
not that of an impersonal order; it is that of a personal will.
It is free and spontaneous, and wholly independent of the
merit of its object: "God commendeth his own love toward us,
in that, while we were yet sinners, Christ died for us." Grace
represents this special aspect of it.[1] Such love is not limited
in its range, as friendship necessarily is; it goes out to all. All
this Paul saw in Christ and his cross. The cross, the seeming
contradiction of that power and wisdom which had always
stood first in the concept of God, became the revelation of this
agape, a love at which he never ceased to wonder, but which,
when received, he saw to be the true wisdom and power which
put all else to shame.[2]

(2) This love, however, which is so gracious, which goes out
to all and stops at nothing, is never for a moment conceived by
Paul as a morally indifferent "good nature." It is *good* will,
that is, it wills only and always the morally good, the highest
good, for its objects. Just because it is this kind of love, holy
and redemptive, it can never be indifferent to evil. It hates
evil and is set against it to destroy it: it involves inexorable
moral demand and inevitable judgment. To believe in a moral
God is to believe in a moral universe. Such a universe must be

[1] Rom. 5:8.   [2] I Cor. 1:22–25.

one not merely of demand, but of appropriate consequence. A moral faith is not possible unless the universe, not obviously at the moment or in the particular instance, but basically and in its final issue, supports the good and is destructive of evil. The idea of judgment is as basic here as is that of saving love; and it rests, with the latter, upon the character and attitude of God. All this is present in Paul's concept of God: his judgment upon evil, now and at the end; his opposition to evil; his idea that "to them that love God all things work together for good"—significantly he does not say here "to them that God loves." And here comes in again the much-debated and difficult term, "the wrath of God", and our earlier conclusion that, while we must be careful not to lower it to the human level, nor oppose it to the love of God, still it stands, not simply for the final judgment ("the wrath," or "the day of wrath"), but for something in the attitude of God toward evil and impenitent men.

(3) In one place, however, Paul seems to depart from this ethical conception of God, subordinating his moral character to sovereign power and will, while at the same time shifting the responsibility of man's being saved or lost from a human decision to a divine and arbitrary determination. The passage is Romans 9: 12–23, but three chapters, 9 to 11, should be read together. The whole matter calls for more thorough consideration in the chapter on Paul's doctrine of God. Paul is discussing the fate of Israel and indirectly defending his mission to the Gentiles. Israel is the people of God. But Israel has rejected the Messiah and thus refused the salvation of God. Has God then rejected Israel? Paul's answer is the flat declaration that the sovereign God does what he wills, and his way has always been that of selection: "they are not all Israel, that are of Israel."

The God who chose one son of Isaac and rejected the other is now choosing among the sons of Jacob. Then he goes on to declare, however, that this choice has no reference to the present or future character of those chosen: it is as arbitrary as the potter's decision as to the kind of vessel he will make out of his clay. Nor does the decision rest with men: "he hath mercy upon whom he will, and upon whom he will he hardeneth." Here, then, is not merely arbitrary will placed above the ethical in the character of God, but the denial of moral freedom and responsibility in man.

If this were all that Paul said we should have no alternative in interpreting him but to follow John Calvin, who accepts this teaching as basic for his idea of God and salvation and balks at none of its implications.[3] What we need to do is to recognize that there is in this passage a flat contradiction of what we have found to be Paul's dominantly ethical conception of God and man and the way of salvation. If we are to be true to the gospel which Paul elsewhere clearly and consistently proclaims, we shall have to reject the declarations to which his apologetic has led him in this passage.

2. At no point is the nature of a given religion more clearly evidenced than in its doctrine of salvation, and that is especially true as regards its success in bringing the religious and ethical into unity. Our study of Paul's teaching as to salvation has already brought this out. Its results can be briefly summarized. Paul protests against a moralistic way of salvation (legalism)

[3] "Everything which he wills must be held to be righteous by the mere fact of his willing it. God not only saw the fall of the first man, and in him the ruin of his posterity; but also at his own pleasure arranged it." Since God "arranges all things by his sovereign counsel," it follows that individuals are born, who are doomed from the womb to certain death, and are to glorify him by their destruction." *Institutes of the Christian Religion*, Vol. II, Book III, Ch. xxiii.

because he knows it can secure for man neither the religious good of fellowship with God, nor the moral result of a true righteousness. But he is as truly concerned with the ethical as Jesus was, and the ethical enters in at every point. (1) The faith which he demands is not simply belief or even trust; it involves an act of moral obedience, the surrender of one's whole life to God. The surrender itself, however, is not blind submission; it roots in insight and conviction and thus is moral in character. (2) God's forgiveness is an ethical deed; it is not a passing over of sins but rather an overcoming of sinfulness. God's grace is a morally creative act. (3) The new life of this sinner has an ethical quality. It is a life of reconciliation; that is, we accept God's love and his will and live in fellowship with him. The life with such a God is necessarily ethical in its demand because he is a righteous God. (4) Paul's idea of salvation as remaking is similarly ethical. To be saved is to be a new creation, that is, to be made over in the spirit of Christ which is the spirit of love. (5) Finally, it is ethical in its means.

On this last point more needs to be said, for the sacramentarians have always found in Paul the biblical foundation of their system, and certain historical students have insisted that at this point Paul has simply taken over the teaching of the mystery religions. But even if we recognize in Paul's conception of union with Christ and in his idea of baptism an element of mystical realism which departs from the dominant ethical-personal viewpoint, one need only look at classical mysticism, at the mystery religions of his day, or at later sacramentarianism, to realize the fundamental opposition between these and Paul's teaching.

For classical mysticism the presupposition of salvation is an ultimate identity of nature between God and the soul of man; for Paul, while there is, even with the sinner, a kinship of being that makes it possible for God to speak to man and for sinful man to know God, yet always the Creator stands above the creature and the Holy God over against sinful man even after man is forgiven. In mystical salvation the soul loses its distinctive selfhood and is merged with God; with Paul the I and Thou always remain. The contrast with the mystery religions has already been pointed out: in them salvation is union with a finite hero-god bringing deliverance from death; with Paul it is a spiritually transforming fellowship with the transcendent God, the Lord of heaven and earth. In both cases Paul, by contrast, stands clearly for the personal and ethical elements in salvation.

As to the sacramentarian system of salvation as developed later in the Church, it cannot secure the support of Paul by quoting Paul's references to baptism, even if it be taken in a realistic sense and not simply as symbol when he speaks of dying with Christ and of being buried with him in baptism. For the essence of the sacramentarian conception of salvation lies in the idea of an impersonal process, in which the divine nature or substance, holy and immortal, is infused into the human nature, sinful and mortal, through the necessary operation of what is impersonal—water of baptism, bread and wine. And the essence of Paul's doctrine of salvation is personal and ethical: a personal God by his grace wins a personal response in faith; by this reconciliation there is established a personal fellowship; through that fellowship, always contingent upon continued faith and obedience, the sinner receives a new spirit and the power of a new life. Further, this new life is shaped and lived in the Church, which is conceived, not simply as divine creation and presence, but as a human-historical fellowship and thus as personal and ethical.

III. THE CHRISTIAN WAY

We have been considering how Paul's ethics entered into his theology. We must inquire now what his theology meant for ethics. Given this faith in God as revealed in Christ and this conception of the way of salvation, what did it mean for human conduct? Granted that he presents us no ethical "system," what are the ethical principles which guide him as he meets the many problems of the Christian life which his work as missionary-pastor forced upon him?

1. Paul's ethics is an ethics of inwardness, an ethics of the spirit. It is like the higher righteousness upon which Jesus insists in the Sermon on the Mount. Paul is opposed to legalism ethically as well as in respect to the way of salvation. It is the inner spirit that makes the Christian man; it is having "the mind of the Spirit," "the spirit of Christ," instead of being "flesh-minded." [1] An ethics of rules cannot meet such a situation. Rules prescribe the external; they cannot reach the inner life. But Paul knows, with Jesus, that abstinence from adultery will not condone the impure heart, and that out of the evil heart will come the evil deed. Such an ethics is simpler than one of rules which attempts to cover all situations and prescribe all duties, as with Pharisaism.

2. This means an ethics of freedom and, in a double sense, freedom from external rules and the freedom of inner unity and self-mastery. There is the freedom from rules which Paul warned the Galatians not to lose when they lightly began the

[1] Rom. 8: 5–9.

acceptance of prescription as to meat and drink and sacred days. It is not a freedom from obligation; that remains for the ethics of the spirit and is nowhere else so all-demanding. The spiritual man has seen the heart of the Eternal, the meaning of life and of all being, of his own true nature and of the highest good; and he has made the supreme choice, the great surrender. He owes not less, but more; his every deed, his inmost thought, his final loyalty, all belong to God. But his obedience is not to something external to himself and foreign. It roots in inner conviction. It involves a true autonomy as man finds in God his own true life. He gains here a real freedom, for the life becomes the expression of the inner spirit. He knows the meaning of Augustine's "Love and do what thou wilt." It is in direct contrast with the self-will of sin which begins with seeming freedom and ends with servitude. For in sin a man divides himself against himself, choosing the lower against the higher, and making himself more and more the slave of the lower which he has chosen. Servant he must be, one way or another. To be human, to be something more than the animal whose rule of life is the impulse of the moment, means to find some goal or good or ideal to which to give allegiance. What Paul saw was that one way meant life and freedom, the achievement of self, and the mastery over self and the world, while the other way meant servitude and death. It was not simply freedom from a system of law that Christ gave, but the freedom which came through "the law of the spirit of life."

3. This ethics of the spirit, because it is an ethics of freedom, means a growing ethics. The ethics of legalism is static. At best it can do what the scribes attempted, by every means of interpretation and extension to make the inadequate letter of the old cover the changed conditions of the new. Paul's ethics had

no such dead system of law to contend with. It was his task in his churches to find out what the new spirit meant in one situation or another. And with this went his doctrine of the indwelling Spirit of God which gave men a living guidance and a growing insight. It will not do to say that there were no remnants of the old authoritarianism with Paul; a man is not so easily freed from the heritage of his race and the training of youth, and Paul is not above the appeal to the letter and rabbinic modes of interpretation if some word of the Old Testament will support his position.[2] But alike his principles and his dominant practice point the other way. And it is important for the Church to see that Chrstian ethics has place for free inquiry, new insights, and every aid which experience and research and experiment can bring.[3]

4. For Paul the ethics of the spirit means the ethics of the spirit of Christ. "Have this mind in you, which was also in Christ Jesus" is the appeal that Paul makes to the Philippians as he calls them to unity, humility, love, and unselfishness.[4] The reference to the spirit of Christ as the norm of the Christian life is not often made in so many words, yet the idea appears again and again. "Let each one of us please his neighbor for that which is good unto edifying. For Christ also pleased not himself." When he wants to "prove the sincerity" of the love of the Corinthians, he appeals to "the grace of our Lord Jesus Christ, that, though he was rich, yet for your sakes he became poor." "Be ye imitators of me, even as I also am of Christ." "For me to live is Christ." "Christ liveth in me: and that life which I now live in the flesh I live in faith, the faith

[2] See pp. 19–21 above.
[3] For an able presentation of this element in ethics, see I. G. Whitchurch, *An Enlightened Conscience.*
[4] Phil. 2:5.

which is in the Son of God, who loved me, and gave himself up
for me." "As ye received Christ Jesus as Lord, so walk in him."
"Put on the new man . . . where Christ is all in all. . . . As
the Lord forgave you, so also do ye . . . Let the peace of
Christ rule in your hearts . . . Do all in the name of the Lord
Jesus." "The Lord direct your hearts into the love of God,
and into the patience of Christ." [5] To be a Christian, in brief,
is to think and feel and act according to, or after (the Greek is
kata), Christ. "To be of the same mind one with another according to Christ Jesus" is his prayer for the Romans.[6] This is
the same as "after the Spirit" in Romans 8:4.

What is much more important than these specific references
to Jesus is the obvious fact that in the large sections which
Paul devotes to ethical matters, using that term in the broad
sense as including matters of personal religious living, his
method is not that of citing some authority or setting up rules
of his own, but rather that of inquiring what the Christian
spirit demands in the given instance. And the Christian spirit is
the spirit of Christ; that is, the spirit of the historic Jesus as
known in his life and death. The problem of the eating of meat
which had been offered to idols, as treated in Romans 14, gives
an excellent example. The Christian life means freedom from
rules, freedom from such superstitions as the belief that an
idol is anything at all or that there are ceremonially clean and
unclean foods, freedom to act according to one's own conscience. But higher than freedom is love, the love which led
Christ to die for men. Hence the conclusion: "Destroy not
with thy meat him for whom Christ died," and the words of

[5] Rom. 15:3; II Cor. 8:9; I Cor. 11:1; Phil. 1:21; Gal. 2:20; Col.
2:6; 3:5–17; II Thes. 2:5. Cf. Eph. 4:13, 15, 20–24, 31, 32; 5:2.
[6] Rom. 15:5–7. Cf. II Cor. 11:17; Col. 2:8.

15:1-3, following this discussion: please your neighbor for that which is good, "for Christ also pleased not himself." Gospel and ethics are one here. The gospel is the word of the forgiving love of God as seen in Christ: the ethics is the rule of this same spirit as the way of life for men.

Here Paul is clearly at one with Jesus, though his appeal, characteristically, is to the spirit instead of the words of the Master. The fifth chapter of Matthew emphasizes the righteousness of the spirit as against obedience to the latter. The spirit that is to rule in us is to be nothing less than the spirit of God: "Ye therefore shall be perfect as your heavenly Father is perfect." That is what it means to be "sons of your Father," Jesus says.[7] Paul points us to the Son as at once the revelation of what God is and of what his sons should be. Paul's great hymn of love in I Corinthians 13 is the most notable evidence in point, though he makes no specific reference to Jesus. Kept on the loftiest ethical level, lyrical in form, it is yet eminently concrete and definite. And that is because it is not the abstraction of the thinker but the picture of something seen in life; it is this same spirit of Jesus which is here his inspiration and guide, as it is in all his ethical teaching.

But this appeal to Christ is not a new legalism or authoritarianism. Only on rare occasion does Paul appeal to a word of Jesus. Nor is the imitation of which he speaks a slavish copying of Jesus' earthly life, as, for example, in terms of poverty or celibacy. He does not refer to particular acts of Jesus but to the one great deed, the giving of himself to the obedience of God and the service of men.[8] And the reference is to "the *mind* of Christ," the spirit that was shown in the deed.

5. Love is Paul's great word for this spirit, the spirit of Christ

[7] Mt. 5:43-48. [8] Phil. 2 and elsewhere.

which is the way of life for men. His teaching can only be
understood as we grasp the distinctive Christian use of this
word. The Greek language has three words which may be
translated love: *eros, philia,* and *agape* (pronounced ăg′a-pā
in English, á-gä′pē in the Greek). *Eros* does not occur in the
New Testament. It denotes the love of desire. It may mean
sentiment or passion or, as with Plato, refer to the higher long-
ings of the soul. *Philia* corresponds most nearly to our word
friendship. It may mean simply to have pleasure or satisfaction
in. With us it usually involves a basis of common viewpoint and
interest, and rests upon a personal preference. It is limited in
scope by this fact as well as by the nature of the case, since
we can take but a limited number into such a relation. *Agape*
as a noun is not found in classical Greek, though it occurs in
verbal form. It first appears in the Greek translation of the
Old Testament, but it is in the New Testament that it comes to
its high and distinctive meaning. It is the Christian meaning of
this term as found in Paul that we now consider.

Love in this sense, *agape,* is the simplest and truest expression of the distinctive nature of Christianity. Here was the
great insight of Jesus: the God of the universe is the Father
of infinite good will; to have faith in his mercy, to lose all
anxiety by trusting in his care, to let this love become the rule
of our life, this is to be children of the Father. The great deed
of Jesus was to incarnate in his life this love that was God,
and through his life and death to make it redemptively effective in the world. Jesus showed how all-inclusive this love was
in its scope, how free in its mercy, how searching in its demand,
and how strong in its transforming power. At all of these points
Paul was a follower of Jesus. He has other words for other
aspects of God's nature, but this free love or grace which asks

not as to human desert, this is the heart of his gospel. And this love is "a most excellent way" for man, Paul holds, without which, indeed, nothing else can avail.[9]

6. Is this love an inclusive principle? Does it take in the whole field of human relations? Is it true that the whole law is fulfilled in this, as both Paul and Jesus say? What about other principles of action in relation to this principle of love? And what about other relations in life besides this one which asks only about giving and does not concern itself with returns? What about ties of friendship and the relation of man and wife? And what of man's obligation to himself? The Swedish theologian, Anders Nygren, has given a history of the Christian idea of love in his work, *Agape and Eros*. He has rightly apprehended two great Christian insights: the ethical insight, that *agape* is wholly free, unselfish, and not determined by merit in its object; the religious insight, that this love is God's love and is found in man only as God's gift. But he finds no place within the Christian idea of love for self-regard, for the love of self in any sense, no place for the thought of human self-perfection or self-achievement, or aspiration for the highest as set forth, for example, by Plato, or even by Augustine when he depicts the soul's hunger for God, no place in the motivation of love for the idea of the sacredness of human personality, no place for those other human ties represented by *eros* and *philia*, even when taken on their highest levels.

To discuss this position at all adequately would take us too far afield. Back of it is Nygren's desire to conserve the distinctive character of Christian love. But more particularly there is the fear of humanism, of reducing this love to something

[9] Gal. 5:13, 14; Rom. 13:8–10; I Thes. 3:12, 13. Cf. Mt. 5:43–48; 22:36–40; Lu. 6:36.

natural, to a merely ethical ideal, to human self-perfecting, instead of seeing it as that which has its true being only in God and which comes only as he gives it. But, in fact, it is not so much the New Testament which determines Nygren's treatment at this point. Rather it is the dualistic-absolutistic theology which sets God over against man as the totally other and makes the relation between God and man, whether in revelation or salvation or ethics, a one-way movement in which God determines all things directly and absolutely. From this standpoint it will not do to find in natural impulses or desires, even in the highest human aspirations, or in natural ties such as those of husband and wife, or parent and child, any real point of contact for God or material with which God's grace works, or even evidence of that grace. The only true love is that which God directly works in man, and works by an absolute determinism. And in God himself there must be no motive for this will; with Calvinistic insistence upon sovereign and arbitrary will, even the idea of worth in man as human personality is excluded, alike with reference to divine love and to human.

That is hardly the New Testament position, whether of Paul or of Jesus. Paul can use the relation of husband and wife as analogy for that of Christ and the Church. Jesus illustrates God's attitude to men by referring quite simply to the way in which fathers give good gifts to their children. As for human desire and aspiration and effort, Paul urges men to work out their own salvation. He speaks of himself as fighting, as running, as pressing on that he may lay hold. He urges men to desire the higher gifts. The human-ethical emphasis here is frank and positive. There is no anxious fear of humanism and moralism for the simple reason that Paul derives everything from God who "works in us both to will and to do." It is the same way with Augustine. He speaks of the soul's longing for God, desiring completion, restless till it rests in him; but he finds the ground for this in God—"Thou hast made us unto thyself," he says.

Nor is it necessary in order to conserve the sovereignty of God to exclude all reference to the rational and ethical in God's action, making it merely the deed of arbitrary will. God is a moral and rational being, the ground of all reason and order as he is of all goodness. And he himself is under the holy obligation of reason and love, not because these form a power above him, but because they are his nature. All of which does not change, but simply emphasizes, the fact of our dependence upon him and of his undeserved mercy toward us.

7. If love with Paul is the all-inclusive principle, does it have place for any obligation toward ourselves? Shall we who are called to love God and our neighbor love ourselves also? We all recognize the deep-seated human impulse, or drive, aiming at self-assertion, self-preservation, satisfaction, or self-completion. We know that it may issue in the sin of selfishness, that it may appear as greed, lust, anger, and in the endless ways in which men oppress and exploit their brothers. We know also that it may take another form, such as that aspiration for the highest good which Plato saw in the nobler type of *eros.* Are we dealing then simply with an evil impulse which is to be extirpated, or can it be informed by the Christian spirit and taken up into the Christian way of lfe? And, if so, does it come under the law of love, a Christian love for ourselves? Paul's teaching, I think, would say yes to this, though Nygren, in the work cited above, vigorously denies this.

We note first that Christian love, *agape,* whether in God or man, though it is not dependent upon the merit and desert of its object, is yet conditioned by the fact that its object is a personal being. God's love goes to men as it does not to sticks and stones, to flowers or stars, or to beasts of the field. That is not due to their merit or achievement, but to that love of God which has created these beings in his image and has made them for fellowship with himself. I am, therefore, under a law of reverence and regard toward all personal beings, irrespective of race or color, of station or even of character.

But I, too, am a personal being, created by God's grace in his image. And so I am under this same law of reverence and regard in relation to myself as in relation to other human beings. I must see myself as God sees me; my attitude and conduct must ever have reference to his end for me. This I take to be the meaning of the phrase, "as thyself," when Jesus bids me love my neighbor as myself, instead of saying, "Thou shalt love thy neighbor, and not thyself." Love, *agape,* let us recall, is good will. It is something purposive, active, creative; it may involve denial of our desires, even a certain severity in treatment. It is thus that God loves, and his love is the norm and creative source of ours. Is not just this the attitude to take toward ourselves? Is not such love, indeed, a holy obligation? The trouble arises from a misconception of this "love thyself," a confusing of it with selfishness, self-assertion, self-indulgence. But these do not belong to *agape*; they deny its spirit and defeat its end.

Man's impulse, then, to seek life for himself is not evil. What is evil is to seek it selfishly and on the lower level; and that is folly as well as sin. There is a divinity of discontent. There is a beatitude for those who hunger and thirst after righteousness. There is praise for the man who learns of a great treasure and sells all that he has that he may obtain it. And in this Paul is at one with Jesus. He has found the supremely excellent and he gives up everything else that he may attain. There is a prize that he wants to get and he presses toward it. He urges the Corinthians to run for this prize.[10] There is a place for aspiration with Paul as with Jesus; and Plato, with his higher *eros,* is not so far from the kingdom of God. Similarly, we may sin against ourselves as against our brothers by a lack of that regard or reverence which is due to every person as person, as one whom God made for himself, one for whom Christ died.

A word more needs to be said as to how this Christian *agape* solves the conflicts which seem to arise between these three forms of love, that for God and neighbor and self. There is first, the seeming conflict between the demand of God and my neighbor. A mediaeval mystic thanked God that, now that the last of her relatives had died, she could give herself solely to the service and love of God. Paul's position is not so much expressed as implicit: it is in our fellow men that we serve God and show our love for him. Of distinctive "religious" duties and practices Paul has little to say. Here, too, he is in line with Jesus' teaching in the great parable of judgment.[11]

The second point of possible conflict would be between love of God and love of self; but that, too, is resolved when we keep to the Christian concept of love. We are to love God absolutely and utterly, with all our heart and soul and mind and strength. But the God who thus speaks is himself the God of love. He brings no selfish and competitive demand—so much of time, so much of goods, so much of ritual and sacrifice. He asks in order that he may give. In him is our true life, our highest good; to love him, to give ourselves thus in utter devotion, this

[10] Phil. 3:8–14; I Cor. 9:23–27.   [11] Mt. 25:31–46.

is to find our life. The fault is not in the search for life but in taking the wrong way and seeking the wrong end.

The third point of conflict offers more difficulties, that between love of self and love of neighbor; and there remains, indeed, a certain tension here under the conditions that obtain in a finite and sinful life. For the individual life needs quiet and meditation and the chance for communion with God—"the nurse of fullgrown souls is solitude"; but love of neighbor is a demand which might well require the full measure of thought and strength. One might answer briefly: what we are conditions the measure of love and service which we can bring; we must be in order to serve. To neglect health of body, to be indifferent to enrichment of mind and spirit, to be less than our best self in any aspect of our nature, this may be disservice to our brother rather than service. Conversely, the love of our brother is the open door to a fuller life for ourselves. But we may well go farther and point out that on every level the achievement of life is always through relations with others. You can be a whole only as you belong to a larger whole, as you give yourself to it and find your own life in its larger and richer life. Love is the way to attain life as well as the call to give one's life. The Church is for Paul the supreme illustration of this. It is more than an aggregate of individual disciples. In its rich and significant corporate life, there is more than any individual can achieve by himself. In and through this larger life God can give most fully; in it we find the fulness of our own life as is not possible outside the fellowship. This is the truth expressed by Paul in such concepts as that of the indwelling of the Spirit in the Church, and that of the Church as the body of Christ.

While the Church is the supreme example here, it is not

alone. Every human association which is normal and necessary illustrates the same fact: life is essentially organic, and the individual reaches the higher and richer life only as he enters into the life of a greater whole. Home, friendship, recreation, labor, science, art, political association, all illustrate this. But all such associations need redemption by the spirit of Christ, alike as animating the individual in relation to the whole, and as determining the spirit, the ends, and the ways of the social whole. That takes us beyond our limits of Pauline study. Here it is enough to indicate how Christian love, and this alone, can solve the conflicts which threaten humanity's very existence, and can lead us to our own true goal—as individuals and nations—by calling us to give ourselves unselfishly to others.

Chapter Eleven

SOCIAL ETHICS

AT NO POINT are we more concerned today as to the meaning of Christianity than in relation to social ethics. What do the principles of our faith mean for the associated life of men? Our work so far, aside from the study of the Church and of history, has been with man's life in the three aspects his inner and individual life, his relation to God, his life with his fellows in direct, personal relation. But our human life involves much more. Its largest area is that which has to do with group life in its varied forms, with the thoughts and ideals and interests of these groups and with the institutions in which this associated life takes form. Family, community, the Church the state, the economic order in its many and varied expressions, the international order, these illustrate the variety and inclusiveness of this life. Every human interest finds expression here. At every point our life is conditioned by these social groupings for good or ill. We can no more escape them than we can escape the atmosphere we breathe. They are, indeed, the very atmosphere of human living.

Every one of these social relations or institutions presents a problem of living and Christian ethics is concerned with them all. All this life of humanity belongs to God. It must all come under his will. It is all under the rule of sin and needs to be redeemed. And there is no hope for it, as our international situation makes increasingly plain, except as it comes under the law of Christ. That is more true today than ever before. Due very largely to our technical development, the area of these relations has increased at every point—political, economic, cultural, in travel and communications; willy-nilly, we think and feel and act in the mass as never before. Intensively as well as extensively, we are more and more one world. That the threat to human life has grown steadily is obvious; the forces of evil have here had a rich field and have grown mighty. And the forces of the spirit are under a peculiar handicap; for their sphere is the inner and personal, and our social life today grows constantly more institutional, more impersonal, more the life of large masses, and thus farther removed from the individual and the distinctly personal. It is not that the individual life as such is intrinsically better than the social, for, as we have seen in our study of the Church, the highest life is achieved in social relations. "Moral man and immoral society" is a specious phrase. But it is certainly more difficult to see how this group life and its institutions can be brought through repentance and faith into the life which God wills for it; and it is not easy to know what the will of God and the way of Christ mean in all the complex social situations of our day. What has Christianity to say as to social ethics?

I. HAS PAUL A SOCIAL ETHICS FOR US?

When we turn to Paul, however, to inquire as to his social ethics and its value for us today, our quest seems to be a hopeless one. Bluntly stated, the problems which concern us did not exist for him and some of his words on social matters raise questions in our mind. Yet while some would counsel us to leave him entirely to one side at this point, it has been pointed out by others that Paul's ethics is in fact definitely and inescapably social ethics and that he has a significant contribution for our day, despite the changed social setting. One fact, however, is clear: we cannot simply ask what Paul teaches about family, community, state, industry, and international relations. The course indicated is rather different from that in our other studies. We will begin, somewhat negatively, by pointing out the conditions which make it fruitless for us to seek direct answers to our modern social problems, noting how different from ours the situation was in which Paul and the primitive Church found themselves. We shall need to consider next the influence upon Paul of the social traditions in which he was nurtured and how these affected his statements about such matters as the family, the social status of woman, and the relation of the Christian to the state. Then we shall be ready to inquire what help we can gain from Paul's interpretation of the Christian ideal and way of life, especially as illustrated in the Christian fellowship.

The difference between Paul's situation and ours as this affected his social teaching appears especially at two points. And first the social setting. Paul belonged to a small and scattered religious group living under a great imperialism. He could not speak to a monarch or a people as the Hebrew prophets did in pointing out social evils and calling for repentance. His situation differed even more radically from ours today. The Christian community, it is true, is still a minority group and we can hardly call our western governments Christian nations in any real sense. Yet we do have a real measure of democracy. Under this Christian men and women can influence thought and action, and the Church in the name of God can bring a Christian judgment upon evil and voice the Christian demand. But the complex questions of public order, thus raised for Christian ethics, obviously would have had no relevancy for the groups whom Paul addressed in his letters.

In the second place, Paul believed that this age was near its end. Soon the Lord would return. Then the whole fashion of the world would change and the things about which men were now so much concerned would pass away. "The time is shortened," he writes. Those that have wives should be as those that had none; "and those that buy, as though they possessed not; and those that use the world as not using it to the full: for the fashion of this world passeth away." [1] This is not asceticism or dualism. It was not that Paul shared the view, quite widespread at that time, that redemption was the soul's escape from the imprisoning world of the material into the spiritual. He was not without the healthy Hebrew realism here. It was part of his faith: "The earth is the Lord's and the fulness thereof." [2] Yet his eschatological outlook inevitably so set the spiritual and eternal in the foreground that all else tended to recede. "We look not at the things which are seen, but at the things which are not seen," he declares: "for the things which are seen are temporal; but the things which are not seen are eternal." [3]

II. PAUL ON MARRIAGE, SLAVERY, AND THE STATE

There are three points, however, where Paul does touch upon broader social matters and at all three of these he has been subjected to criticism. And first as regards woman and marriage. He seems to speak of marriage as a concession to human weakness. "It is good for a man not to touch a woman."

[1] I Cor. 7: 29-31.   [2] I Cor. 10: 26.   [3] II Cor. 4: 18.

"I would that all men were even as myself," that is, unmarried; but not every one, he suggests, has this gift. "Because of fornications, let every man have his own wife." As to woman's place, he declares that "the head of every man is Christ; and the head of the woman is man; and the head of Christ is God." "Neither was the man created for the woman; but the woman for the man." "The husband is the head of the wife, as Christ also is the head of the church." [4] Here are teachings which the Church of today cannot well make its own though they have strongly influenced the Church of the past. Paul reflects here the common conception of antiquity, reaching down indeed to our own time, of the inferior nature and status of woman. He is, in fact, untrue here to the Christian principle which he himself enunciates, that in Christ there is neither male nor female.[5]

As regards marriage, it must be made clear that Paul is not influenced in his negative attitude by the idea, far too common in his day and in the thought and practice of the later Church, that there was something evil in the flesh as such in contrast with the Spirit, and particularly in all that concerned sexual relations. Significantly he speaks of fornication not as a sin of the flesh against the spirit but as a man's sin against his body, the body which should be the temple of the Spirit; nor did he for a moment think of sexual union within marriage as sin.[6] In part Paul is influenced in these advices by the shortness of the time before the end, in part by his own ideal of absolute devotion and undivided attention to the work of the Lord. The married man, he says, thinks about pleasing his wife, the unmarried man about pleasing the Lord. In both cases, practical considerations are determinative, not principles.

---

[a] I Cor. 7:1–7; 11:3–12; Eph. 5:22, 23.
[5] Gal. 3:28.   [6] I Cor. 6:15–20.

A second social situation upon which Paul touches is slavery. The material in point is found first of all in the beautiful letter which he sends to the Christian Philemon by the hand of the runaway slave Onesimus, now returning to his master under Paul's influence. Why, it is asked, does he here accept slavery without protest instead of suggesting to Philemon that it was inconsistent with Christian principles? Further, in I Corinthians 7:20–24, he lays down the general principle which would seem to rule out all correction of social injustice: "Let each man abide in that calling wherein he was called. Wast thou called being a bondservant? Care not for it." Here again we must put ourselves back into Paul's situation. So doing, we can understand why Paul did not essay the rôle of social revolutionary—and can be glad that he did not do so. But when Paul declared that in Christ there was neither bond nor free, and when he said to Philemon that Onesimus was to be to him "no longer as a servant [slave], but more than a servant, a brother beloved . . . both in the flesh and in the Lord," then he laid the foundation for a new order which was bound to come.

The third social problem to which Paul makes reference is that of the state.[7] The disciple is to be "in subjection to the higher powers," for these are ordained of God. To resist them is to "withstand the ordinance of God." The ruler is "a minister of God, an avenger for wrath to him that doeth evil." If we do what is good we need have no fear. And Paul says this not of a Christian state but of Rome, though we must keep in mind that this was not the later Rome of the Christian persecutions. In part this represents sound practical advice to the weak Christian communities as to their relation to civil authority. In part it reflects his appreciation of the Roman state as the source

[7] Rom. 13:1–7.

of that stable order which made possible the peaceful spread of the Christian movement. Clearly the evil world needed such a power to maintain order, and that meant the Roman way, that of force. Of course, when the new age came with Christ's return, then all would be different. Thus the Christian for Paul seemed to be living in relation to a threefold social order. (1) He was the subject of an imperial state, Rome, an earthly rule made necessary by the evil among men and one which had a certain providential rôle so that in some measure God's will was to be recognized in this. Yet this after all remained something external to the disciple and relative in its authority. (2) The Christian's real citizenship was in heaven.[8] There was his supreme loyalty and there his highest treasure; and while Paul did not raise this question, there is no doubt as to where he would have stood in case of a clash between Rome and the will of his Lord. (3) Meanwhile the Church, the fellowship of the believers, represented in anticipation and in partial realization the rule which was to come. And this was the point, as we shall see, where Paul developed his real social ethics.

III. THE SOCIAL MEANING OF PAUL'S CONCEPT OF GOD

But while we understand how Paul takes this position, it is obvious that we cannot transfer his conclusions to our time, particularly as regards our conception of the state and our relation to it. In any case, here as elsewhere the value of his teaching is to be sought in his underlying religious concepts. His social contribution is to be found at four points: his vision of God and of God's purpose for man, his conception of man

[8] Phil. 3:20.

and of man's true life, his portrayal of the spirit which should rule life in all its relations, his conception of the Church as a fellowship controlled by this spirit. Our task then is to see the social significance of Paul's ideas as to God, man, love, and the Church.

The social weakness of our age lies in its loss of faith in God. Our western world has developed science and techniques; it has discovered man's power through his control of nature, it has made its own the kingdoms of this world and rejoiced in its possessions; it has forgotten God where it has not denied him. But when it has met the deeper problems of life, how men and nations might live together instead of destroying each other in this quest of wealth and ease and power, it has either swung to cynicism and despair or taken refuge from its despair in the false gods which offered themselves for deliverance. We do not need to follow the pattern of Paul's apocalypticism in order to gain his faith in God and see its meaning here. There is a God of judgment upon evil, of mercy for the sinful, of saving presence and power, a God of high purpose working to good ends. We shall not escape pain and struggle, we shall need to bring loyalty and self-sacrifice; but we know that defeats are temporary, that the whole structure of life is against evil and for good, that God's end is sure, and that therefore we may fight on in faith and courage.

One thing we cannot do and that is to assign to religion and the Church the spiritual life of man, with some attention to social benevolence, and leave all other interests to secular control. How fateful such a conclusion could be we see when we observe its later influence, especially as illustrated in Luther and the Lutheran movement in Germany. Here Church and state were set side by side as coordinate divine institutions. The rulers of the state presumably were to obey God and the Christian was to obey the state in all matters that concerned government and the affairs of "the world." True, Luther stressed the religious significance of the daily vocation, but about the total social order within which the vocation was carried on, the Church had no word to speak. But in the meantime, while the Church concerned itself with the inner and individual life, the modern age brought far-reaching changes. Industry and the nation-state grew and became mighty. Over against them the Lutheran Church with its quietism, with its separate "spiritual" sphere in which it preached the "pure Word," made no pretence of challenge to the growing paganism of the social order in the name of the God who was Lord of all life. And the Roman Church, with its idea of a *corpus Christianum*, a Christian "culture" under direction of the Church, was increasingly helpless and increasingly ready to accept the autocratic state, provided the latter recognized the Church as a privileged institution in its own field. Now the last stage of totalitarian statism has made plain to us that its triumph would mean the destruction of the Christian religion. Unfortunately the elements of fascism were present in western lands even before the name was coined or its logical conclusions drawn. They appeared with those who claimed for state or business a control which recognized no authority of God, no relevancy of the way of Christ, and no right of the Church to speak in regard to the social-political order.

But these limitations which we find in Paul are, after all, a secondary matter. It has been necessary to point them out in order to guard against the error of seeking in Paul specific rules or patterns for our social life.

This God of Paul's faith meets a second urgent need, that of an authority which stands above the warring forces of classes and nations and economic groups. At times our day pays a lip service to moral ideals, but these are usually interpreted to square with the desire. More often all this is pushed aside in the name of "realism," political or economic. With the lack of any common authority or of any rule of conduct higher than self-interest and the power to enforce it, the world has moved on in endless conflict. What we must recover is the faith in a higher order which has the right to command, the belief in eternal differences between right and wrong which we disregard at our peril. And such a moral faith must rest upon a religious faith, where right is grounded in the will of a righteous God in whom goodness and power are one. The God of Paul confronts alike men and nations with a righteousness which means mercy to those who answer in faith and obedience and judgment to those "who hinder the truth in unrighteousness." [1] The loss of faith in the reality and power of a righteous order which exists independently of man's will and above men and nations, this is the root of all social disorder, and the end of this disorder is destruction. Whether the terrible tuition of war will lead men back to such a faith remains to be seen.

IV. THE CONCEPT OF MAN

Paul's conception of man in its social significance is second only to his concept of God. It does come after this, not before, because it roots in his belief in God. Not what man is in himself is decisive here, not his innate goodness, for Paul is a realist here. Nor does Paul classify men and divide them, setting good

[1] Rom. 1:16–18; 3:21, 22.

against evil, the elect or select above the masses, or one race above another. "All have sinned and come short of the glory of God." But all belong alike to God's purpose of love; all have been made in God's image and for fellowship with God. Paul knows no greater sin than the sin against love, the sin against the brother for whom Christ died. And Christ died for all men. Paul knows himself therefore as debtor to all.[2] Here Paul follows Jesus, for whom no man lay outside the sphere of God's love and whose wrath was kindled against those who injured or despised or disowned the least of his brethren among the sons of men.[3] So Paul's concept of man stands against all racism, all pride of class, all exploitation of man by man, of backward races by "superior" races. So far as this earth is concerned, the end of God's creation, the end of his work of redemption with all its cost, is to be found in man—not in a few men or in one race of men, but in all men. The great sin of man is to use his brother man as possession or tool to minister to his own pleasure or pride. That which God has set as his end, man may not use as means.[4]

One other element in Paul's concept of man is socially significant. Paul knows the evil that is in man, but he knows what man can become when he finds his true life in God. He believes

---

[2] Rom. 1:14; 14:15.

[3] Rom. 1:14; 14:15; Mt. 18:1–14; 25:34–46.

[4] We have often applauded Terence's noble words: "I am a man, and nothing which concerns man is foreign to me." (*Homo sum, nihil humani a me alienum puto.*) And Cicero has a striking phrase about taking away from a man what really makes him a man: *hominem ex homine tollere.* But to give a full depth of meaning to such humanism we must see man as a being who belongs to the Eternal, having his origin in God and his true destiny in the purpose of God. And without this we shall have no secure defense against that obscene degradation of man, that dehumanizing of classes and races of human beings, which is so terrifying a social portent today.

that man can know the truth and follow it. Sentimentalism turns from realities and builds on dreams; its sin is that of wishful thinking. Paul is a realist, but his realism includes the fact of God as well as the facts about man; it includes the realities and the power of grace and truth and love as well as sin and ignorance. And so he holds his high ideals with hope, a contrast to the cynicism and pessimism which mark too much of the "realism" of our day. We are coming to see that democracy must be a social philosophy, or faith, not merely a political or even an economic order. A truly democratic social philosophy will have this faith in man but will need equally the faith in God who alone can furnish ground for the democratic faith in man.

V. THE PRIMACY OF THE SPIRIT

Central in Paul's individual ethics, as we have seen, is his emphasis upon the inner spirit and attitude. His ethics is made up of these two elements: the vision of this right spirit and the effort to see what this spirit requires of us in the concrete situations of life. Here is Paul's third contribution to social ethics. It is obvious that the social life needs organization and must create for itself institutional forms. These multiply as man's associated life becomes more complex in its nature and more inclusive in its scope. In both respects the growth has been at an increasing tempo during the last hundred years and particularly the last generation. We are now facing the necessity of creating global institutions for a new global life, an almost impossible task. What Paul tells us is that the primacy here, as in every human relation, belongs to the right inner spirit. "Europe needs a new heart," wrote Sir Philip Gibbs, the distinguished journalist, at the close of the first world war. We need to see now that the world needs a new heart, to realize the futility of plans for a new world order, or a new economic order, if there should remain only the old individualism and selfishness, the old pride and hate and fear. That does not mean that we must wait for a "converted" world before we can work for needed change in the social order or for international organization. It does mean that the inner spirit will always have the primacy, that we must turn to leaders who are touched with that spirit, that the new spirit must be fostered by the Church within its own fellowship and must be constantly held before men, and that men of good will everywhere, in the Church and out of it, men who are touched by the Spirit of God even if they do not name his name, must work to create this spirit in every group to which they belong. To create men in that spirit must be the Church's task.

But what is decisive for Paul's ethics is the character of this spirit. That is what makes Paul's ethics social in its very nature. For his is no mere individual ethics of self-achievement, no legal ethics concerned with rules and divine exactions, no asceticism, whether in search of merit or of escape from evil; it is the ethics of self-giving love, of *agape*, of love as seen in the spirit of Christ who loved men and gave himself for them that they might have life. There is no solitary religious life for Paul any more than for Jesus. It is life with our fellows and in the service of our fellows—not just of our family or our group or those of our faith, but, as with Jesus, the service of those that need by those who have. God is love. Christ is God's love in action. They are Christ's who have his spirit. That spirit is forth-going, self-giving, serving, creative. Paul's ethics at its center and in all its outreach is social.

But just as Paul did for his time in the narrower sphere of more individual relations, so we must ask what this spirit requires of us in regard to the larger problems of the social life of today. Can this creative good will for men be squared with national selfishness, seeking its own and indifferent to the needs of other lands? "The pitiless poverty, the animal-like existence, and the seeming hopelessness of nearly one billion human beings in India, Burma, Malaya, Thailand, Indo-China, and China," [1] can this be of no concern to those who make Christ's *agape* the rule of life? Can we of America acquiesce in a situation in which normally five to twelve millions in this place of plenty are shut off from land and tools and other means of earning a livelihood? Can we acquiesce in an international order, or lack of order, which calls for the slaughter of millions of youth in recurring world wars? The Church is not the technical adviser of society in these matters, but it must be the conscience of society, and in the spirit of Christ it must voice the judgment of the God of love and bring his demands. If the Church accepts this love as the will of God it cannot remain silent in the face of a society whose institutions are still so largely pagan in their indifference to human well-being.

VI. THE SOCIAL SIGNIFICANCE OF THE CHURCH

Paul's greatest contribution in social ethics is in his conception of the Christian fellowship. The primary meaning of the Church for Paul is religious; the Church is a divine creation whose life is from God, a body whose head is Christ, a temple in which God's Spirit dwells. But it has a historical-social

[1] Leland Stowe in *They Shall Not Sleep*, p. 50.

aspect. It is a human fellowship, and Paul's letters treat no theme more frequently than the life of the disciples as lived together within this fellowship and the principles which should govern this life. We have considered in an earlier chapter what these mean for the Church. Now we need to ask whether they can be applied to other forms of our social life and what value they may have.

Now, it is easy to rule out such questions at the start. Is not the Church different from all other social institutions? Is it not a society of the saved, a company of saints? Will not its life be under a wholly different order? Must we not face the fact that the Church represents a minority group today even in so-called Christian nations, and that the avowed basis of action in industry and state is never even nominally Christian? How then can we bring Christian principles to bear upon this life? To this a threefold reply must be made.

1. The Church as a human fellowship is not a world apart. Its members are not "saints," they are saints in the making. The ethical problems which Paul discusses with them are in large measure such as appear in every human group. They belong in the main to human relations as such. Ethically considered, human life is one, whether you view it in home or Church or state. As there is no separation between individual and social, so there is no separation between these various spheres. The same moral laws and the same possibilities apply to all because they all concern human beings. One need only consider the sins against which Paul warns his churches: selfishness, pride, division, contention, anger, bitterness, malice, and sexual immorality. There is a distinction between Church and non-Church, between saints and sinners, between sacred and secular, but there is no separation. All this life belongs to

God, all of it is imperfect and sinful and in need of redemption.

2. As the world outside the Church is not apart from the rule of God, so it is not without his presence and direction and help. We dare not minimize the strength of the forces of evil in the world or the pagan character of much of our institutional life; and we recognize how this life, growing ever larger and more complex, has been increasingly depersonalized. It seems at times like a Frankenstein creation which now threatens to destroy its maker. We wonder how it can ever be reached by any personal-ethical appeal. But the problem is not impossible of solution. It is, after all, the problem of democracy, and there is no reason why democratic peoples, while frankly facing realities, should revert to cynicism and pessimism; nor is there reason why Christian people should say, here is a realm in which we cannot appeal to Christian ideals, for which Christian ethics has no relevance, in which we must rely upon force, where we can hope for no more than a measure of rude justice. If there are forces of evil at work in society, so also in the individual life. If in the individual life the redemptive powers of the new age are now working, so also in the larger human scene. War itself has revealed the strength of unselfish devotion to the common good which appears, not simply on occasion, but in great masses of the common people. War is bringing some realization of the wickedness and futility of the ways which the nations have been following, whether in imperialistic domination, in militant aggression, or in selfish isolation. More and more leaders have expressed a conception of a world order which includes mutual good will, creative cooperation, and a regard for men as men the world around, even though nationalism and power politics are still the more

common viewpoint. And the meaning of all this is that here too God is at work, and here, too, in this larger world, the Church must hold up the Christian way.

The growth of materialism, on the one hand, and the recrudescence of a militant paganism on the other have led many to overlook the extent to which Christian thought has shaped the social ideals of the common man. Jacques Maritain has recently pointed out how "the secular conscience" has been influenced by "the hidden work of evangelical inspiration." He recognizes the imminent danger of our day in his repeated phrase, "if it does not veer to paganism," but notes some of the powerful convictions which are moving and growing everywhere in the common man, seeing in them the working of the Christian tradition: the dignity of the human person as person transcending the state, justice as the needed foundation for the common life, the idea of a community of free men as against the dominance of any caste or race or class, faith in the brotherhood of man and a sense of social duty. Rightly he not only holds to the Christian source of these ideals historically but asserts that they can be effectively maintained only as we believe in God and see man in his relation to God.[2]

3. Finally it must be said to society as to the individual: there is none other name whereby men may be saved. There is no hope for our social order, economic or political or international, except in the way of the spirit of Christ. The principle of selfishness, the reliance upon force, the propaganda which suppresses the truth, the denial to men of their real humanity, these are the ways of death. Whether or not the end of humanity is to be a common destruction, as some hold, so much is sure: the hope of humanity cannot lie anywhere

[2] See his chapter on "Evangelical Inspiration and the Secular Conscience" in his volume, *Christianity and Democracy*.

else except in the spirit of that fellowship which was created by Christ. The universe has only one order of life and that is revealed in him. Individually and socially, mankind can have life, true and abiding, only in the measure that it finds this way.

VII. CONCERNING INDIVIDUAL AND SOCIAL

Deeply significant for social ethics is the way in which Paul unites individual and social and shows how each comes to its own within the Christian fellowship. The basic social problem to which he thus contributes is peculiarly urgent today and calls for some analysis at this point.

To realize the significance of the individual human being, of man as man, has been one of the supreme ethical achievements of history. It has taken nearly three millennia to win this insight; it will take longer still to win general recognition for it and to embody it in social institutions. Its first clear expression is in the Hebrew prophets. In discovering a God who was righteous and merciful, they found the true nature of man. This righteous God cares for all men: for the fatherless and widows, for the farmer being crowded off his bit of land. Religion is kinship of spirit with this God in justice and mercy. Neither group ritual on the one hand nor tribal mores on the other any longer sufficed. Becoming ethical, religion necessarily became individual and inner. More and more the individual came to his own in religious significance and social regard. Before that he had been lost in the tribe or nation; not by himself but only in such relation did he count. Now God cared for each man and each man in reverence and personal trust could come to this God. The movement, of course, was not in Israel alone, but in Israel it was rooted in religion and here it came at last to its fullest and surest expression in Jesus. Jesus bade men believe in a God of personal concern and care for whom the very hairs of their head were numbered, who heard when the single soul lifted his voice in the secret place of prayer, who rejoiced when the one lost sheep returned.

But the concern with the individual, cut off from these roots and taken by itself, may grow into an individualism which is destructive of all social life and in the end of the individual himself. On the one hand it means the failure to see the significance of that corporate life without which man cannot be truly human. Socially, such an atomism means anarchy. On the other hand, morally considered, it is the spirit of selfishness. Here the individualism appears not merely in the individual but in class and race and nation. It is the denial of brotherhood, the refusal of obligation, the single insistence upon the right of the individual, of self or group, of country or race. In the world scene it appears today as that thorough-going nationalism which will surrender no iota of its authority or privileged position for the sake of peace or a larger welfare, while reserving the right to profit from others in trade or imperialistic control. But it appears *within* the nation too. Our democracies today find their greatest peril not from foes without but in aggressive and consciously selfish interests in their own midst. And these in turn are made possible by the individualistic attitude of the masses, by apathy and selfish indifference, clamorous of rights but refusing to accept the obligations of citizenship or any concern with the needs of others. Thus social control falls to political organizations and to pressure groups representing various organized interests, while vast numbers in the unorganized groups suffer under race discrimination or as the economically disinherited. This philosophy of individualism is defended under such terms as common-sense realism, rugged individualism, the liberal tradition, or the American way.

But there is an equal threat to our social life today coming from its corporate aspect. The corporate is an inescapable element in human existence. Life on the plane of the human is necessarily life in group relations: family, community, Church, state—biological, social, religious, economic, political. The question as to corporate, or group, life is not that of whether but of how. On the lower levels of human culture, group life was almost the whole life; the individual came but slowly to his own. Now the movement has come around again full circle and the organization of the corporate life endangers the free and full life of the individual; that is, it tends to destroy human life in its highest expression or at least to hinder it. The extreme expression of this is the totalitarian state, which arrogates to itself absolute authority and seeks to dominate all life, inner and outer, individual and social. But aside from this there is danger to a rich and free individual life from the strong tendency to what we may call mass existence. It is the result in large part of technological development, of the machine age. In any case, the movement is from the individual to the group, from the personal to the impersonal: mass production in industry, mass aggregations of capital with absentee and so impersonal ownership, massed population in the city, mass recreation made technically possible by radio and screen, our very sports becoming passive and impersonal as professional agents perform for us in great stadia and our opinions being molded for us wholesale by news associations, columnists, and radio commentators. So the mass life produces the modern mass man.

Much of this associated life is necessary. We may be able to decentralize industry in some measure, we may encourage a larger rôle for smaller groups in social and political life; yet it remains true that we are bound together in new ways and larger measure and we must accept social planning and social control. Totalitarianism is simply the wrong answer to a very real problem. The crucial question is, what shall be the nature of this larger corporate life? As the real life of the individual may be lost in individualism, so the real group life may be lost in the existence of mere masses, or aggregates, under external control. How can the individual maintain the true and free life of a man and yet be a living member of the group and its servant? And how can you have the needed social unity and control while yet conserving the free life of the individual?

Needless to say, Paul does not give us specific directions which we can apply to our problem of economic organization or world relations. But his conception of the Christian fellowship does point the way to a true ideal of both individual and corporate life and of that relation between them in which each contributes to the realization of the other.

And first as to the corporate life: the Christian fellowship shows the way to unity without compulsion. There is a certain compulsion in life which we cannot avoid. We are bound together whether we will or no by the very conditions of human existence, and civil society, because of this as well as because of ignorance and evil, will always require a degree of external control. But if there is only this, then there is likely to be ceaseless and destructive strife, made the more serious because we are so inescapably bound together. Our salvation must be in having unity within union, a unity of spirit and life. The Christian fellowship shows the way to such unity. It must come from the inner cohesion of a common spirit, not from external compulsion. There must be ideals which we share in common, a common confidence or faith, common goals which we seek, a common welfare to which we are devoted. Such unity in its fulness can only come where there is a common faith in God and when his creative Spirit works in men; yet in a measure these unitive forces can be seen at work in the world today. They are most easily called forth in time of war as against a common danger, but they can be mobilized for the high creative tasks of peace. The whole movement of thought in our western democracies has been toward an increasing recognition of the need of these ideal elements and the realization that political organization is only the first step toward a democratic society.[1]

[1] A pertinent illustration is the following statement by Charles E. Merriam in "The Meaning of Democracy," *The Journal of Negro Education*, 1941, p. 309, quoted by Gunnar Myrdal, *An American Dilemma*, Vol. I, p. 8. Having indicated the political form of democracy, Professor Merriam lists its postulates:

"(1) The essential dignity of man, the importance of protecting and cultivating his personality on a fraternal rather than upon a differential basis, of reconciling the needs of the personality within the frame-work of the common good in a formula of liberty, justice, welfare.

"(2) The perfectibility of man; confidence in the possibilities of the human personality, as over against the doctrines of caste, class, and slavery.

"(3) That the gains of commonwealths are essentially mass gains rather than the efforts of the few and should be diffused as promptly as possible throughout the community without too great delay or too wide a spread in differentials.

"(4) Confidence in the value of the consent of the governed expressed in institutions, understandings and practices as a basis of order, liberty, justice.

"(5) The value of decisions arrived at by common counsel rather than by violence and brutality.

"These postulates rest upon (1) reason in regarding the essential nature of the political man, upon (2) observation, experience and inference, and (3) the fulfillment of the democratic ideal is strengthened by a faith in the final triumph of ideals of human behavior in general and of political behavior in particular."

Cf. *Christianity*, by H. F. Rall, pp. 131–139, and Ch. 9, on "Social Change," in *Religion and Public Affairs: Essays in Honor of Bishop F. J. McConnell*, edited by H. F. Rall.

The Christian fellowship shows how the life of the individual and that of the whole are realized together and each through the other. As we have seen, Paul uses first the biological analogy, that of the body. The figure had been used by the Stoics before him. We recognize its significance today. The part cannot fully achieve except as it shares in the richer life of the whole. To be a whole, man must belong to a whole which is larger than himself. The whole in turn has no life apart from its members. The more adequate illustration, however, is social, not biological, and the simplest analogy is that of the family. The Church is the family of God, and human society can bring individual and social into a life-giving unity only as it approximates the true life of a family. Paul does not develop this thought of the family. The word itself occurs with Paul only in Ephesians 3:15 when he speaks of "the Father [*Pater*] from whom every family [*patria*] in heaven and on earth is named." But the conception is implicit with him as with Jesus in the idea of God's fatherhood, of the kinship of men with God as his children, and of the true relation of men with one another as brethren. In the family each member has his own distinct place and unique significance. The family has its joy and its sorrow in the life of each single member. It is concerned to promote the well-being of each, and upon this its own well-being depends. Here each is for all and all are for each in the fullest sense. That does not mean a total merging of the two. We are dealing here not with an aggregation of units in a mass, or of cells in an organism, or of subjects in a political system. The family, or fellowship, in Christian usage is a society of persons. Each person thus has a life of his own, sacred in its own right. And the group has a common life which can call upon the individual member for sacrificial service. Hence there is always a latent tension and this may easily become real conflict.

At this point the Christian fellowship makes its other contribution and its greatest in the concept of the Christian *agape,* love. It is very well to argue the fact of the solidarity of the race or the social solidarity of a nation, that capital and labor must work together for a shared prosperity or else both will suffer, that no nation can have peace and economic well-being except as these belong to all. One can stress, too, and one must stress, the fact that there can be no freedom in a nation unless we surrender some of our individual "right" to do as we please; that there can be no social rights without social obligations. And we need to make plain that this applies to the nation in the family of nations as truly as to individual men. But in the end all this will be of little avail unless there goes with it a genuine spirit of good will toward others. To rate all men everywhere as men like ourselves and unselfishly and actively to will their good, this is our great need today. Without this our generalizations, no matter how true, are only so many words; and our economic and international plans, no matter how wise, will be without real effect. The Church of Christ must proclaim this way of love in its message. It must exemplify this spirit in its own life, transcending differences of race and class within its own communion and maintaining its fellowship even against the dividing forces of war.

Chapter Twelve

GOD

THEOLOGY usually begins with the doctrine of God. There is good reason for this, for what we think of God determines all else, our conception of the world and man, of sin and salvation, of the Church and the Christian way of life, and of our hope for the future. There is good ground, however, for putting last a statement of Paul's doctrine of God. For Paul's approach, as we have seen, is not theoretical or systematic. What is new and distinctively Christian in his concept of God is not something which he posited at the beginning and out of which he drew his conclusions as to salvation and the Church. Rather his vision of God came out of his experience in relation to Christ and salvation and the Church. His method was neither speculative or dogmatic, after the common manner of theology; it was that of insight and faith and experience as he responded to the revelation in Christ. Thus we have been getting Paul's idea of God as we went along in our study of salvation and the Church, of Christ and the Spirit. In all these we have had to refer constantly to the conception of God. What we need to do now is to bring this together. The summary of the Christian elements can be quite brief. We shall need to give somewhat more space to what precedes and follows this: first, to the Old Testament idea of God which Paul brought with him, then, at the close, to certain conclusions which theology has drawn from Paul, particularly as to the doctrine of the Trinity.

I. THE GOD OF THE PROPHETS

Paul's God is no new God, any more than was the God of Jesus. The God of the early Christians was the God of Israel. We must first then recall the main elements in this conception. Hebrew thought with the prophets had won its way through to a clear ethical monotheism: there is one God, the creator of heaven and earth, the ruler of all nations. He is "the living God," not abstract idea, or impersonal order, or spiritual essence, but the God of purpose and action. He is the revealed God, or, better, the self-revealing God, not known by mystical vision or philosophic insight, or even by divinely communicated ideas, but rather making himself known by his mighty deeds. He is the God of righteousness and mercy, an ethical God. This is his character in his relation to men; this is seen in his attitude toward his people and in his purpose for men. In all this we have an intensely personal conception of God, one might say anthropomorphic; for anthropomorphism was not left behind when its cruder forms were discarded. You cannot have an ethical God except as you have a personal God, and that means the higher anthropomorphism. When you conceive a God of moral character, of action shaped by purpose, a God who draws near in mercy, who speaks to his servants and enters into covenant relations with his people, then you have a personal God. It might be misleading to speak here of the immanence of God, for the background of that term is more philosophic and its association is more with the static, while the prophetic approach is intensely religious and the association is with the active and dynamic. Let us say rather that this is the God who is present in action, who draws nigh in mercy, and with whom fellowship is possible because he is Person dealing with persons.

But there is another aspect to which justice is not always done, either in relation to prophetic thought or to that of Paul; that is the transcendence of God. Here again it is better to use the more distinctly religious term and speak of the holiness of God, using that in the primary sense. Rudolf Otto in his *Idea of the Holy* has helped us to a better understanding of the unique religious factor here involved. Significantly it is described by Otto primarily · in terms of the feelings evoked rather than of a rationally defined concept. There is that in the divine, in Otto's term the numinous, which calls forth awe, fascination, fear. It is that which makes God God and not man. Power and glory and majesty enter in, but beyond these there is the idea of the hidden, the mysterious, that which transcends human comprehension. That is why we understand it best, not by attempted definition, but through the feelings which it calls forth.

The primitive idea of the holy was markedly modified, as we know, in prophetic thought, particularly by the elements of the ethical and the rational. The unknown and mysterious God now appears as the one who speaks and asks men to understand. He is the self-revealing God, the God who can be known. The God of majesty and power, the inscrutable or arbitrary sovereign, now becomes the righteous God, dependable and faithful. Here, as Otto does not sufficiently recognize, is not just something added to the idea of the holy; here, in a measure, is its transformation. God's righteousness and mercy become now the very point at which his transcendence, or "otherness," is to be discerned as over against man. Just because he "is God, and not man: the Holy One in the midst of thee," he will have mercy.[1]

[1] See the deeply significant and epoch-making passage of Hos. 6:8–11, and compare Isa. 55.

But this does not mean that the distinctive quality of "the holy" in its primary sense has disappeared. There is the attitude not just of reverence but of awe and wonder; there is "the fear of God." The glory, the majesty, the power, the unfathomable in God's nature and will still remain. It has been described as paradox: but paradox points more to error or limitation in human thought, that is, to a contradiction which is real and thus absurd, or else one which is due to our faulty apprehension. Here is something that is better described as a duality (not dualism) or polarity which is not just in our thought but is in God himself.[2] Paradox moves in the realm of thought and is settled, if at all, by reason. Polarity is a dynamic term; it deals with a duality of movement, or forces, and the problem which it poses is met by attitude and action rather than argument.

This duality in the concept of God appears with Paul in certain notable passages. The God of Paul, on the one hand, is the God revealed, the God of mercy who has drawn nigh to men. In Christ he has shown us his heart of love. His will for men has been made plain—they are to be sons in the likeness of the Son; his purpose for history is revealed—the redemption of a people of God and the establishment of his rule with the overthrow of evil. Not only has he drawn nigh to us in Christ; he has come by his Spirit to dwell in men. God has brought us into the likeness of children who share the spirit of the Son and through God's Spirit can cry, Abba, Father. No one could assert more strongly than Paul the God of kinship and fellowship and the primacy of the ethical and personal in God.

The other aspect of this duality, however, is equally present

[2] See H. F. Rall, *Christianity*, pp. 25–28, 40–42, and note the earlier discussion in the chapter on Ethics.

with Paul as it is in the Old Testament. There is a hidden God as well as a God revealed, a God who determines all things by his sovereign power, whose wisdom is inscrutable and whose ways are past finding out. In the assertion of this point of view, however, there are places in which Paul seems to deny flatly, not only his declaration of the revealed God whose essential nature is mercy, but even the righteousness of God in what seems to us the clear meaning of that term.

The relevant passages are those upon which traditional theology of the Augustine-Calvin succession has built its doctrines of divine determinism and the predestination of man. God chooses whom he wills to be saved, and the choice rests upon the will of God and that alone. "He hath mercy upon whom he will, and whom he will be hardeneth." It does not depend upon what men do, good or bad; he chose Jacob as against Esau before they were born: "Even as it is written, Jacob I loved, but Esau I hated." Has not the potter absolute right over the clay, he asks, and so makes from the same clay "a vessel unto honor and another unto dishonor"? So it is at present with Israel: there is a remnant being saved "according to the election of grace"; "the election obtained it, and the rest was hardened." [3] The picture that we have here seems quite clear: a God of sovereign power decides the lot of men, not by consideration of their character (justice), nor under the influence of mercy (for he could save whom he willed), but by arbitrary determination; and men are determined in action and character by the power of God, some to faith and obedience, some to hardness of heart.

If this were all that we had of Paul the problem of interpretation would be simple. But we must not forget a directly

[3] Rom. 9:11–23; 11:5–8.

contrasted point of view which has appeared in all our studies up to this point. Everywhere Paul has assumed man's freedom and responsibility. He summons men to accept the gospel: "we beseech you on behalf of Christ, be ye reconciled to God." [4] He uses every basis of appeal, every mode of argument. He admonishes his followers to be faithful, he calls them to watchfulness. In his appeal to the Galatians, he recognizes that, though set free by Christ, they might again become enslaved, that is, they might fall away from grace.[5] He faces the fact that, though he has preached to others, he must use every effort if he himself is not to be rejected.[6] There is no suggestion here that everything is settled by the determination of God, and that, having been foreknown and foreordained, the calling and justification and final state of glory are all inalterably fixed.[7] Everywhere the moral elements in the situation are assumed: men know the truth, men wilfully reject the truth, men are therefore rejected of God. Nowhere, except in these two chapters of Romans, does he indicate that men are lost because God has shaped them on his wheel as "vessels of wrath fitted unto destruction." Israel is rejected, not because of the inscrutable decree of arbitrary will, but because "they did not subject themselves to the righteousness of God," because "they did not hearken." [8] And so with individuals, both Gentiles and Jews; judgment awaits them because they knew the truth and did not obey it.[9] If their minds have become darkened and their hearts hardened and their life one of corruption, it is because of disobedience and rejection of God.[10] Paul's argument is constantly punctuated by "wherefore," "for this cause," "that

[4] II Cor. 5:20.
[5] Gal. 1:4.
[6] I Cor. 9:24–27.
[7] Rom. 8:29, 30.

[8] Rom. 10:3, 16.
[9] Rom. 1:18–23; 2:1–29.
[10] Rom. 1:18 to 2:1.

they may be without excuse." More important even than this constant assumption of human freedom and responsibility, is the gospel itself, Paul's gospel of the God of grace and of a salvation offered to sinners, to all sinners. And this is repeated in the very heart of this other presentation, that of Romans 9 to 11. Confess Jesus as Lord and you shall be saved, he says. The Lord "is rich unto all that call upon him. . . . Whosoever shall call upon the name of the Lord shall be saved. . . . There is no distinction between Jew and Greek." [11]

How then did Paul come to set forth this argument of chapters 9 and 11, which seems to assert an arbitrary sovereignty to which justice and mercy alike are subordinated as God predestines men to death or life, and a determinism which supplants human freedom and responsibility? Several elements enter in here. (1) There is a religious motive, uniting the old and the new in Paul's faith. The old was the confident Hebraic faith in the one God, "a great God, and a great King above all gods," an absolute monotheism in which all depended upon the will and power of this God. The new was the defense of his gospel of grace, whose confidence rested not in man's achievement but wholly in the God who called men and justified men and glorified men. The clue to the motivation and intention of Romans 8:26–30 is found in the words which follow: "If God is for us, who is against us?" This is what he is trying to say to them: "Let us draw comfort and courage from the fact that our salvation rests upon God's purpose, rather than our deed." (2) There is an apologetic motive, relating to the apparent rejection of Israel and to his right to preach to the Gentiles. Here, for the time being, he turns aside from the idea of a God of grace offering his mercy to all men, Jew or Greek,

[11] Rom. 10:9–13.

and of a line drawn solely by men themselves through their acceptance or refusal of this grace. He appeals rather to God's sovereign right to choose, a right which man may not question. This right God exercised in choosing Israel, taking Jacob instead of Esau. Now he is illustrating it again, choosing in Israel a remnant to be saved, but calling his people also from among the Gentiles.

These passages have been fateful for traditional theology, proceeding, as it did, from the assumption of Paul's doctrinal infallibility. It mattered little for Augustinianism that this was really an excursus in which, for apologetic purposes, Paul carried the common Jewish conception of divine sovereignty to its extreme, with results which, strictly taken, would have cut the ground from under his preaching. Paul himself let this stand, without effort at reconciliation, side by side with his dominant religious message. The Augustinian-Calvinistic theology, in its thorough-going form, made these words the determining viewpoint for its doctrinal structure, where divine sovereignty, absolute predestination, total depravity, and strict determinism went together.

Religious speech will always include an element of paradox, that is, of statements that stand in apparent contradiction. It must not be strained after, as has been the modern vogue, where, in the reaction from the superficially rational, paradox has been assumed to be the hall-mark of truth. Paradox belongs rather to form; the essential matter is the fact of the polarity of life. It is not that life is irrational or that we have a contradiction of mutually exclusive principles; it is rather that there is in all concrete existence, from lowest to highest, a certain duality of movement or of forces. If there were direct opposition it would mean deadlock; actually, though it involves a certain tension, it is rather the condition of life and growth.[12] All this is exemplified in the problem with which Paul was struggling, that of divine sovereignty and human freedom. We all know the duality of human life that is here involved: on the one hand a sense of dependence, of an all-encompassing Cosmic Order, of a Power that rules our life; on the other, the consciousness of individual and autonomous being, a life set apart from all else as by "a salt, unplumbed, estranging sea," and a power to determine our reaction toward that which is without, of which Augustine and Calvin themselves freely take account when they entreat and exhort or when they assert moral responsibility. And here the relation of the ethical to the religious comes to a head. Knowledge of the truth as that which reveals the meaning of our life, freedom of choice and action, and consequent responsibility, these are the core of the moral life. The awareness of a higher Power, the feeling of dependence, the sense of awe and reverence and absolute obligation, these are at the heart of religion. Taken separately, the one may lead to a passive fatalism, the other to moralism or shallow activism, deficient alike in respect of adequate goal and of power of attainment.

Now Paul has a real contribution to make here, though it is not found in the one-sided philosophy of Romans 9 and 11. It is suggested in Philippians 2:12, 13, with its surface paradox and its profound insight. Here is the moral earnestness of true prophetic religion. This is right and good, it says, this is your task; sense its seriousness, give yourself to it, "work out your own salvation with fear and trembling." But there is something more, something which gives courage and confidence for the moral effort. It is the realization that God is working in us;

[12] See *Christianity*, by H. F. Rall, Ch. III.

God supplies the willing and the doing and everything else, including faith itself. Only, this work of God is not mechanical or magical or compulsive. It means, not bondage, but a new and real freedom: a religious freedom, that of faith, and a moral freedom, that of a new spirit and power within. It is "the law of the Spirit of Life in Christ Jesus," at once God's presence and our own conscious, purposive life. It is strength, freedom, peace.[13] Hence, so far from being excluded or submerged, the ethical comes here to its own. But this is possible only because the God of our faith is something more than an all-determining Power, because he is a merciful God who takes men by his grace into life-giving fellowship with himself. And this is Paul's supreme word about God. That this God is a God of power and purpose who will ultimately work out his ends and upon whose power we can rely, this does not contradict the former faith but rather gives it a basis of assurance and courage: "If God is for us, who is against us?"

II. THE CHRISTIAN CONTRIBUTION

But while the basic conception of God with Paul is prophetic, there is a distinctly Christian development which requires consideration. It is to be sought, not in specific doctrinal statements, but in Paul's experience of God and in the gospel which he proclaimed. We can deal more briefly with this here because of the discussions of the two preceding chapters. The God of Paul is the God whom he knows through Christ. He is "the God and Father of our Lord Jesus Christ," and that phrase is a summary of Paul's doctrine of God. Even here Paul is moving forward on the prophetic line. It has little kinship with the

[13] Rom. 8: 1–17.

efforts of later theology which sought, with the help of philosophical concepts, to define God metaphysically and to determine his nature in and by himself as transcendent and ultimate being. It is the God revealed, the God made known by action, the God coming into our history and related to human life. The character of God is here the first concern; he is the God of righteousness and mercy. And the second concern is the purpose of God and his way with men. The first is known through the second: Christ is the deed of God revealing his character of love; Christ is the way of God, the way of forgiveness and reconciliation by which God achieves a rule of righteousness which the law could not bring to pass. It is not some proposition about God that is decisive here, whether spoken by Christ or heard by Paul in some direct communication. It is revelation by action: Christ himself is God's Word to us, through what he was and did and said. That is "the light of the knowledge of the glory of God in the face of Jesus Christ," discerned by Paul in his Damascus road experience but not a mere matter of ecstatic vision. The term Son of God finds its meaning here. Whatever further meaning it has for a doctrine of the person of Christ, it is first of all not so much a declaration about Christ as about God. To call Christ Son in this preeminent sense is to say that God is the Father whose character is known in the Spirit of his Son. So Paul dares to correlate, or even equate, the Spirit of God with the Spirit of Christ; and Paul's greatest single contribution to the Christian doctrine of the Spirit is the realization that it is the Christlike Spirit, just as God is the Christlike God. What God is and what God wills and how God works, all is known in Christ.

Next in importance in Paul's thought of God is the idea of the Holy Spirit. God is one who is present as living and life-giving Spirit, transforming men by "the law of the Spirit of life" and creating the Fellowship which is the communion of the Holy Spirit. Here again the God who is known is the God of experience. In the Old Testament the creative-redemptive work of God is seen primarily in nature and history. Here God is seen as creator in the sphere of man's inner life. The deepened and enriched concept of God which comes from this new experience is clear on almost every page in the New Testament, though especially with Paul. Neither the personal nor the ethical aspects of God are lost in this mystical emphasis. On the contrary, it means that God is more richly known in personal fellowship; it is through the Spirit in us that we cry, Abba, Father. And the Spirit as thus shared is ethical in its nature and in its fruits. Above all, the experience of God as indwelling Spirit brought to the early Church the deep sense of the reality of God, of his living presence, and of their participation even now in the gifts of that kingdom for whose coming they waited.

III. AS TO THE TRINITY

Paul's God is the God who is revealed in Christ and is with men as indwelling Spirit, redeeming and re-creating: does this mean the trinitarian God of later theology? It may be answered that this depends upon how that doctrine is formulated. The average churchman today either passes it by as a puzzle belonging to theologians or, disregarding the term itself, appropriates the religious content which we have found in Paul's teaching. Very simply he thinks of God in threefold manner: as the God and Father of all, Creator and Redeemer; as the God who in Jesus Christ has come to men for their salvation and thus revealed himself; as the God who dwells with men through his Spirit as living and saving Presence and Power, transforming human life, creating in the Church a new people of God. His actual concept of God is thus determined by the fact of Christ and the experience of the Spirit.

The traditional creedal formulation, however, and notably as expressed in the Athanasian Creed, goes definitely beyond this. The Athanasian is distinctly the theologians' creed. It has, of course, the practical purpose of warding off error and preserving the faith; but it moves in the realm of abstract thought and formal definition, not of religious experience and personal faith. One ignorant of the Christian way might read this and not gain any real knowledge of the historic Christ and his meaning as Revealer and Redeemer, or of the nature of God as indwelling and life-giving Spirit. There is no effort whatever to connect the doctrine with the historical Jesus or with Christian experience.

So far as Paul is concerned, the problem may be approached in two ways. First we may inquire whether what Paul says concerning Christ and the Spirit indicates that he placed these two on a level with the Father as three coordinate or equal divine beings. That can be definitely negatived. Over and over again his position appears. "For us there is one God, the Father, of whom are all things." He does not speak of Christ as God. Our Father is likewise the Father of Jesus Christ. The distinction which he gives to Christ as Son and Lord does not alter this. For Paul, as for John, he is the Son whom the Father has sent into the world, who receives from God his power as Lord and at the end returns it again to God.[1]

It is much more difficult to state Paul's position as regards the Spirit. We have seen his ambiguity at this point. Of the

[1] I Cor. 6:8; Phil. 2:9–11; I Cor. 15:27, 28.

reality of the Spirit with Paul there is no question, nor of his conviction that this is indeed the Spirit of *God* which is present, and not some emanation or "power" or mere influence coming down from God. But it is not clear how he thought of the Spirit as distinct from Christ, or in its relation to Christ, or as a third in relation to God and Christ. For there was no historical personality here as in the case of Christ. It is this ambiguity which explains why the Church did not take up the question of the "Three" until long after its consideration of the Relation of Father and Son, and why its concept of God moved so long in binitarian rather than Trinitarian lines. The Old Testament had not reached the idea of the Spirit as a Being to be distinguished from Jehovah; it speaks simply of the Spirit of Jehovah. It is not clear whether Paul moved beyond this. Even Christ and the Spirit, though distinguished, are terms used by him at times almost interchangeably. Perhaps his thought is something like this: There is one God, source of all being and life, who in his Son has come to men, and who as Spirit is in the Son and as Spirit gives himself to men. This Spirit is present in the corporate and historical life of the Church and in the individual life of the believer. God and Christ and Spirit are thus one sphere of divine life, which appears to us historically in Christ and is shared by us experimentally in the Spirit. But the essential part with Paul is no such construction of theory, even assuming that he held it. It is the simple declaration of faith as related to living experience: there is one God who brings men salvation through Christ and dwells in them by his Spirit.

The other approach to our question is to inquire whether Paul does not give us the Trinitarian conception in germ when he associates the three together in a single expression,

Father, Son, and Spirit. Most familiar is the apostolic benediction: "The grace of the Lord Jesus Christ, and the love of God, and the communion of the Holy Spirit, be with you all." [2] It is interesting to note that Paul's salutations at the beginning of his epistles almost all have the twofold form: "Grace to you and peace from God our Father and the Lord Jesus Christ," while the benedictions at the close refer simply to "the grace of the Lord Jesus Christ." The threefold benediction occurs only in the passage just mentioned. Only a few other passages contain a threefold reference. Two are in the deutero-Pauline epistle to the Ephesians. "Through him [Christ] we both have our access in one Spirit unto the Father." [3] In the fourth chapter he speaks of "the unity of the Spirit" (later of the "unity of the faith"), of "one body, and one Spirit," and then, summarizing the "one hope of your calling," he refers to "one Lord, one faith, one baptism, one God and Father of all, who is over all, and through all, and in all." Here clearly we have no more than we have found elsewhere with Paul: the Christian experience of the one God who is over all and in all, of one Lord through whom the salvation of God has come to men, and of the Spirit in which they are united in the Spirit-created Church and in which they "have access unto the Father." It is a declaration of faith, not a doctrinal formulation. This is certainly Pauline in thought even if the critics are right in calling this letter deutero-Pauline.

Turning to unquestioned sources, we have in I Corinthians 12:4–6 the same threefold reference to the Spirit, the Lord, and God. Here clearly the emphasis is upon the many gifts as having but one divine source, referred to now as Spirit, now as Lord. It is the same with the apostolic benediction

[2] II Cor. 13:14.   [3] Eph. 2:18.

quoted above. It is easy to read back into this the later Trinitarian definitions and conceptions, but taken by itself it suggests the twofold way in which the Christian has knowledge and experience of the one God. The terms are not Father, Son, and Spirit, but God and the Lord and the Spirit. It agrees with the other and more specific declarations noted above: "To us there is one God, the Father, of whom are all things, and we unto him; and one Lord, Jesus Christ, through whom are all things and we through him." "In one Spirit we were all baptized into one body."[4]

It is, then, generally recognized today that the doctrine of the Trinity at the very least is not explicitly declared by Paul or elsewhere set forth in the New Testament.[5] Shall we say then that there is a Trinitarian form of experience? This is nearer to the truth, though the expression may be misleading if we do not keep in mind that this is also a unitary experience. If we were to state this in Paul's own language and form of thought, it would be somewhat as follows. There is for us one God and Father, the living God, God of righteousness and mercy. He has come to us in Jesus Christ, the Son of his love. Through him we have grace unto salvation, in him as Son we know the Father, and he is our Lord. And God has given himself to us in his Spirit, the creator of the Church which is the communion of the Holy Spirit, and the power of a new life in each one of us.

Dr. H. Wheeler Robinson has well stated the matter in a comment on Ephesians 2:18, which speaks of our access through Christ in one Spirit unto the Father. "Here we see

---

[4] I Cor. 8:6; 12:13.
[5] This is admitted even by Karl Barth. See his *Dogmatik: Die Lehre vom Worte Gottes*, 1932, p. 330.

the unity of the approach to God which the Christian experiences. . . . Paul did not conceive Father, Son, and Spirit as three *hypostases* and one *ousia,* three 'centres' on one plane equidistant from the believer. Paul conceived of a line of intensive approach, always in the Spirit, always through Christ, always to the Father, even though he may not always express this as explicitly as he does in the passage quoted. This unity of the Godhead in the Christian experience of the New Testament is of primary importance and remains true for all unsophisticated reproduction of that experience. The unity of God is as clear to the normal faith and experience of the Christian as it is to the philosophical theist. Any attempt to differentiate Father, Son, and Spirit must be made within an already existent unity of experience." [6]

[6] *The Christian Experience of the Holy Spirit,* pp. 230, 231.

Chapter Thirteen

EPILOGUE

1. The purpose of this study has been a double one: to inquire historically as to Paul's interpretation of Christianity, to ask critically as to the validity of its teaching and its value for us today. But before we attempt a summary of our conclusions we must meet the sweeping charge which is constantly made against Paul. Claiming to be a loyal follower of Jesus, it is said, Paul was really an innovator. It is Paul, not Jesus, who founded the elaborate system which has been known as Christianity. What we need is a return to the simple piety and the lofty ethics of Jesus. The humble teacher of Galilee, we are told, represented Jewish piety stripped of all ceremonialism, and religious belief freed from all superstition. He asked men to live in simple trust and obedience with the Father God and in love to treat all men as brothers. Fatherhood, sonship, brotherhood, this was the triad of his religion. He was not a reformer, least of all a revolutionary. He had no thought of founding a new religion or of establishing a Church. He was a teacher of truth and a noble example. Paul changed all this. He substituted a religion about Jesus for the religion of Jesus. Under the influence of the mystery cults he introduced the idea of the dying and rising Savior-God and of a sacramental salvation. Under the influence of the concepts of the older legalism and the sacrificial system, he brought in the idea of Christ's death as a substitutionary sacrifice necessary if God was to forgive. Though he did not develop all this, he initiated the movement and planted the germs out of which grew the

doctrinal theories, the authoritarian creeds, the political-ecclesi-
astical institution, and the sacramentarianism of later days,
in other words the Catholic Church. And when the reformers
purged the Church of its greater evils and grosser superstitions,
under the dominance of this same Paul Christianity still remained a system of dogma.

Much of this attack has been discredited by more careful
critical study. Jesus was far more than the simple teacher of
ethics and religion; he knew himself as the herald of coming
judgment and redemption and as serving God in some unique
manner, probably as Messiah, to bring in the new age. A truer
statement of Paul's own position has been set forth in our
studies. Yet there is an element of truth in what is said as to
Paul's rôle in relation to the emergence of Christianity. Paul
did stand at the turning point of the new movement. Not
alone, but more than any other, he guided the new movement
into the ways which it was henceforth to follow, so that it
became not a passing reform in Judaism, but a universal and
spiritual faith finding expression in the historic Church. In so
doing, however, he did not defeat that which Jesus represented
but rather had the insight to discern its meaning and the devotion to give it effect. This must now be indicated, and first
by a truer appraisal of the significance of Jesus.

2. The question for Christian thought is not that of the cen-
trality of Jesus, but where his deepest significance is to be
found. Is it in his teaching, his character, or in something more
than these? Certainly his teaching is not to be underestimated.
He came in prophetic spirit declaring that the kingdom of God
was at hand, calling men to repent, and bidding them even now
to live as children of the kingdom. His teaching had the simplicity which belongs to those who can pass by the incidental

because they see what is essential. He called men to see God in his holiness and turn from their sins, to see him in his goodness and power and learn the life of trust and peace, to see his purpose of redemption and rejoice, and to live as children in the spirit of the Father. But his words were not those of a mystic or a philosopher standing aside from the turmoil of life ; they were the summons of a prophet pointing to great events and asking men to prepare for their coming.

Nor are we to underestimate the significance of his spirit and life. It is true that our gospels do not give us a biography of Jesus in any modern sense, and that words and deeds are here recorded in terms of the significance which they had come to have for the faith and life of the later Church. Yet it is equally clear that Paul and all the others of his day are dominated by the figure of Jesus. Theirs is, indeed, the risen Lord but their Lord is one who thus lived and wrought and spoke and loved and died, and in so doing showed men at once the heart of the Eternal and the true life of man. As against the mythical savior-gods of the mystery religions and the abstract ideals and principles of the philosophers and the Stoic preachers, in Jesus truth and life were one, and his greatest teaching was that which he lived out before the eyes of men. In him the Word of God had become flesh and dwelt among men.

But we must go farther still. The truth which he proclaimed and the life which he lived must never be left behind, but Jesus entered into history in a way which cannot be determined simply by a study of his life and teaching. We must keep clearly before us the fact that Christianity is not primarily a system of ideas or an ethical ideal ; it is a historical movement into which ideas and ideals enter, but which is first of all the redemptive action of the Eternal working in time. Jesus' message of the kingdom of God was concerned with this. He went to his death believing that by his obedience he was serving this saving purpose of God.

The question then is not merely what Jesus taught. "It is what Jesus did to human history by his life and death rather than what he said about it that matters when we come to define Christianity." [1] The question whether Jesus intended to found the Church is debatable; the incontrovertible fact is that he did found it. He did call a company of disciples about him, the "little flock," to whom it was God's good pleasure to give the kingdom.[2] By word and life and death and by his living presence he created the growing company which was the Christian Church. To them he gave a faith and a spirit which set them apart even before they recognized the divine logic of what was happening. The early Church did not have to go back to specific words of Jesus. He was always more to them than his words. In him God had acted even while Jesus was on earth; the "mighty works and wonders and signs" were what "God did by him." Now God had made him Lord and Christ and through him God was working with even greater power in the forgiveness of sin and healings and the gift of his Spirit.[3] There never was any Christianity for which Jesus was merely a teacher and example from the past.

3. From this point of view we must consider the question of the relation of Paul to Jesus. Paul never conceived of this as being merely that of a disciple repeating the words of the Master with the scrupulous verbal fidelity which was the ideal

---

[1] John Macmurray, *The Clue to History*, p. 4.
[2] Lu. 12:32.
[3] Acts 2:22, 33, 36, 38; 3:16.

of the Jewish disciple in relation to his rabbi. Paul's task was to interpret to men who Christ was and what God purposed to do through him and what he was doing even now. Nevertheless, Jesus was a teacher and Paul was a teacher, and what they did and what they hoped for rooted in the deep convictions of their faith. It is interesting, therefore, to note their essential agreement in teaching. In part that was because both were in the same great prophetic succession; it was even more because Paul was a true disciple of his Master. The agreement is evident as we turn to the central doctrines.

(1) We meet with Paul the same God of love whom Jesus proclaimed, no mere rewarder of the righteous but the one who goes forth to seek and to save that which is lost. For Paul this vision of the free love of God has its supreme expression in the sending of his Son. Paul has no other God than the God and Father of the Lord Jesus Christ. (2) With Paul as with Jesus religion is a life of fellowship in which the son lives with his Father in trust and obedience. (3) Paul is equally one with his Master in his ethics, especially in the primacy which he gives to the spirit of love and in his conception of that spirit. (4) With Jesus Paul proclaims the coming kingdom of God, holding as Jesus did that the sons of the kingdom were already sharing in its privileges and living by its laws. For both, the kingdom means not merely the breaking of the power of evil which held men in bondage but something spiritual and ethical, the power of God within men and a rule of love and righteousness and peace.

4. Recognizing this deep agreement of faith between Paul and Jesus, we must see clearly, too, the differences between them. And the principal difference comes from this: Jesus stands for the fact, Paul for the interpretation. The criticism

of Paul, when he is conceived in opposition to Jesus, rests upon the assumption that Christianity is a matter of ideas; the whole problem is altered when the central element is seen as the living God known in historical events. Even though Christ was the center of Paul's message, his message differed because he spoke to a situation quite other than that in which Jesus had found himself. The "fact of Christ" included now not only Christ's person and word, but his death and resurrection, the new Fellowship that had arisen, and his presence and power working in that Fellowship. From his very loyalty to Christ there came the new themes to which Paul addressed himself: Christ and his redemption, faith and forgiveness, the Church and its living head, the Holy Spirit and the new life in man, the return of Christ and the final redemption. We must still ask as to the adequacy of Paul's interpretation but our general attitude toward it will rest in the main upon our answer to the crucial question: Was Jesus the last and noblest of the prophets but only a prophet, or was he God's supreme word to men, God's saving deed of love, God's instrument for the establishment of his kingdom? If we hold to the former we will agree with Johannes Weiss that it was "a fateful happening that Christianity did not develop directly from the prophetic preaching of Jesus concerning the kingdom of God as a religion of pure monotheism, but that the idea of the Messiah, even during the lifetime of Jesus, and then completely after his death, entered into an indissoluble union with the person of Jesus." If we hold to the latter, we will think of Paul as true follower of Christ and not an innovator.

5. There are certain further facts, however, which we must take into account in considering Paul's interpretation of Christianity. (1) Paul does not stand alone within the New Testa-

ment. Though united in their central faith, the New Testament writers offer a wide variety of interpretation. We think of the synoptic gospels and the Johannine literature, of the outlook of the primitive Church and of the letter to the Hebrews, of Paul and his conflict with the Judaizing Christians, and of "little apocalypses" found in the synoptic gospels as well as the apocalyptic book of Revelation. (2) Christianity is greater than any one of its interpreters or all of them together. Each of these, including Paul, represents a human effort to interpret the divine meaning of great events and, first of all, of Christ and his way of salvation. (3) Paul himself, like the other interpreters, was a child of his age, and its many interests and influences appear in him. That was not a sign of weakness, for he was no mere composite, nor was his gospel a syncretism; syncretisms are external combinations and lack in power, while his words have the unity and power which come from life. But he was the more effective because he knew the needs of his day and used its language. In his early training, his situation in life, his outlook, his modes of thought and expression, he differed from Jesus. Even more does he differ from us at many of these points: his apocalyptic mood and imagery, his social outlook as subject of the great Roman *imperium,* his Jewish background influencing him even when he reacted from it, the forms in which, for example, he clothed his thought of the death of Christ and of the person of Christ. (4) The Christian movement, which grew so quickly in those first years, has not stood still since Paul's time. There have been nineteen centuries of divine action and Christian experience. With all that Paul brings, using all that the past offers, knowing itself in the great Christian tradition, the Church of today under God's guidance still has the responsibility of understanding the faith for itself and of interpreting the way of life to its generation. Christ is still the Lord of its life and faith, but it is a living Christ, and its God is the God who is still at work and who still by his Spirit guides us into the truth.

6. It is not easy now to state what we owe to Paul. We are so familiar with his great conceptions, they have so entered into our Christian heritage, that we do not particularly associate them with his name. We cannot, of course, give Paul individual and sole credit for these doctrines: it was part of his unique fitness for his task that he was able to take up into himself so much of the best insights of his day. We can say that he was foremost in formulating these great Christian truths and in bringing them into unity. So, without trying to adjudge the matter of credit or originality, we may note here those great religious conceptions of Paul which have become the enriching and abiding possessions of Christian thought.

(1) Paul has made plain for us the nature of Christianity as a historical religion in contrast with all abstract systems of thought, achieved by pure reflection and having no necessary relation to historical events. His God is the God of history. He sees Christianity in relation to a given past, to the revelation of God in Israel. He links the Christian faith inseparably to the historical Jesus of Nazareth. Central for him is not a doctrine about the person of Christ, not a theory about the two natures or about the status of a preexistent *logos;* it is the belief that in this Jesus of Nazareth, living, loving, dying, risen from the dead, the eternal God has spoken to us and wrought for our salvation. But the history is not one which belongs simply to the past. Christianity stands for a great tradition, but that does not mean traditionalism; it is not the idea of a Christ of the past, of a God who no longer speaks to men, and

whose creative work has ended. The living God is at work now in men and in the Church. By his Spirit he leads men into the truth. And his greatest redemptive work is yet to come.

(2) The Christianity which Paul has given us means corporate religion. It is social alike in its religious and its ethical aspect. The purpose of God is social, the creation of a people. The Christian message comes to us through the Church. In its fellowship we are nurtured, and through this the richest spiritual life is made available. Here, too, is the opportunity for the active expression of that life in worship and service. A solitary religion is a contradiction of the God of the Christian faith and of the way of love which is the spirit of Christ. This corporate religion does not mean the Church as authoritarian rule or as dispenser of sacramentarian power, but as the Fellowship which God continuously creates by his Spirit, in which God dwells, of which Christ is the head. With its divine nature the Church at the same time is deeply and richly human, a fellowship of mutual love and service. It is the body of Christ, not simply as deriving its life from him, but as showing him forth visibly to the world and as doing his work in the world.

(3) Paul made the religious life an inner and individual matter. The individual belongs to the fellowship but only in the free and shared life of faith and worship and love. The Church is no institution which simply masters and owns and uses. It is here to serve and only in the life of the members of the fellowship does it realize its own life. Apart from them it has no life, either in the supra-historical-mystical sense of the Orthodox Church or the legal-institutional sense of the Roman Church. The depth and richness of this individual life Paul secured by his doctrine of the personal relation of each

child with the Father, as Jesus taught, by his teaching of the life which God by his Spirit bestows upon each as an inner possession, and by his doctrine of Christian freedom. In his appreciation and understanding of this individual inner life Paul has had many and notable followers, Augustine and Luther, Wesley and Fox, mystics and saints; but he has remained in this field a leader for us all.

(4) Paul established the meaning of Christianity as a religion of salvation. Here was his deepest concern. Here his insight helped the new faith to meet the deeply felt wants of his day. Here he struck the note to which men in their need have answered ever since. The Christianity of Paul offers men not only insight into the meaning of the world and life, a lofty conception of God, and a commanding ethical ideal, but a way of help, of deliverance from evil and strength to achieve and hope for what lies beyond. Here Paul united the elements which so often have been disjoined in religion: moral demand and saving help, forgiveness and healing without abatement of the requirement of righteousness. All the aspects of life are included in his conception of salvation, yet in its essence it is simple. Salvation for him means life; true, there is escape from death and deliverance from the powers of evil, but all this is in order to the real end, that men may have life. As a distinguished New Testament scholar once said: "It can all be put in the words of Romans 8:2: 'the Spirit of life.' For life is last and highest in the goal of religion." [4] This life is first of all the life of fellowship with God, and God is its beginning and end. Its source is his gracious purpose and the love that goes out to men in Christ. Its work is to overcome sin by forgiveness and so to reconcile men to God. Its end is the new

[4] H. J. Holtzmann, *Neutestamentliche Theologie*, Vol. II, p. 157.

and life-giving fellowship with God and the new man in the spirit of Christ who is created by this fellowship. Salvation is not simply creative of the individual, but socially and historically. In the spirit of love and faith it shapes a new fellowship, that of the Church, a new humanity here upon earth; and so it indicates what human life will be in all its relations in the kingdom of God. It thus has a historical-social as well as an individual dimension.

(5) Paul has given to us an ethical conception of religion. He held up the lofty ideal of an inner spirit and attitude, the spirit of love after "the mind of Christ," resisting all temptation to resolve this into a matter of rules. He saw the meaning of Christ and of his spirit of love as a way of life for men. He held to this ethics of the spirit as against the morality of rules. Yet this meant for him no quietism or subjectivism; rather he asserted the lordship of this spirit over all life. And while he laid down no system of rules, his treatment of concrete situations shows us plainly what this spirit of love demands and how it enters in to shape all human relations. His greatest service, however, was to make clear once for all that religion must be ethical and that ethics must be rooted in religion. The Church has not always followed him here. Sometimes it has depended upon rules and external control and then its ethics has become a mere moralism, wanting alike in inner spirit and creative force. Sometimes its idea of salvation has lacked the ethical, reverting to mystery or magic or an extreme mysticism. But the fault does not lie with Paul. For him the life with God is conditioned by a surrender of will and affection; the surrender is not to sovereign Power but to a God who is righteousness and love; and the saving fellowship is ours only as we live with men in this same spirit of love and

righteousness. Through faith, by grace, in love, these are the regnant principles in all his thought of salvation. No ethics without religion, without this fellowship with God as its creative source. And, when once you know what kind of a God this is, when once you have seen God in Christ, then it is equally clear: no religion without ethics.

(6) Paul has given us a religion of freedom. That does not mean a religion without obligation. He knows that freedom comes only through surrender to the highest, that only thus is man freed from the bondage of fear of the world and from slavery to his own lower self. The Christianity of history has not always been a religion of freedom. Sometimes there has been a legalistic bondage with the imposition of rules and prescriptions. It has very frequently been an authoritarian religion demanding the acceptance of doctrines or submission to the rule of the Church. Sometimes the free grace which Paul preached has been superseded as a way of salvation by elaborate schemes of sacrament and discipline.

For Paul the freedom of religion meant the freedom of faith, a simple trust in the God who comes in Christ, arising from an inner conviction and issuing in a willing surrender. Ethically it meant the rule of an inner spirit of love freely expressed in the service of men. As a religion of salvation it meant God's free and forgiving grace receiving men into the fellowship of children with their Father as against the obedience of servants. And with the freedom of faith and grace and love went the freedom of the mind, knowing no God but the God of truth who gives to each the Spirit by which he is led into the knowledge of God and ever richer apprehension of the truth.

A BRIEF LIST OF RECOMMENDED BOOKS

This bibliography is intended for the general student. It makes no pretense to be exhaustive at any point. It comprises works of varying viewpoints, including the distinguished Jewish scholar, Joseph Klausner, and the Roman Catholic, Fernand Prat, S. J. Our first source is Paul's own letters, and our first task is to read and re-read these writings, seeking to enter into the mind and spirit of the great apostle. I have not cited works in foreign languages, but I should like to include here the *Neutestamentliche Theologie* of H. J. Holtzmann, a work which should have been translated into English long since.

GENERAL WORKS DEALING WITH THE EARLY CHURCH

Johannes Weiss, *History of Primitive Christianity,* 1937, (especially Vol. II)

Hans Lietzmann, *The Beginnings of the Christian Church,* 1937

Paul Wernle, *The Beginnings of Christianity,* 1903

Clarence T. Craig, *The Beginning of Christianity,* 1943

P. G. S. Hopwood, *The Religious Experience of the Primitive Church,* 1936

E. F. Scott, *The Gospel and Its Tributaries,* 1935

THE MAN AND HIS WORK

T. R. Glover, *Paul of Tarsus,* 1925

H. Weinel, *St. Paul, the Man and His Work,* 1906

A. D. Nock, *St. Paul,* 1938

A. H. McNeile, *St. Paul, His Life, Letters, and Christian Doctrine,* 1920

A. Sabatier, *The Apostle Paul,* 1906

C. T. Wood, *Life, Letters, and Religion of St. Paul,* 1925

Paul's Teaching

Joseph Klausner, *From Jesus to Paul,* 1943

W. L. Knox, *St. Paul,* 1932

C. A. Anderson Scott, *Christianity According to St. Paul,* 1927

W. Morgan, *The Religion and Theology of St. Paul,* 1917

Otto Pfleiderer, *Paulinism,* 1877

F. C. Porter, *The Mind of Christ in Paul,* 1930

A. Deissmann, *The Religion of Jesus and the Faith of Paul,* 1926

C. H. Dodd, *The Meaning of Paul for Today,* 1922

F. Prat, *The Theology of Paul,* 1926

J. E. Rattenbury, *The Religious Experience of St. Paul,* 1931

A. Schweitzer, *The Mysticism of Paul the Apostle,* 1937

H. A. A. Kennedy, *St. Paul and the Mystery Religions,* 1913; *St. Paul's Conception of the Last Things,* 1904

M. S. Enslin, *The Ethics of Paul,* 1920

J. S. Stewart, *A Man in Christ,* 1935

INDEX OF BIBLICAL PASSAGES

OLD TESTAMENT

NEW TESTAMENT

INDEX OF NAMES

INDEX OF SUBJECTS